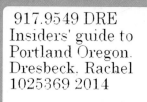

FA MAY 2014

INSIDERS'GUIDE® to
Portland, Oregon

EIGHTH EDITION

D0963897

INSIDERS'GUIDE®

GUILFORD, CONNECTICUT
AN IMPRINT OF GLOBE PEQUOT PRESS

All the information in this guidebook is subject to change. We recommend that you call ahead to obtain current information before traveling.

Photo Credits

Photos licensed by Shutterstock.com: pages i, ix, 17, 19, 23, 24, 29, 37, 43, 57, 82, 102, 118, 125, 126, 129, 136, 153, 154, 161, 163, 198, 205, 213, 215, 218, 220. Photos by Rachel Dresbeck: pages 5, 13, 31, 44, 53, 54, 58, 77, 81, 90, 95, 106, 110, 117, 123, 131, 142, 145, 170, 171, 174, 179, 191, 192, 222, 246.

To buy books in quantity for corporate use or incentives, call **(800) 962-0973** or e-mail **premiums@GlobePequot.com.**

INSIDERS' GUIDE

Author: Rachel Dresbeck
Editor: Amy Lyons
Project Editor: Lauren Brancato
Layout: Joanna Beyer
Text Design: Sheryl Kober
Maps: XNR Productions, Inc. © Morris Book Publishing, LLC

ISSN 1541-7921
ISBN 978-0-7627-9189-7

Printed in the United States of America
10 9 8 7 6 5 4 3 2 1

Contents

Directory of Maps

About the Author

Rachel Dresbeck, a writer and editor, has observed and written about Portland for a variety of publications. She's also an author of the first edition of the *Insiders' Guide to the Oregon Coast,* as well as the *Insiders' Guide to Portland* since the second edition. She was educated at Whitman College and the University of Oregon, has taught writing and literature at Portland Community College and the University of Oregon, and now teaches writing and writes about research at Oregon Health and Science University. She lives with her husband and daughters in the Richmond neighborhood of Portland, where she studies ways in which citizens sustain their civility and community spirit against all odds.

Acknowledgments

Portland is a city of neighborhoods, so first I would like to thank my neighbors for their insight, witticisms, and generosity over the years. I would especially like to thank my neighbors far-flung and close by: the Bancheros, Forrests, Frosts, and Colwell-Averetts, as well as the Gurleys, the Ellises, and the McCollums, and the Passarellis, McFaddens, and Walkers. I am especially grateful for the time shared at Pine Grove and at the St. Walkers Invitational.

Thanks also to my ever-patient husband, Tom, and my daughters, Flannery and Cleo, who make writing anything a more interesting experience, who are my favorite companions for exploration, and who had to make a lot of dinners as I was completing this volume. This book is dedicated to them.

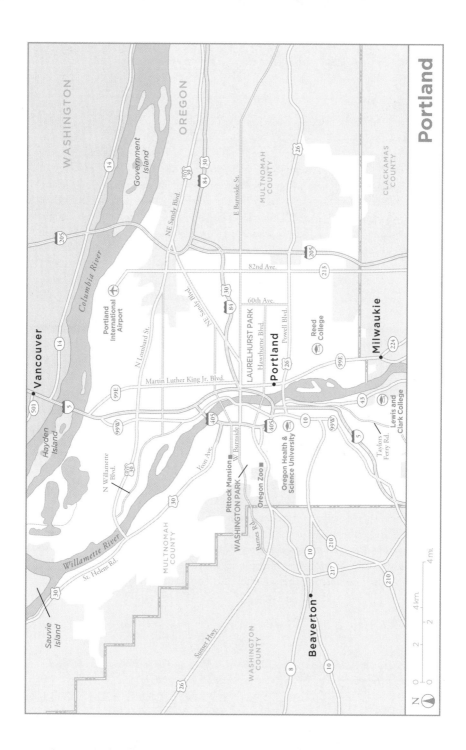

Portland

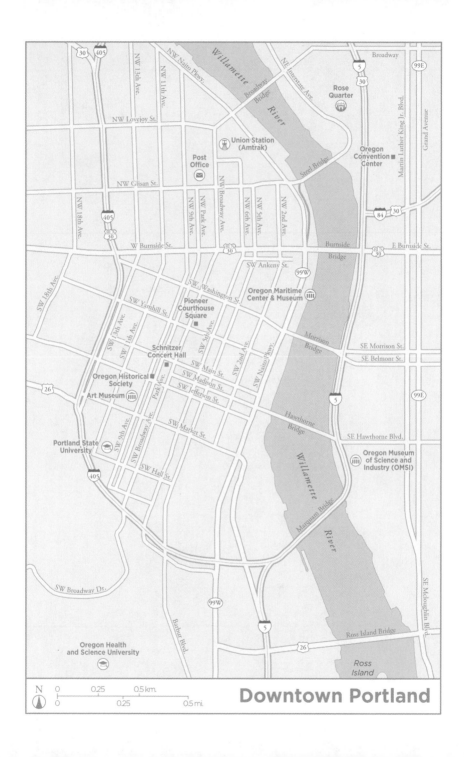

Downtown Portland

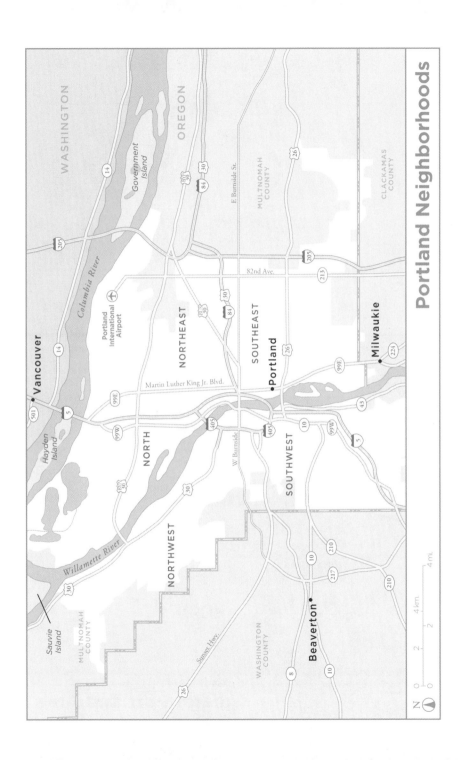

Portland Neighborhoods

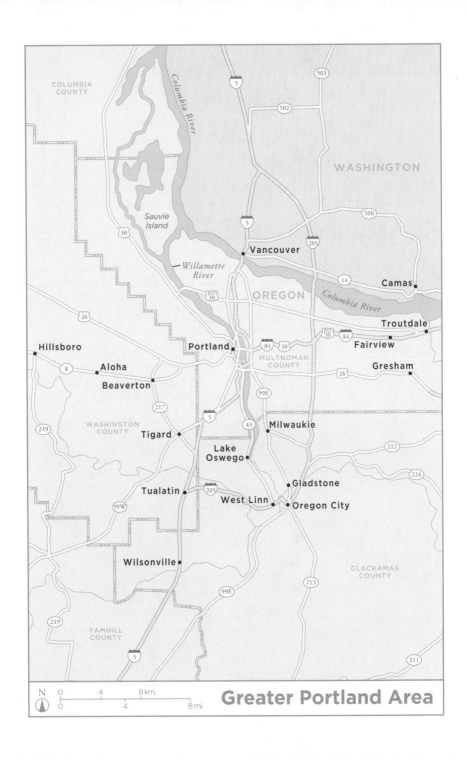

Greater Portland Area

How to Use This Book

Insiders' Guide to Portland, Oregon is designed to allow you to make the most of your time here, however long it is. Our guide is organized into thematic chapters that cover everything from accommodations to well-being. The internal organization of chapters will vary depending on their content. For example, the Festivals & Annual Events chapter is sorted chronologically, but the Shopping chapter is set up alphabetically by topic. Many chapters, such as Accommodations or Attractions, may be additionally organized into geographic areas for easier navigation.

Portland is divided into eastern and western halves by the Willamette River. It is further divided by Burnside Street, which runs east and west, into four quadrants: Southwest, Northwest, Southeast, and Northeast. A fifth "quadrant," North Portland, the portion west of Williams Avenue, extends from the Broadway Bridge to the Columbia River; however, for the purposes of this book, listings in North Portland and Northeast Portland have been kept together. Vancouver, which is immediately north of Portland just across the Columbia River in the state of Washington, is also mentioned frequently in our book, as are the towns that surround the city. Thus you will also find sections for Vancouver and for Outlying Areas, for a total of six basic geographical divisions.

A cyclist climbs the Vista Bridge in southwest Portland.

The first chapters are designed to help you orient yourself to the Portland Metro area by giving you information about transportation and history. The next several chapters concern the exigencies of daily living—where to eat and sleep. Then we devote a large number of chapters to various forms of recreation; these range from telling you how to find a nearby antiques shop or climbing park to securing Blazers tickets. We also include a chapter with suggested itineraries, should you want to go exploring the innumerable attractions of the region within and beyond the city limits.

Moving to the Portland Metro area or already live here? Be sure to check out the pages at the back of the book, where you will find the Living Here appendix, which offers sections on relocation, child care and education, retirement, and media.

Within all chapters, you will find frequent cross-references and even, for the sake of convenience, some cross-listings.

Throughout this book you'll find Insiders' Tips (indicated by an ⓘ), which offer quick insights, and Close-ups, which provide in-depth information on topics that are particularly interesting, unusual, or distinctly Portland.

You'll also find listings accompanied by the ★ symbol—these are our top picks for attractions, restaurants, accommodations, and everything in between that you shouldn't miss while you're in the area. You want the best this region has to offer? Go with our Insiders' Choice.

A few basic maps are included in the guide, but you may also want to purchase a more detailed map of the city and surrounding areas in order to prevent those interesting discussions between driver and navigator about which way to turn.

The Greater Portland Metro area comprises Multnomah, Washington, and Clackamas Counties. You won't notice when you cross from one county into another, but you will need to know which county you are dealing with for the sake of real estate, schools, and government. Where necessary, then, we will point out these distinctions.

Don't just take our word for it: Use this guide to explore for yourself the charms of Portland. Our dynamic city is always changing, adding new attractions and business, and closing others down. You may discover some of these changes in your own travels.

We are glad you are here. Portland is a beautiful city at the leading edge of a new approach to living, one that respects tradition but repurposes it for a future that will challenge all of us. We have an ethos of innovation, DIY, and experimentation. Design is honored and sought after. Craftsmanship is prized—the slow rather than the fast, small-batch rather than mass-produced, micro rather than macro. We are friendly in this pursuit of beauty: Neighbors get together to paint street murals. Sometimes our local favorites go national, like Stumptown Coffee and Voodoo Doughnuts—or even Columbia Sportswear and Nike. But this only demonstrates that the particular has appeal that is universal.

The Portland Metropolitan area is home to nearly two million people who live, work, and play in one of the most beautiful urban zones in the country. It comprises Multnomah, Washington, and Clackamas Counties, as well as the southern edge of Clark County in Washington State across the Columbia River to the north. The city itself is organized into quadrants: Southwest, Northwest, Southeast, and Northeast. There is also a fifth "quadrant," North Portland, but for the purposes of this book, we will include that in the Northeast neighborhood quadrant. These areas of the city refer to their position along the Willamette River, which marks east and west, and along Burnside Street, which marks north and south. Understanding this orientation will make getting around Portland much easier.

SOUTHWEST PORTLAND

Southwest Portland encompasses **the downtown area,** stretching west beyond Washington Park and south along the Willamette River. The downtown area is composed of short and easily walkable blocks. Here you will find hotels, retail, and many of the attractions featured in this book—for example, Pioneer Courthouse Square, the Portland Art Museum, and Portland State University. Above downtown are affluent neighborhoods with lovely houses lining hillside streets, and along with these, Washington Park, Forest Park, the International Rose Test Garden, the Japanese Garden, and the Oregon Zoo.

Along the Willamette River lies Tom McCall Waterfront Park, and farther south is the South Waterfront area, a district rising atop old shipbuilding yards. This neighborhood features sleek high-rises built alongside a verdant greenway.

Portland Index

- The Portland Metropolitan area has more than 2 million people.

- The city of Portland covers 145 square miles.

- The average rainfall in Portland is 35 inches per year.

- Portland residents enjoy an average of 128,618 minutes of sunshine per year.

- Portland has 2,450 wetland acres and 19,515 acres of forest and woodland areas within its city limits.

- The number of hens a Portland household may keep without a permit: 3. No roosters, please.

- The median age in the metro area is 35.

- The mean time for commuting to work is 24 minutes.

- The largest private employers in the Portland area are Intel (15,000), Providence Health System (14,000), Oregon Health and Science University (14,000), Fred Meyer Stores (9,900), Legacy Health Systems (9,700), Kaiser Foundation Health Plan (9,000), and Nike (7,000).

- There are 52 microbreweries in Portland, more than anywhere in the nation.

- Portland has more than 40 different coffee roasters supplying local caffeine addictions.

- You can still find iron horse rings in front of many neighborhood houses. Sometimes they have toy horses tied to them.

- Portland is the home of Powell's City of Books, the largest independent bookstore in the world.

It is the home of one of the campuses of Oregon Health and Science University and the lower landing dock of the Portland Aerial Tram, accessible by streetcar.

NORTHWEST PORTLAND

Northwest Portland is characterized by its creative energy, both in its industrially chic **Pearl District** and in its beautiful **Victorian district, Nob Hill. Pittock Mansion** is also in Northwest Portland. This area is also the home of Chinatown, with its entrance at 4th Avenue and Burnside Street, an Asian-American neighborhood with shops, restaurants, and art galleries. The **Portland Classical Chinese Garden,** a standout in the district, is one of the few authentic classical-style Chinese gardens in the United States.

Northwest Portland is the site of **Powell's Books,** one of the largest bookstores in the world. Powell's marks the outer edge of the Pearl District, a reclaimed industrial area that is now home to art galleries, luxury condos, upscale shops, art schools, and fine restaurants. Across from Powell's is the historic Blitz-Weinhard Brewery building, which is now part of the Brewery Blocks development and home to swanky shops and condominiums.

Along 21st and 23rd Avenues, you'll find boutiques, antiques shops, and bookstores in renovated Victorian houses. The street life along both avenues is bustling and vibrant, and it's a city favorite for window-shopping and people-watching.

> **i** Portland has a number of nicknames: the City of Roses, Bridgetown, and PDX, our airport code. And we are still known as Stumptown, from the hundreds of fir stumps left in the streets by 19th-century builders. Hinting at our future commitment to good public transportation, early city officials painted them white to warn wagoneers out after dark.

SOUTHEAST PORTLAND

Southeast Portland is a sprawling district characterized by parks, funky residential neighborhoods, Reed College, a riverfront industrial area, and an emerging indie business scene. **Lower Burnside** is the epicenter of new urban energy and its attendant development. The **Hawthorne, Belmont, Division,** and **Clinton** Districts are filled with single-family homes and apartment buildings mixed with shops, music stores and bookstores, coffeehouses, microbrew pubs, food carts, and restaurants geared to every palate. Southeast Division is the site of some of the trendiest and most influential Portland restaurants and coffee shops, including Stumptown and Pok Pok.

Further south, **Sellwood,** a historic district annexed to Portland in 1893, features **Antique Row,** more than 50 antiques stores tucked into the neighborhood of Victorian homes and turn-of-the-20th-century architecture. The **Oaks Bottom Wildlife Refuge,** home to bald eagles, herons, beavers, ducks, and other marsh animals and birds, is found in Southeast Portland, while nearby **Eastmoreland's** tranquil residential neighborhood features beautiful houses, bordered by the public **Eastmoreland Golf Course,** the brick campus of **Reed College,** and **Crystal Springs Rhododendron Garden.**

Area Codes & 10-Digit Dialing

When you make a call in the Portland area, you will need to dial the area code first—all 10 digits. (It won't be a long-distance call unless you dial a "1" first, which would make 11 digits.) The area codes that serve Portland are (503) and (971). These are also codes for Salem and northern coastal towns. Area codes (541) and (458) will give you access to southern, central, and eastern Oregon, including the central and southern coasts.

Area code (360) serves Vancouver; calls from Portland to Vancouver, however, are long-distance calls.

NORTH & NORTHEAST PORTLAND

Northeast Portland and its neighbor North Portland are home to a blend of industry, commerce, culture, and houses. Beautiful older houses line tree-shaded streets in neighborhoods such as **Laurelhurst, Irvington,** and **Alameda.** The popular **Lloyd Center** is the largest single shopping destination in the quadrant (see Shopping). By light rail, Lloyd Center is just minutes from downtown.

Portland's Convention Center lies between the Lloyd District and the river, its 150-foot-high twin spires stamping their distinctive profile on the city's skyline. The MAX line stops outside the center's north entrance and also serves the adjacent **Rose Quarter,** a 43-acre complex, featuring the **Memorial Coliseum** arena, the **Moda Center** arena, **One Center Court** entertainment complex, and four parking garages. The streetcar serves this area as well. The

Rose Quarter hosts a variety of sports events, including those of the **Portland Trailblazers,** as well as rodeos, circuses, concerts, ice shows, and other spectacles. Other popular neighborhoods farther north, such as **Alberta** and **Mississippi,** offer their own charms: It is here you will find reclaimed houses and many creative small businesses, excellent shopping, and inventive restaurants.

Our Relocation chapter provides more details on these neighborhoods.

VANCOUVER

Vancouver was originally settled to supply the vast Hudson's Bay network of fur trappers. This scenic Northwest city, named after British explorer George Vancouver, has 55 parks and playgrounds inside city limits, including the **Burnt Bridge Creek Greenway** and the **Discovery Trail.** The **Vancouver National Historic Reserve** is a partnership that manages historic sites at **Fort Vancouver, Columbia Park,** and **Pearson Field,** one of the oldest operating airfields in the nation. Vancouver is also known for its celebration on the Fourth of July, when it stages a large fireworks show.

OUTLYING AREAS

You will also find charming towns throughout the greater Portland area, including **Beaverton, Lake Oswego, West Linn, Tigard, Tualatin,** and **Hillsboro** on

The Pearl District's newest green space, Fields Park

Close-up

How to Talk Like a Native

While Oregonians, especially natives, don't have any revealing regional accent, we do have a vernacular. To aid you in communicating effectively here in Portland, we offer the following list of local phrases and pronunciations.

The Banfield: I-84, which runs east from Portland to eastern Oregon and beyond. A major commute route.

The Coast: The beaches along the Pacific Ocean anywhere between Astoria, Oregon, and the California border.

Couch Street: Pronounced *"Kooch."*

Glisan Street: Pronounced *"Glee-son."*

MAX: More formally the Metropolitan Area Express, this is the light-rail system operated by Tri-Met. The system runs from Hillsboro to Gresham, to the airport, and to North Portland. Do not get caught riding MAX without a ticket or valid transfer.

OHSU: Oregon Health and Science University.

OMSI: Oregon Museum of Science and Industry. Pronounced *"AHM-zi."*

Oregon: Correctly pronounced *"OR-uh-gun,"* never *"OR-uh-gone."*

PDX: The airport code for Portland International Airport, frequently used as shorthand for the city.

The Schnitz: The Arlene Schnitzer Concert Hall, named after the grande dame of one of Portland's most prominent families.

The Sunset Highway: US 26, which runs west from Portland to the Oregon coast. Another major commute route and perpetual construction zone.

Willamette: The Willamette River. This river divides Portland into east and west neighborhoods before flowing into the Columbia at Kelley Point. Residents on each side have strong opinions about the other's attitudes, political perspectives, lifestyles, and personalities. The correct pronunciation is *"wil-LAM-et,"* not *"WILL-a-met."*

the west side, and **Troutdale, Fairview, Gresham, Milwaukie,** and **Oregon City** on the east side. These growing communities tend to have more new houses and strip malls than Portland proper, but their rural roots are evident if you know where to look. These towns are technically considered suburbs, but they also have their own distinctive economic centers and personalities. These areas and others are profiled in greater detail in the Relocation chapter.

GETTING HERE, GETTING AROUND

Navigating the Area

Portland is not difficult to navigate once you understand its idiosyncrasies. The city is divided into east and west by the Willamette River and north and south by Burnside Street. These serve as your orientation marks, and addresses and street numbers are organized around them. If you're on Southwest 5th Avenue downtown, you'll know that you're 5 blocks west of the Willamette River. Similarly, Burnside Street is the starting point for street addresses, and these rise in number the farther north or south that you travel from Burnside. So if your Southwest 5th Avenue address happens to be 423, you'll know that you're about 4 blocks south of Burnside.

Arriving by Air

PORTLAND INTERNATIONAL AIRPORT, 7000 NE Airport Way, Portland, OR 97218; (503) 460-4234, (877) 739-4636; flypdx.com. Portland International Airport—which we call PDX (its aeronautical code)—is notably clean, light, and pleasant, with food that is actually good and shops, like Powell's and Pendleton, where you want to buy things. Free wireless Internet access is available throughout most of the main terminal level of the airport. Security is functional and efficient. The airport's crews are experienced in responding to the Oregon winters, and the airport is rarely closed. The airport is 10 miles from downtown Portland, and it's easily accessible via public transportation, as detailed below. Airlines that serve PDX include the following:

Air Canada, (888) 247-2262, aircanada.com

Alaska Airlines, (800) 252-7522, alaksaair.com

American Airlines, (800) 433-7300, aa.com

Delta Air Lines, (800) 221-1212, delta.com

Frontier, (800) 432-1359, flyfrontier.com

Hawaiian Airlines, (800) 367-5320, hawaiianairlines.com

Jet Blue Airways, (800) 538-2583, jetblue.com

Seaport Airlines, (888) 573-2767, seaportair.com

Southwest Airlines, (800) 435-9792, southwest.com

Spirit, (800) 772-7117, spirit.com

United and United Express, (800) 864-8331, united.com

US Airways, (800) 428-4322, usairways.com

Virgin America, (877) 359-8474, virginamerica.com

Ground Transportation

Transportation from the airport is available by light rail, taxi, and other ride ser-vices. You can, of course, also rent cars. Car rental agencies are on the terminal grounds, though several of them have only kiosks there.

Light Rail: The Red Line. Portland's light-rail system, MAX, is a conve-nient way to get downtown from the airport. The Red Line serves downtown and PDX: It takes about 40 minutes and costs $2.50, one-way. Trains are just outside the baggage claim area, and they are well marked with prominent signs. To take the Red Line into town, purchase your ticket prior to boarding the train at one of the vending machines inside the terminal, near the doors leading to the trains or outside near the track. You'll need to buy an all-zone ticket. The vending machines will accept $1 bills, change, and—for several tickets—credit cards. (You can buy tickets ahead of time online and have them mailed to you, if you are well organized; see trimet.org/store/index.htm.) Once you've bought your ticket, be sure to validate it in the machine prior to boarding, and hang onto this ticket for your entire ride—it acts as proof of payment. Cheerful TriMet transit authority employees are usually standing by to help you figure out tickets, destinations, and other problems. Trains to downtown leave about every 15 minutes at peak times and slightly less often at other times. See the TriMet entry later in this chapter for more information on the MAX line.

Other Ground Transportation: For other means of transport, you will find the Ground Transportation Center across the first roadway on the lower level of the airport in the parking garage, just across from the baggage claim area. Posted signs will tell you whether you are in the right section for your chosen mode of transport; you can also ask the airport service personnel who are always in attendance to direct you. They can also help you get a taxi—only certain companies can serve the airport, so they'll make sure you are in one that's legitimate. Taxis to downtown Portland should cost about $30; the trip downtown takes from 20 to 40 minutes.

You will also find a number of other shuttle and towncar services in the Ground Transportation Center. The prices for these will vary depending on the number of passengers, the distance you will travel, and the luxuriousness of the vehicle. Shuttles and towncar services, unlike taxi service, are not as tightly regulated, so be sure to clarify the price before you begin your journey. The best way to find a shuttle service is to use the widget on the PDX website: portofportland.com/PDX_ Grnd_Trnsprtn.aspx. PDX maintains this comprehensive website and includes links to all shuttle and towncar services, as well as to taxi service, to Portland and beyond, so ground transportation should be pain-free to find and easily arranged online or by phone.

> **i** The best bargain for transportation from PDX is the light-rail MAX line—just $2.50 for a ride into the center of Downtown Portland.

Rental Cars

For car rentals at the airport, go to the parking garage's first floor. The on-site agencies include **Avis Rent-A-Car,** (503) 249-4950, **Dollar Rent-A-Car,** (503) 249-4793, **Hertz Rent-A-Car,** (503) 249-8216, **Enterprise,** (503) 252-1500, and **National,** (503) 249-4900. Agencies that have shuttle service to PDX include **Alamo,** (503) 249-4900, **Advantage,** (503) 284-6064, **Budget,** (503) 249-6331, and **Thrifty,** (503) 254-6563.

Once you've left the airport, it should take 20 to 30 minutes to reach downtown, and there are clear directions to the freeways from the airport access roads. Airport traffic is funneled onto I-205. To reach downtown, you will take I-205 South to the I-84 West exit. Follow I-84 to I-5, where you should follow the signs to City Center. When you return to the airport, take the Airport Way

> **i** Oregon is one of two states in the country that prohibit self-serve gas stations. Don't try to fill your tank yourself, or irate attendants will descend upon you. Unfortunately, our laws do not mandate oil checks or cleaning of windshields; these you may have to do yourself.

West exit off I-205, which leads directly to the airport terminal, the car rental lots, and hotels on the airport's property.

Arriving by Train

AMTRAK AT UNION STATION, 800 Northwest 6th Ave., Portland, OR 97209; (503) 273-4865 (station information), (503) 273-4866 (daily arrival and departure information), (800) 872-7245 (reservations and schedule information); amtrakcascades.com. One of Portland's most charming, classic views is Union Station, with its brick clock tower that has been keeping the trains on time since the 1890s. Because Union Station is part of the downtown Portland transit mall, you can take a bus or MAX train from the train station to downtown Portland with supreme ease.

Arriving by Interstate Bus

GREYHOUND LINES, 550 NW 6th Ave., Portland, OR 97209; (503) 243-2361, (800) 231-2222; greyhound.com. Portland's Greyhound Lines bus station is a clean and modern terminal on the far northern end of the city's transit mall adjacent to Amtrak's Union Station, both of which are a short walk from downtown. Greyhound is the only transcontinental bus line serving Portland. The Greyhound terminal is connected with city buses and the MAX line.

BOLT BUS, boarding at 647 SW Salmon St., Portland, OR 97205; (877) 265-8287; boltbus.com. This comfortable and modern bus line runs between Portland and Seattle multiple times each day, and between Portland and Vancouver, B.C., with stops in Bellingham, WA, and Seattle, twice daily. The trip to Seattle takes a little over three hours; the wireless access will keep you entertained for the duration, and your blood pressure will not go up when you hit Tacoma, as it would if you were driving.

Arriving by Car

Bear in mind a few things as you travel the city. The downtown area is laid on a grid of one-way streets, so look carefully before making a turn lest you find yourself heading straight into traffic. The major southbound street is Broadway; the major northbound street is 4th Avenue; 10th and 11th Avenues are also important north- and southbound streets. Naito Parkway runs along the Willamette River; it permits both north- and southbound traffic. Important eastbound streets are Market, Alder, and Columbia; westbound arterials include Clay, Washington, and Jefferson. Burnside allows both east- and westbound traffic, but the places where you are allowed to make a left turn off Burnside are rare in the downtown area.

Two major streets, 6th Avenue and 5th Avenue, are the arterials for the bus and light rail system downtown, making up a large component of the transit mall. This is helpful to know if you're driving downtown because you must be alert to the traffic markings. Some blocks along these streets are for mass transit only, some blocks allow cars, and some blocks funnel cars right into "turn only" lanes. Car drivers should also pay attention to the signs that warn you not to turn on red lights, because these signs prevent cars from being hit by MAX trains. Furthermore, you must allow buses the right-of-way if you are driving behind them and they are signaling to pull into traffic. A flashing red YIELD sign on the bus will let you know if you are hogging the road illegally.

You should know a few other important streets and highways in the area. I-205, the freeway that takes you to the airport, will also take you south around the eastern edge of the city of Portland to communities such as Oregon City and West Linn before it reconnects with I-5 just south of Lake Oswego. To the north, I-205 takes you across the Columbia River into Washington State, hooking up with I-5 north of Vancouver. SRs 99E and 99W are also critical roads. They are the eastern and western sides of SR 99, the principal thorough-fare of Oregon before I-5 was built, which splits in two just north of Eugene. The directions "W" and "E" designate which side of the Willamette River you are on. South of Portland, SR 99W is also called the West Pacific Highway, but in the city limits it has several names. In order, from south to north, they are Barbur Boulevard, Naito Parkway, and, when it finally crosses the Willamette again, North Interstate Avenue. Similarly, the East Pacific Highway, 99E, is also called McLoughlin Boulevard from Oregon City until just north of the Ross Island Bridge. At that point, SR 99E splits into a northbound arterial called Grand Avenue and a southbound arterial called Martin Luther King Jr. Bou-levard (or MLK). These two rejoin north of Broadway to form Martin Luther King Jr. Boulevard. Both SR 99W and 99E merge into I-5 immediately south of the Columbia River.

Driving east and west over the hills that divide the city from the western suburbs can present some difficulties. The main route, US 26, is responsible for some of the worst traffic in the city, just west of downtown, where it is called the Sunset Highway. This is the principal highway between downtown Port-land and the west side of the metro region, and it gets backed up in the Sunset Tunnel, which takes cars under the west side of the hills, backed up again as it climbs the Sylvan Pass, and backed up yet again at the interchange with SR 217. To travel east and west, you might try a couple of alternative routes. Burn-side will take you over the hill into Beaverton from downtown; when it splits in two, follow Southwest Barnes Road to SR 217. The Beaverton-Hillsdale Highway, or SR 10, can be a good choice; you can also take I-5 south to SR 99W or to SR 217. But all these routes will present the driver with traffic, and they might take you well out of your way.

Another caveat: US 26 turns into a business route when it hits downtown Portland's west side. To follow it east through town, on your way to Mount Hood, for instance, you must be attentive to the signs that direct you toward the Ross Island Bridge, where the highway turns into Powell Boulevard for miles until it passes through the eastern Multnomah County town of Sandy and becomes a proper highway again.

Broadway can also be confusing because it extends from Northeast Portland (where it is called "Northeast Broadway") across the Broadway Bridge to downtown Portland, where it is technically named "Southwest Broadway." But nobody calls it that—downtowners call it just plain "Broadway." While Broadway passes through downtown, it takes the place of 7th Avenue, so you will find it between 6th and 8th Avenues. And after it passes through downtown, it turns into Broadway Drive. Look carefully at the street address of your destination.

Portland's Bridges

Portland is a city of bridges: More than 10 span the Willamette River, from the St. Johns Bridge at the north end to the Sellwood Bridge at the south. Because Portland is a deepwater port, the five bridges in the heart of downtown are drawbridges, letting large ships pass through. Our bridges are a distinctive feature of our cityscape—but you will need to know how to negotiate them. You may also notice a new bridge under construction south of the Ross Island bridge; that is a planned light rail and bicycle bridge scheduled to open in 2015.

Here are Portland's bridges, from north to south.

The St. Johns Bridge links outer Northwest Portland with the North Portland community of St. Johns.

The Fremont Bridge carries traffic from I-405 and US 30 to I-5.

The Broadway Bridge extends Broadway across the river from Northeast Portland to downtown.

The Steel Bridge has two decks: The lower accommodates Amtrak and freight trains, as well as cyclists and pedestrians, while the upper deck carries light rail, trucks, and cars.

The Burnside Bridge is the conduit for car and pedestrian traffic along Burnside, one of the city's most important streets.

The Hawthorne Bridge—a popular route for pedestrians and cyclists—is Portland's oldest.

The Morrison Bridge links downtown and the east side with entrances to I-5 northbound and exits to downtown and the east side for commuters traveling south on I-5.

The Hawthorne Bridge connects downtown and Southeast Portland and it's a designated bike bridge. On the east side of the river, the Hawthorne Bridge leads to Hawthorne Boulevard, but on the west side, Hawthorne turns into Main and Madison Streets.

The Marquam Bridge carries I-5 traffic across the Willamette.

The Ross Island Bridge carries US 26 over the Willamette, connecting to Arthur Street on the west side and to Powell Boulevard on the east. The westside approach, which connects to Barbur Boulevard, SR 43, and Arthur Street, can be confusing.

The Sellwood Bridge allows just two lanes of traffic to flow from SR 43 on the west side to the Portland neighborhood of Sellwood on the east side.

Road Safety and Regulations

Oregon law requires you to drive according to the conditions, regardless of the posted speed, so bear that in mind. Driving on the freeways through Oregon rain requires particular attention. At higher speeds, hydroplaning on a sheet of water can occur, and stopping distances stretch when roads get wet. Please don't drink and drive. If your trip calls for a visit to wine country and a tasting of the vintages, take along a designated driver or limit your imbibing. It is illegal to have an open container of an alcoholic beverage in your vehicle. Distractions should be kept to a minimum. It is illegal to operate a motor vehicle while using a mobile communication device—phone or text—unless you have a hands-free adapter. Both hands, in other words, must be kept on the wheel.

In Oregon, bicyclists have an equal legal right to the road, and drivers of motorized vehicles are required to stay out of marked bicycle lanes. Special green pavement markings alert drivers to places where they must be particularly watchful of bicycle right-of-way. It is legal for motorized wheelchairs to travel in bike lanes. And in downtown Portland you'll also find marked skateboard routes; you'll need to share the road with them too.

Parking

Parking on downtown streets during business hours takes some patience. Meters generally cost $1.60 per hour and allow parking for periods of time between 15 minutes and 5 hours. Cars are frequently monitored to make sure drivers don't overstay their welcome. Parking after 7 p.m. is free in most areas, but in some—for example, near the Rose Quarter and at the Convention Center—metered hours extend to as late as 10 p.m. The meter will indicate the hours of enforcement. Portland was an early adopter of SmartMeter stations, so you will find few coin-operated meters. These central pay station machines work by issuing paper stubs that you adhere to your curbside window. The SmartMeters are convenient; you can pay with coins or with debit or credit cards.

Municipal parking garages are an alternative to on-street meters. There are six clearly marked Smart Park garages in downtown Portland, where parking is $1.60 an hour for the first two hours. On the weekend you can park at Smart Park for $4 to $6 for the whole evening when entering after 6 p.m. Many downtown merchants will validate your Smart Park ticket for two hours of free parking if you spend $25 or more in their stores. Private garages are also an option, of course.

Public Transportation

TRIMET, (503) 238-RIDE (trip information); trimet.org. TriMet is Portland's award-winning mass transit system, comprising the bus, light-rail, and streetcar systems, and it is noted for its efficiency, comprehensiveness, and accommodation. Operating in three counties (Multnomah, Washington, and Clackamas), TriMet's buses are scheduled on routes that cover almost 600 square miles. The downtown transit mall extends all the way to Union Station for connections to Amtrak and to Greyhound bus service. You will pay $2.50 for an adult fare, which is good for 2 hours and on any part of the transit system: bus, MAX, or streetcar. Keep your ticket or transfer; it serves as a receipt, and the drivers will check. On the bus and streetcar, unless the rider has a pass or transfer, fares are paid upon boarding, but on MAX, they must be purchased and validated before boarding. MAX tickets are available from machines at every station. After you purchase your ticket but just before you get on the train, insert your ticket into the validator machines at the MAX stops. These machines stamp your ticket with the date and time. Bus drivers cannot give you change, so exact fare is needed—or you can download an app and pay with your smartphone (trimet.org/mobiletickets/index.htm).

Fares are discounted for senior citizens and youth. Children 6 and younger ride for free. A day ticket ($5) can also be used on buses, streetcars, and light rail, and you can also get discounted fares if you buy weekly or monthly passes. These passes are widely available throughout the city at many drugstores, grocery stores, and bookstores. The TriMet website has a comprehensive list of outlets.

MAX has four lines: the Blue Line, which runs east and west between Gresham and Hillsboro via downtown Portland; the Red Line, which runs from the Beaverton Transit Center through downtown to the airport; the Yellow Line, which travels north and south between downtown and the Expo Center, along Interstate Avenue to Portland State University; and the Green Line, which runs from Portland State University east to Clackamas Town Center. Trains run approximately every 15 minutes. In addition, the WES (Westside Express Service) commuter line links Wilsonville, Tigard, Tualatin, and Beaverton with downtown Portland and beyond. It runs each weekday in the morning and afternoon, every 30 minutes.

In addition to light rail, Portland also has a streetcar system with two lines: the Central Loop line, which travels from Southwest 10th and Clay to Southeast Water at the Oregon Museum of Science & Industry, and the North-South line, which extends from Good Samaritan Hospital in Northwest Portland to the South Waterfront district in Southwest Portland. Both lines travel via Portland State University. Streetcars stop every 2 to 3 blocks—although to disembark, you must push the yellow strip to let the driver know you want off—and they run from 5:30 a.m. to 11 p.m. Mon through Thurs and until 11:45 p.m. on Fri. Sat hours are from 7:15 a.m. to 11:45 p.m. and Sun from 7:15 a.m. to 10:30 p.m. They arrive every 12 to 15 minutes during peak hours and a bit less frequently at other times. Well-marked, glass-covered streetcar stops, however, are equipped with electronic screens that helpfully note when the next streetcar will arrive. If you are only riding the streetcar, you can purchase a ticket for $1 at any streetcar station or from the machine on board (note that the machines on the trains themselves take cash only—$1s, $5s, and coins). If you already bought a bus or MAX ticket, then your streetcar fare is covered. Streetcars are technically owned and operated by the City of Portland, not TriMet, but they have been integrated so seamlessly that you should not really know the difference.

The bus lines are the heart of the TriMet system. Bus routes vary in frequency and in how early and how long each bus travels its route, but during peak times on the most traveled routes, buses run at least every 15 minutes if not more often. Schedules for individual bus lines and the light-rail lines are free and commonly available at banks, stores, post offices, bookstores, and dozens of other locations, or accessible on the web at trimet.org. But TriMet was also an early adopter of computer tracking; their "transit tracker" service (tri met.org/arrivals/index.html) allows you to check real-time arrivals for any bus from your desktop or laptop—a real blessing on rainy winter evenings. They have also made this system available to app developers, who have responded with much creativity, so you can download free apps for tracking, route planning, and other useful information from the TriMet website.

All bus stops are marked by blue and white signs displaying the route numbers of the buses serving that line. Many are well lit, with covered bus shelters to protect you from the rain and wind, but not all stops are so well equipped. On the transit mall, there are more elaborate shelters with route maps and video screens displaying information and arrival times for the next bus. The system is divided into regions, designated by regional symbols; these symbols mark service to specific areas from the transit mall. Be observant when boarding buses: Those marked with an "X" or "L" are express buses that most commonly run during commute hours. After leaving the transit mall, they will stop only at major stops until they reach a local transit center. Most drivers are very careful to announce that they are driving an express route. If in doubt, ask. TriMet's drivers, with rare exception, are courteous and knowledgeable and recognize the long-term value of being helpful to all riders.

PORTLAND AERIAL TRAM, 3303 SW Bond Ave., Portland, OR 97239; (503) 865-8726; portlandtram.org. The Portland Aerial Tram ferries passengers from the South Waterfront up to Oregon Health & Science University on Marquam Hill, 3,300 feet above, offering splendiferous views of Mount Hood,

The Portland Aerial Tram connects Oregon Health and Science University with the South Waterfront district.

Mount St. Helens, and the city. Tickets cost $4, though children age 6 and under ride for free, as do patients, visitors, and employees of OHSU. The tram operates weekdays from 5:30 a.m. to 9:30 p.m., on Sat from 9 a.m. to 5 p.m., and on Sun from mid-May through mid-Sept from 1 to 5 p.m. It's closed on legal holidays.

C-TRAN, 2425 NE 65th Ave., Vancouver, WA, 98661; (360) 695-0123; c-tran.com. C-Tran is the bus service for Vancouver and Clark County, Washington. By arrangement with TriMet, C-Tran also offers service across the Columbia River to downtown Portland. To get from Vancouver to Portland, the ticket price is $3.50. C-Tran and TriMet honor many of one another's tickets, so a TriMet ticket can be used on C-Tran local and limited bus routes; an exception is the Portland Express; the fare for this convenient trip is $3.50.

Taxis

Portland, Oregon, isn't New York City or Washington, DC, where taxis are a way of urban life. Good luck trying to flag one from the corner: They will rarely, if ever, stop. However, you can telephone for one. Fares start at $2.50 and go up $2.60 per mile; you'll also pay an extra $1 per additional passenger and a gate fee of $2.50 if you are going to or from the airport. Cab fare from the airport to downtown for two passengers and their luggage should run a little over $30. Portland cab companies include the following:

Broadway Cab, (503) 227-1234

Green Cab, (503) 252-4422

New Rose City Cab, (503) 282-7707

Portland Taxi, (503) 256-5400

Radio Cab, (503) 227-1212

Sharing a Car

Portland is a great city for those who like to walk, bike, or use public transportation. Yet even if you have liberated yourself from car ownership, you may find yourself needing to use a car occasionally. That's where car sharing comes in, and in Portland, we have three different options: **Zipcar** (zipcar .com) and **Car2go** (car2go.com/en/portland), which are cooperatives that allow members access to cars across the city, distributing the cost and hassle of owning a car among all its members, and personal car sharing. With both ZipCar and Car2Go, members are charged for time they use the cars and, in the case of ZipCar the number of miles they drive them, portioning the fees for insurance, gas, repair, and cleaning among everyone. ZipCar has hundreds of cars, trucks, minivans, and even cute Mini Coopers and other sportscars are available all day, every day, at specific locations around town. To use a car, you call ahead to make a reservation, pick up the car at the designated spot, and return it to the same location at the time you have arranged. Car2go is a "point to point" car sharing service: you are charged by the minute but you don't have to return the car to the same location, and there are no late fees. The catch is that you drive your Car2go vehicle, usually a tiny electric Smart-Car, to your destination and then leave it for the next person who needs it, which might be you or someone else. Fortunately, there are enough of these vehicles around so that you can find another one nearby. Finally, there is personal car sharing: The California-based Getaround (getaround.com/pdx) established a Portland outpost in 2012. This peer-to-peer rental company allows you to rent your neighbor's car (or rent out your car to your neighbors) by the day or the hour.

Bicycling & Skateboarding

More and more people are riding their bikes in Portland, and many of these people are commuters. The city estimates that nearly 15,000 bicycles cross the Hawthorne Bridge each day, compared with 200 in 1975—representing almost 20 percent of all vehicles that cross the bridge. Cyclists are allowed on most of Portland's downtown bridges. The city—which has developed a comprehensive Bicycle Master Plan—has established nearly 200 miles of bikeways that include both off-street paths and bike lanes along streets. Special blue zones warn motorists that cyclists have the right-of-way in these lanes and that cars must yield to bikes when cars are attempting to turn a corner. Bright green boxes painted on the pavement at intersections tell drivers that bikes have the right of way. Such attention to bicycle riding has earned Portland accolades across the nation, and it is routinely touted as an unusually bike-friendly big city, likely the most bicycle-friendly urban area in the country.

Portland has a vigorous city-sponsored bicycle office. Check them out online at portlandonline.com/transportation. This office can provide maps and other information about bike routes, bike parking, safety, and commuting. The City of Portland Bicycle Program continues to expand and improve

A 4-story mural in downtown Portland proudly claims our status as Bicycle City USA.

the region's network of bike paths, and they have posted signs all over town that tell cyclists how far, and in which direction, their destinations are. Bike storage lockers may be found in many parts of the city, and all TriMet's buses and MAX light-rail trains are equipped with bike racks. Portland's reputation is in part due to the efforts of the Bicycle Transportation Alliance (BTA), founded in 1990. This advocacy organization works closely with city planners to make walking, biking, and even driving safer and more sustainable for everyone. BTA may be reached at (503) 226-0676 or by visiting their informative website, bta4bikes.org.

Bicyclists aren't the only ones using human-powered wheels to get to work, school, and beyond. Skateboarders have joined them, having won a victory in 2001, when the city of Portland allowed them access to downtown and added their rights and responsibilities to the bicycle code. Now that skateboarding has become decriminalized, preferred skateboard routes have been designated, which you will find on green signs throughout the 200 blocks of downtown. Those who wish to ride their skateboards through town must follow a few strictly enforced rules: They must wear helmets if they are younger than 16, and they must wear lights at night, among other things. And tempting though it is, they must refrain from skating on the sidewalks. To learn more about biking and skateboarding in the Portland area, see the Recreation section in the Kids chapter.

Walking

Walking in Portland is one of the city's chief pleasures. Miles of paths line the waterfront, inviting pedestrians to ramble. Not only is the downtown area clean and well maintained, but the little villagelike neighborhoods that make up the city encourage residents to walk to the store, the bank, the library, dinner, even work. The city has found that promoting foot traffic is a smart business move, and neighborhoods that feature services and retail that are easily accessible by foot have high property values in Portland. If you're thinking of relocating, you might consider the walking potential of any prospective neighborhoods by visiting Walk Score (walkscore.com). You might even find a great job in your own neighborhood and be able to walk to work.

History

But for the toss of a coin, you might be reading the Insiders' Guide to Boston, Oregon. Early settlers Asa Lovejoy and William Overton brought their canoe ashore at a clearing in the woods along the Willamette River. Both men agreed that it looked like a promising site for a town. But Overton, a drifter from Tennessee, lacked the 25 cents he needed to file a land claim. So he struck a deal with Lovejoy: They would share the 640-acre site if Lovejoy would put up the money, and the two filed a claim in 1842. But Overton tired of the pioneer's life, and he sold his half of the claim to Francis Pettygrove. By 1845 the settlement in the clearing in the woods had grown enough so that it demanded a name. Pettygrove, a native of Maine, favored the name Portland, while Lovejoy, who was from Massachussets, preferred Boston. The two men agreed to settle the matter by flipping a penny. Pettygrove won, and you can still see the "Portland Penny" on permanent display at the Oregon History Center.

EARLY HISTORY

Of course, the story of Portland and the surrounding area begins thousands of years before these 19th-century events, and well before Europeans ever touched Oregon's shores. Historians believe that the first Native Americans, including the Klamath, Modock, Bannock, Nez Perce, and Chinook tribes, came to Oregon between 10,000 and 12,000 years ago. The coastal tribes relied heavily on abundant salmon, shellfish, seals, and the occasional stranded whale. The tribes farther inland lived on game and altered the landscape as they burned forests and grasslands to attract their prey. The Native Americans that lived in the area that would become Portland—the Kalapuyas, the Clackamas, the Molalla, the Tualatin, the Chinook, the Multnomah, and the Wapato, among others—had sophisticated, multifaceted cultures well supported by the area's abundance. Many of the tribes were quite wealthy. Some of these groups were river tribes, who built large dwellings along the Willamette, Clackamas, Pudding, and other rivers. Other tribes—the Molalla, for instance—lived farther upland, in the foothills of the Cascades. The Molalla were a more nomadic hunting tribe, riding horses east and north toward the Columbia.

While there were occasional conflicts among these different groups, it was largely a peaceful region, with little war. Instead, these tribes had elaborate networks of trade, both within and among all the tribes in the region, as well as with the Eastern trappers who began to show up in the early 19th century. They had a lot to trade too. Though these tribes did not plant crops, many engaged in protoagricultural practices. For example, they burned the grassy fields to harvest grasshoppers, to flush out camas seed, and to ensure the health of the meadows. Division and specialization of labor was common, as were advanced systems for storing the roots, berries, nuts, elk, bear, and salmon that they gathered, hunted, and fished. And much legend and ritual were dedicated to thanksgiving and appreciation for all that the gods had given them in this beautiful place. Hundreds of thousands of people lived here for 10,000 years before Eastern settlers had ever heard of the place, dwelling in villages large and small, speaking a variety of languages, living out their own histories.

The first European to see the Oregon coast was probably Juan Rodriguez Cabrillo, a Spanish sea captain who attempted to map the Pacific coast in 1543; however, he did not set foot on land. Sir Francis Drake is said to have had that honor in 1579 when he claimed the area for England in the name of Queen Elizabeth. That claim, however, was hollow, for it would be another 200 years before the next English vessel reached Oregon. Numerous European ships landed on the Oregon coast in the late 16th century and the early 17th century; however, those expeditions revealed little about the inland regions. By 1750 Russian trappers had worked their way down through Alaska and Canada to the Oregon shoreline in search of otter, but they did not establish a colony, choosing instead to build Fort Ross along the northern California coast in 1812. In fact, no less than four nations laid claim to Oregon—Spain, Russia, Britain, and the United States—but not one built a single settlement to signify a legal presence.

In 1788 John Meares sailed right past the mouth of the Columbia River, and in 1792 Captain George Vancouver also missed it, leaving the second largest river in the United States to be discovered by Captain Robert Gray of Boston, who named it after his vessel, the USS *Columbia*.

The Lewis & Clark Expedition

President Thomas Jefferson planned a secret mission in 1803: to send a small party of men overland to the Pacific—a bold venture that no one before had attempted. Congress covertly approved the trip, along with its budget of $2,500, because these explorers would be venturing outside US jurisdiction into British territory. Jefferson was looking for an expeditious water route to the Pacific via the Missouri River, its tributaries, and a legendary River of the West said to flow down from the Rockies to the Pacific, hoping that the distance between the east- and west-flowing rivers would be a one-day portage. It would be a simple route west for traders, emigrants, and adventurers.

Jefferson also charged the group with collecting scientific information about the region's interior.

President Jefferson chose his neighbor, longtime friend, and personal secretary, Meriwether Lewis, to lead the contingent across the Louisiana Purchase and to the Pacific coast. Lewis, in turn, wisely selected frontiersman and mapmaker William Clark to be his coleader.

In the spring of 1804, Lewis and Clark, along with 31 men and the intrepid Newfoundland hound, Seaman, left St. Louis and started up the Missouri River heading west. Over the next two years the group—eventually christened the "Corps of Discovery"—would traverse present-day Missouri, Nebraska, the Dakotas, Montana, Wyoming, Washington, and Oregon. The journey took so long that the few insiders

Portland's history is revealed in architectural details throughout the city.

who knew about it feared that the members of the expedition had perished. But on December 5, 1805, Lewis and Clark reached the Pacific Ocean and Clark wrote in his diary, "We now discover that we have found the most practicable and navigable passage across the continent of North America."

The route discovered by Lewis and Clark was too difficult for others to follow. In fact, Lolo Pass, where their expedition crossed the treacherous Bitterroot Mountains in western Montana, is a rough haul even today—two centuries later. But because their detailed maps and notes provided a wealth of scientific data, the West was no longer an uncharted mystery, and their expedition was celebrated as a success. Although they examined only a small portion of the Northwest Coast and the Columbia River, they gathered much valuable and accurate information about the rest of the Northwest from friendly native peoples. Their reports stirred excitement in the East; their vivid descriptions of a land of bounty created an "Oregon fever" among fur traders who had previously trapped and traded in the Rocky Mountains.

The Fur Trade & Fort Vancouver

The second major westward expedition was not funded by a government but was backed by one of the world's richest men—John Jacob Astor, who whetted his appetite for adventure by reading about Lewis and Clark's journey. By 1810 Astor saw an opportunity to make a new fortune: a fur-trading enterprise at the mouth of the Columbia River. In 1811 he dispatched an overland party to follow the trail of the early explorers and to establish trading posts. He also sent another party there by sea, in a ship traveling around Cape Horn. The ship arrived safely but was destroyed afterward in a skirmish with Native Americans.

John Jacob Astor's Pacific Fur Company did eventually establish a presence in the area, but it was not as great as that of its competitor: the Hudson's Bay Company, run by the British. The Hudson's Bay Company, established in 1670, was an experienced operation. It had many outposts west of the Rocky Mountains from Alaska to Mexico. But supplying them was expensive and difficult (as Astor too discovered). Thus, the company decided to build a settlement that could sustain itself and perhaps produce enough surplus to furnish other outposts in the West, reducing the need for the costly ships that the company used to bring supplies to its people.

The Columbia River is central to Portland's history—and the history of the west.

In 1825 the Hudson's Bay Company sent Dr. John McLoughlin to build a fortified settlement along the Columbia: Fort Vancouver, on the north side of the river. Its location was ideal—it was close enough to the sea that it could receive trading ships and send them back laden with pelts, and it was on a beautiful, richly soiled plain well out of the dangers of annual flooding.

Fort Vancouver became the administrative site and supply depot for the Columbia Department of the Hudson's Bay Company. Mills were built for processing lumber and grain. Barrel-makers, bakers, and blacksmiths were hired and brought to the fort. Schools and churches were formed, and a hospital was built and maintained. By the time the first pioneers stumbled out of the mountains in 1842, Western civilization was well established.

McLoughlin was the chief administrator of Fort Vancouver for nearly 20 years, and without him, it is hard to say how the American pioneers would have fared. McLoughlin was a fascinating figure. He had good relations with the native peoples, and his principled administration was admired by many, though—like that of any good administrator—it was not without controversy. He enforced the company policy of protecting its interests while respecting the trade-friendly Native Americans and making no attempt to convert them into Europeans. But the American emigrants were a different story: They posed a direct threat to the comfortable monopoly that the Hudson's Bay Company enjoyed. McLoughlin was dismayed by them, yet he could not keep them out, since the legal claim of the British to the territory had not been established. At the same time, he felt compelled to help the pioneers as they arrived, sick and starving. His solution was to attempt to bring them into the fur trade, and to this end, he helped these emigrants establish themselves in the Willamette Valley, a difficult choice that was often in conflict with his duties to the Hudson's Bay Company.

No good deed ever goes unpunished, and McLoughlin's good deeds were no exception. He wisely governed Fort Vancouver; he was respected by the native nations; he had helped hundreds of pioneers; he was a prudent and farsighted steward. Naturally, then, he developed new political opponents once the territorial dispute was resolved, in 1846; they convinced the US Congress to block any claim to land that he had cultivated for more than 30 years. He died in sorrow and in poverty in 1857. Later Oregonians regretted his treatment, restoring some of the property to his heirs in 1862. In 1953, Oregonians sent a statue of John McLoughlin to represent the state in the National Statuary Hall Collection in the United States Capitol in Washington, DC, officially recognizing his contributions.

AGE OF PIONEERS

Explorers who followed Lewis and Clark, such as John Frémont, were often so upbeat that they made the trip west seem easy and enjoyable, which it definitely was not. They were encouraged in their reports by the US government, who wanted to make sure these resource-rich lands stayed out of the hands of the Russians and the British.

Oregon Trail

Driving this great movement was more than just positive reports. In 1843 the federal government allotted 640 acres of land to every adult homesteader and 160 acres to every child, with hopes of anchoring the United States' claims to the Northwest Territories. Most of those who came as far west as Oregon made the land trip. However, some came by water and did so even before a land route was established. The sea route never was a popular choice, though. The fare was costly, and most westward-bound pioneers came from central states far from seaports. Also, the sea journey often took up to a full year compared with the wagon journey, which took five to eight months.

The first organized party of emigrants to actually reach the Oregon Territory came with the American pioneer physician Elijah White. Under the leadership of John Bidwell, an Ohio schoolteacher, this group loaded their wagons and left Missouri in 1841 and in 1842 reached Oregon. The terminus of their journey was the future site of Oregon City; later settlers would head for the verdant Willamette Valley. During the 1840s thousands of pioneers settled there, where wheat, fruits, and vegetables thrived. Others settled higher up, for gold prospecting and to harvest Oregon's bountiful supply of Douglas fir trees.

The Oregon Trail directed the flow of westward expansion and permitted the settlement and development of the Pacific Northwest. Before the completion of the first transcontinental railroad in 1870, an estimated 350,000 pioneers followed the Oregon Trail westward, more than all the other routes combined.

In Oregon, the trail's route has remained a principal course of east-west travel to the present day, though it lies buried beneath I-84. The road crosses a diverse range of terrain—the rugged Blue Mountains in northeastern Oregon, the dry plateaus between Pendleton and The Dalles, the Cascade Mountains and Columbia Gorge section, and even the geographic end of the trail in Oregon City, where the Willamette Valley settlements all began.

> **i** Of the estimated 350,000 settlers who migrated west on the Oregon Trail, at least 20,000 died en route. Cholera was the most common cause of death.

PORTLAND'S EARLY DAYS

As the Native American way of life was disappearing, the settlers were busy creating a new one. Gradually the Oregon Territory began to acquire the sheen

> **i** Oregon's pioneering spirit extends to many areas. Among other firsts, it was the first state to officially register all its voters, the first to elect US senators directly, the first to create an initiative system—and in case none of the above worked out—the first to develop a system for recalling public officials.

of Western civilization. A pristine tract of forestland in 1844, Portland boasted 821 residents by 1850, making it the region's most populous community. Mail arrived by steamship, which took the route around Cape Horn, and was distributed to the 40 post offices in the area. And thanks to the vision of New England sailor Captain John Couch, who chose Portland over Oregon City as a deepwater harbor for his shipping, the city soon became known as a port deserving its name.

The city gained its most enduring nickname in 1889 when local artist, writer, and bon vivant C. E. S. Woods called for an annual rose show. The Portland Rose Festival was launched that year in what would soon be known as the "City of Roses."

The Lewis & Clark Centennial Exposition

Lewis and Clark shaped Portland long after they departed the quiet native trails that lined the Columbia. Portland derives much of its appearance—even today—from the successful, extensive world's fair held here in 1905 to celebrate the 100-year anniversary of their expedition. The Lewis and Clark Exposition drew thousands of visitors to Portland and precipitated an economic boom, accompanied by a wave of building and development, especially in Northwest and Southwest Portland. Hotels and other civic buildings were constructed to capitalize on the wave of visitors. Few of the fair's actual structures remain—most of them were dismantled, and more than a few burned down. The fair's buildings were beautiful but not designed to last. Yet the hotels, department stores, and other pavilions that were built throughout the city remain today, furnishing the architectural bones of the city.

The Lewis and Clark Exposition also changed the appearance of the nation: It was here that plywood was introduced.

THE WAR YEARS

World War II forever altered the shape of the Portland area. Henry J. Kaiser's Oregon Shipbuilding Corporation began building freighters of the famous Liberty Ship class when World War II was less than a month old. The first Kaiser shipyard in the Portland area was the St. Johns Yard. At the end of one year, it launched 36 ships. By war's end, the yard had built 141 vessels, including Liberty Ships and their successor, the Victory Ship.

> **i** Lone Fir Cemetery, on Southeast 20th between Morrison and Stark, holds the earthly remains of early Portlanders. These Oregonians—some with important historical names, some with ignominious ones—lie side by side, speaking eloquently of our common fate.

The Rise & Fall of Vanport

Portland's new residents included large numbers of emigrants from the deep South. They arrived by the trainload, lured away from poverty and oppression to work in the wartime shipyards of Henry Kaiser. Between 1940 and 1945 Portland's African-American population surged from 2,100 to 15,000.

The state was not always hospitable to minorities, and over the course of its history had created laws limiting the freedoms of everyone who wasn't white and Protestant. But the war efforts and the workers needed to sustain them created a dilemma. Henry Kaiser was busy building the Liberty Ships for the war effort, yet these new workers had nowhere to live. The sudden increase in population strained the city's ability to meet even the most basic needs of these war workers. The city authorities in Portland dragged their feet, not wanting to create housing for this influx of workers—who might then decide to stay. So Kaiser went around the city authorities and applied the same rapid building techniques to housing war workers as he did to making warships, assembling practically overnight the city of Vanport, just outside the city limits of Portland. It was built to sustain the workers, including providing for their families: It had schools, medical clinics, shops, even 24-hour day care, since many of Kaiser's employees were women with children. Nearly 70,000 workers and their families lived in this city. The major drawback was that it was built on a flat floodplain between the Willamette and Columbia Rivers.

Rapidly, Vanport became the state's second-largest city. Three years after the war, about 19,000 people still lived there. On Memorial Day, 1948, the rivers, swollen by rain and melting snow, broke the dikes protecting Vanport and swept the town away, killing 18 people. The city's entire population, then about one-fourth African American, became homeless.

Vanport was never rebuilt and today West Delta Park stands on the site of this former community.

POSTWAR PROSPERITY

War's end brought more changes to Portland and Oregon. Returning veterans enrolled in large numbers at colleges, started families, and bought houses. During the postwar years, Portland prospered, like most of the nation. Wood products and fisheries filled the state's coffers in the postwar building boom, and Portland, as the major city in Oregon, benefited greatly. In the late 1960s and early 1970s, Republican governor Tom McCall, a true visionary, guided the state through a challenging phase by making controlled growth and environmental protection the top priorities of state government. One of his many important achievements was to lead a controversial but farsighted legislative effort to keep the coastline open to the public—an effort significantly contributing to making Oregon the tourist mecca that it is today.

"The past is not dead. It isn't even past," observed William Faulkner. He was talking about the American South, but it's also true in Portland, even in ways that we may not notice. We drive down McLoughlin or Pettygrove, we visit the Multnomah or Clackamas County libraries, we rush by an old pioneer cemetery or restored farmhouse from the 19th century, but rarely do we give thought to the people who walked here before us—pioneer, fur trader, or Native American. Yet our lips echo with their names and our feet tread the same earth. Their spirits live on.

The clock tower of the historic Portland Telegram *building, an evening paper established by magnate Henry Pittock*

Accommodations

Visitors to Portland will find a variety of accommodations, from the basic to the sublime. They range in style, in price, and in location, but no matter where you plan to stay, you should be able to find a place to lay your head and suit your needs. You will find certain chains well represented throughout the Portland Metro area. We figure you know about these reliable places already, so in this guide we have concentrated on the standouts in the area, including some in these chains where appropriate. We also focus on the hotels in the center of town, but we've included some options for other parts of town as well. Do note that the area around the Convention Center and Lloyd Center has large Doubletree and Holiday Inns that are well attended and host many meetings and events.

As Portland's star as a destination for tourism rises, new hotels, guesthouses, and vacation rental services have arrived to meet the demand for rooms. Many of these, but not all, are found downtown. Not surprisingly, it is expensive to park your car downtown, where hotels charge about $30 per day. Some hotels do offer free parking for guests. Some provide valet parking at their own facilities or nearby garages; others offer their guests discounted parking at local garages. Parking outside of the downtown area is less expensive. Whether you stay downtown or elsewhere in Portland, however, you may not need a car at all. Downtown is well served by the MAX line from the airport, the train station is a short cab ride to the downtown core, you can easily get around downtown by streetcar, and it may be simpler just to be car-free.

Price Code

The following price code for hotels, motels, and bed-and-breakfasts in this chapter is based on an average room rate for double occupancy during high season. While there is no sales tax in Oregon, there is a room tax of 12.5 percent.

$	Less than $90
$$	$90 to $150
$$$	$150 to $200
$$$$	More than $200

Please note that many hotels and motels change their room rates frequently, so the ranges we have quoted in this chapter are meant simply as a guide to point you in the right direction, not as the final word on the cost of

A view of downtown Portland's hotels and office buildings

your stay. Most hotels have a range of room prices; this code is meant to reflect a typical weekend rate for a double or queen room for two adults, unless otherwise noted.

Quick Index by Cost

$$$$

ACCOMMODATIONS

Vacation Rentals

With its renowned restaurants, proximity to the Willamette Valley wine country, and energetic cultural scene, Portland is becoming a vacation destination—and that means an emerging market for vacation rentals. Some good sources? Try Historic Hawthorne Rentals (historichawthornerentals .com) for its stylish eastside locations and longer-term rentals. Vacation Rentals by Owner (vrbo.com/vacation-rentals/usa/oregon) and the very popular Craigslist (portland.craigslist.org) are also reliable sources as well, though the former has more Portland-specific rentals. Consider renting in the Pearl District and skipping the car rental: You can easily get there via train or MAX; it's got terrific restaurants, shopping, nightlife, and even drop-in babysitting services; and it's well connected to the rest of the city by the streetcar.

ACE HOTEL, 1022 SW Stark St., Portland, OR 97205; (503) 228-2277; acehotel.com/portland; $$$. This Ace Hotel is very Portland, with an indie aesthetic and an attitude to match. It is named after the card, which can be either high or low; its stylish 79 rooms vary widely in standards of luxury. The Ace is going for something other than the standard hotel experience, so adjust your expectations accordingly—for example, you will not find free coffee or newspapers, though delicious coffee is available next door at the excellent Stumptown coffee shop. It may not be the ideal choice for a romantic honeymoon or a tense business trip, but it could be ideal for a weekend getaway with friends.

> **i** Try the Portland Visitors Association website for deals on hotel rooms and help with planning your meeting: travelportland.com.

THE BENSON HOTEL, 309 SW Broadway, Portland, OR 97205; (503) 228-2000, (888) 523-6766; bensonhotel.com; $$$$. A grand and historic Portland building, the Benson has been the hotel of choice for visiting US presidents and other dignitaries since 1912. Its builder, lumber baron Simon Benson, spared no expense, importing rare Circassian walnut paneling, Austrian crystal chandeliers, and Italian marble to adorn this beautiful hotel. This commitment to superior quality remains, and the Benson's furnishings and service offer a fine balance of warmth and elegance. Its downtown location is convenient to galleries, theaters, restaurants, and shopping, and the convention center is a short MAX ride away. Even if you don't stay here, drop by the lobby bar for a drink.

> **i** Traveling with Fido? The Ace Hotel, the Sheraton Four Points, and numerous others are proud to accommodate your dog. Some charge fees, while others do not: The Hotel Vintage Plaza and the Fifth Avenue Suites even have complimentary dog treats. For a list of more dog-friendly hotels in Oregon, visit Portland Pooch at portlandpooch.com.

ACCOMMODATIONS

EMBASSY SUITES PORTLAND DOWNTOWN, 319 SW Pine St., Portland, OR 97204; (503) 279-9000; embassysuites.com; $$$. The Embassy Suites is a beautiful, modern luxury hotel sited in the historic Multnomah Hotel. It offers guests 276 2-room suites. The east-facing rooms afford views of Mount Hood, 60 miles distant. A full breakfast and a nightly hosted manager's reception are included in the room rate. The building has a colorful history: It has served as an airport, twice. As part of the 1912 Rose Festival, Silas Christopherson flew his Curtiss pusher biplane off the hotel's roof. Then, in September 1995, when the building was being remodeled, pilot Tom Murphy, with permission from more than two dozen government agencies, duplicated the flight.

THE FULTON HOUSE, 7006 SW Virginia Ave., Portland, OR 97219; (503) 892-5781; thefultonhouse.com; $$$. The Fulton House offers 2 guest suites in a lovely 19th-century house near Willamette Park along the river, as well as near the Portland Aerial Tram. Breakfasts are served buffet style, and treats are offered every afternoon. The Fulton neighborhood is one of Portland's oldest—indeed, it used to be a separate town—and it is filled with pretty houses and cute shops, as well as offering plentiful, free, and safe street parking. Its proximity to the Willamette greenway means that it is well situated for walking and biking along the river, but it is just a few minutes' drive from all the downtown attractions as well.

THE GOVERNOR HOTEL, 614 SW 11th Ave., Portland, OR 97205; (503) 224-3400, (800) 554-3456; govhotel.com; $$$$. The historic Governor Hotel is an inviting luxury hotel rooted in the past but offering every modern convenience. In the lobby are early-20th-century murals depicting the travels of Lewis and Clark. The beautiful stained-glass dome in the adjacent restaurant captures the grandeur of the building, which is a National Historic Landmark. You'll find a Starbucks in the lobby, and just outside the door is the Portland Streetcar line. The Governor is ideally situated close to downtown shops, galleries, and restaurants. Jake's Bar and Grill, a younger sibling of the original Jake's, one of Portland's oldest and most popular restaurants, is adjacent.

THE HEATHMAN HOTEL, 1001 SW Broadway, Portland, OR 97205; (503) 241-4100, (800) 551-0011; portland.heathmanhotel.com; $$$$. This elegant downtown hotel is in a superb location next to Portland's Performing Arts Center. The Heathman is distinguished for its excellent restaurant, for its collection of works by locally and internationally notable artists, as well as for its unique mezzanine library, with signed editions by authors who have been hotel guests. The Heathman also has an outstanding multilingual concierge staff who will find you tickets to local shows, make your dinner reservations, hook you up with sightseeing tours, and fulfill other requests.

THE HILTON–PORTLAND, 921 SW 6th Ave., Portland, OR 97204; (503) 226-1611; hilton.com; $$$$. In the center of downtown, the Portland Hilton is a well lit, contemporary facility with 782 guest rooms and 40,000 square feet of meeting space (the most of any hotel in the city). There is an attractive display of works by regional artists, and just off the lobby there is a warm, dark-paneled bar and restaurant. Serving an international clientele, the Hilton offers foreign currency exchange and a multilingual staff. Here too the concierge staff is remarkably attentive and knowledgeable.

★ **HOTEL DELUXE PORTLAND**, 729 SW 15th Ave., Portland, OR 97205; (503) 219-2094, (866) 895-2094; hoteldeluxeportland.com; $$$. This stylish hotel lies just south of the Pearl District, west of downtown and off the MAX line very near Jeld Wen Field, convenient to everything. The hotel pays homage to the era of the classic studio films, with stills from memorable movie moments lining the corridors and coolly elegant rooms. But its amenities are strictly 21st century. Be sure to check out the hotel bar, the Driftwood Room—a fine spot for a pre-dinner cocktail.

HOTEL FIFTY, 50 SW Morrison St., Portland, OR 97204; (503) 221-0711, (877) 237-6775; hotelfifty.com; $$$$. This urbane and contemporary spot quite near the Willamette is a lovingly upgraded and refurbished hotel in an outstanding location. Hotel Fifty will provide you with the standard amenities of a modern hotel, including free wireless, snug memory-foam beds and cool linens, iPod docks, and large, capacious showers. In addition, all rooms are smoke-free. Parking is $20 per day, but the hotel is very, very close to the MAX line, so in theory you don't need a car.

THE HOTEL LUCIA, 400 SW Broadway, Portland, OR 97205; (503) 225-1717, (877) 225-1717; hotellucia.com; $$$$. The comfortable, well-designed Lucia is well located at the northern edge of the heart of downtown, close to all the major business, tourist, and shopping districts. It features a polished, Pacific Rim aesthetic with contemporary decor. The Hotel Lucia also features a permanent collection of the photographs of David Kennerly, the Pulitzer Prize– winning Oregonian and personal photographer to President Gerald Ford. Of note are the two excellent on-site restaurants, Imperial and Portland Penny Dinner, both operated by Portland chef Vitaly Paley—one of the city's best. See the Dining chapter for more information.

★ **HOTEL MODERA**, 515 SW Clay St., Portland, OR 97201; (503) 484-1084; hotelmodera.com; $$$$. Hotel Modera is a sleek temple of cool comfort. It's well situated at the southern end of downtown, near the Portland Farmers' Market. It's also right on the MAX line and within easy walking distance to the streetcar. The restaurant, Nel Centro, provides a beautiful and unusual view of downtown. A local favorite is the large courtyard—an exemplar of urban landscape design, with a living wall and fire pits. What could be better than a summer evening in a high-design courtyard, with a cocktail, a loved one, and a fire pit, in the heart of Portland?

HOTEL MONACO, 506 SW Washington St., Portland, OR 97204; (503) 222-0001, (888) 207-2201; monaco-portland.com; $$$$. One of Portland's favorite hotels, the Monaco has rooms like French salons, decorated in creamy tones accented by beautiful modern fabrics in complementary orange, periwinkle, and deep browns, with eclectic furniture and opulent linens. There are 229 rooms, a number of them 1-bedroom suites. This hotel occupies a building listed on the National Register of Historic Places. Guests are just a block from Pioneer Courthouse Square, and public transportation, food carts, and shopping are all very near.

★ **HOTEL VINTAGE PLAZA**, 422 SW Broadway, Portland, OR 97205; (503) 228-1212, (800) 263-2305; vintageplaza.com; $$$$. Featuring a wine-country theme that extends to the names of most rooms, to the interior color scheme, and to a nightly tasting of Oregon wines at the lobby fireplace, the romantic Hotel Vintage Plaza is an intimate downtown hotel with an atmosphere that cushions guests from the fatigue of travel. The rooms are private, comfortable, and tasteful. There are "starlight rooms" with conservatory windows that let natural light flow into the room, and some two-story townhouse suites. The hotel, on the north end of downtown, is close to major shopping, cultural, and business districts. We know many people who refuse to stay anywhere else.

THE MARK SPENCER HOTEL, 409 SW 11th Ave., Portland, OR 97205; (503) 224-3293, (800) 548-3934; markspencer.com; $$$. The Mark Spencer is popular for extended stays in Portland, and it has special packages for artists—especially actors, directors, and other performance-art personnel—who are making lengthy visits. More conservative than some of the trendier downtown hotels, the Mark Spencer offers convenience and value in its 101 rooms and suites. Afternoon tea is served daily in the lobby, wine tasting is offered in

The Willamette River

the evening, and a light breakfast in the morning. In the same block as Portland's renowned Jake's Restaurant, the Mark Spencer is just across Burnside Street from Powell's City of Books.

THE MARRIOTT HOTEL–CITY CENTER, 520 SW Broadway, Portland, OR 97205; (503) 226-6300, (800) 228-9290; marriott.com; $$$. The renowned Marriott service is here presented in a boutique hotel setting. This hotel features nearly 250 rooms and 10 suites on 20 floors; it's got a cocktail lounge and a restaurant on the premises; it's in the heart of downtown but close to the Pearl District, the Chinese Garden, and the river. It's a good hotel for the business traveler: The rooms have high-speed Internet access (fee-based), and the hotel provides a generous amount of meeting space. The paneled lobby is quite lovely, with a big chandelier and a sweeping staircase just right for making a spectacular entrance.

THE MARRIOTT HOTEL–DOWNTOWN WATERFRONT, 1401 SW Naito Pkwy., Portland, OR 97201; (503) 226-7600, (800) 228-9290; marriott.com; $$$. Across Naito Parkway from the Willamette River and the Tom McCall Riverfront Park, the uppermost of the Marriott's 503 rooms perch 14 stories above street level, offering fine views of Mount Hood. With one of the largest meeting spaces in the downtown area, this hotel attracts a lot of conferences, and it features organized facilities, attentive service, and super-upgraded Wi-Fi. But since almost every room is designed to have a decent view, the hotel also attracts its share of tourists. The Marriott is convenient to recreation areas along the Willamette River.

⭐ **THE NINES HOTEL,** 525 SW Morrison St., Portland, OR 97204; (503) 222-9995; thenines.com; $$$$. Occupying the upper 9 stories of the 1909 Meier & Frank department store building, the Nines is a gorgeous hotel, balancing its historic exterior with a lovely, modern interior that provides the expected amenities of a luxury operation, such as a VIP floor, spacious and comfortable rooms, cozy beds, soft linens, and a multilingual staff. This LEED-certified hotel is part of the Starwood chain, and in spite of its luxury status, it offers great value; for one thing, it is incredibly convenient to stay there, since the MAX line from the airport stops right across the street.

RIVER'S EDGE HOTEL & SPA, 0455 SW Hamilton Court, Portland, OR 97239; (503) 802-5800, (888) 556-4802; riversedgehotel.com; $$$. River's Edge Hotel & Spa is in an attractive building south of downtown on the Willamette River, in the burgeoning South Waterfront district. Public spaces and rooms alike are outfitted with sleek but comfortable furnishings and plush rugs. Many rooms have balconies that look out on the Willamette, to Mount Hood, and beyond. The hotel is near Oregon Health & Science University's Center for Health & Healing, as well as the many new businesses developing in that area, and the restaurant next door, AquaRiva, is quite good. It also features an excellent day spa on site.

★ THE RIVERPLACE HOTEL, 1510 SW Harbor Way, Portland, OR 97201; (503) 228-3233, (800) 227-1333; riverplacehotel.com; $$$$. Right on the bank of the Willamette River, at the south end of Tom McCall Waterfront Park, the RiverPlace Hotel offers rooms facing the river or with a north view of the city's skyline. The hotel's patio is a good spot from which to view displays of fireworks, runners, in-line skaters, skateboarders, dog-walkers, cyclists, and people out for a stroll—as well as the parade of river craft sailing or rowing by. RiverPlace is close to the Portland Aerial Tram. An excellent restaurant is on site: Three Degrees, which offers regional specialties, beautifully prepared.

THE WESTIN PORTLAND, 750 SW Alder St., Portland, OR 97205; (503) 294-9000; westinportland.com; $$$$. One of the nicest downtown luxury hotels, the Westin features elegant guest rooms as well as handsome meeting space in a very conveniently situated central location. Everything in this hotel feels fresh and modern, as well as comfortable. Best of all, it's right in the heart of downtown, a short stroll or streetcar ride from museums, galleries, shops, and restaurants. The Daily Grill restaurant serves Northwest-inspired traditional American cuisine and is excellent for a predinner cocktail, or any other meal, really. Of course, you will also find all the luscious Westin amenities you have come to expect, such as great workout facilities and comfortable bedding.

NORTHWEST PORTLAND

INN AT NORTHRUP STATION, 2025 NW Northrup St., Portland, OR 97209; (503) 224-0543, (800) 224-1180; northrupstation.com; $$$. The Inn at Northrup Station is a great option in Northwest Portland, where there are few hotels. This stylish place features suites that are brightly colored and filled with modern furniture, with marble and granite in the bathrooms and kitchens. And yes—there are kitchens, making this hotel an excellent value. The Inn at Northrup Station is well located between the lively shopping and restaurant districts on Northwest 21st and Northwest 23rd Avenues—and it's right on the streetcar line, offering easy access to the Pearl District and downtown Portland. There is no restaurant on site, but there is free parking.

SILVER CLOUD INN, 2426 NW Vaughn St., Portland, OR 97210; (503) 242-2400, (800) 205-6939; silvercloud.com/portland; $$. This Silver Cloud Inn is situated in Northwest Portland, at the edge of an industrial area. It is not a luxury hotel, but it is well placed for business travelers, and it is also convenient for anyone wanting to explore Northwest Portland. The hotel is tidy, quiet, and within walking distance of good restaurants, an eclectic mix of small shops, a brewpub, and coffeehouses. The hotel's location allows easy access to the highways following the Columbia River to the Oregon coast and to those leading east to Mount Hood and the Columbia Gorge.

> **i** The root word for hotel is "hostel" and in Portland we have two: in Northwest Portland at 1818 Northwest Glisan St., Portland, OR 97209 (503-241-2783; nw portlandhostel.com) and in Southeast Portland at 3031 Southeast Hawthorne Blvd., Portland, OR 97214 (503-236-3380; portlandhostel.org).

SOUTHEAST PORTLAND

BLUEBIRD GUESTHOUSE, 3517 SE Division St., Portland, OR 97202; (503) 238-4333, (866) 717-4333; bluebirdguesthouse.com; $. Something beyond a hotel but not quite a bed-and-breakfast inn, the Bluebird Guesthouse brings much-needed and novel accommodations to Southeast Portland. The 7 charming guest rooms and the public areas in this repurposed vintage Portland house are decorated with vivid colors and comfortable furniture. It is within easy walking distance of some of Portland's best restaurants, as well as coffeeshops, cafes, and bars. Two rooms have private bathrooms; the others share two and a half bathrooms. Children ages 6 and older are welcome. There are no televisions, but there is free Wi-Fi, and the prices are reasonable.

CLINTON STREET GUESTHOUSE, 4220 SE Clinton St., Portland, OR 97206; (503) 234-8752; clintonstreetguesthouse.com; $$. This 4-room bed-and-breakfast in Southeast Portland is in a pretty, thoroughly refurbished Craftsman-style bungalow built in 1913. The house has a lush and productive garden, with much of its produce—including the fresh eggs from the hens in the back—ending up on your breakfast plate. The decor is simple, serene, and vintage, but the extra outlets so you can keep your laptop charged are a thoughtful nod to the present. The Division Street neighborhood offers some stellar restaurants and coffeeshops nearby—it is centrally located and near the busline, but if you are not used to walking much, you might be happier having a car.

JUPITER HOTEL, 800 E. Burnside St., Portland, OR 97214; (503) 230-9200, (877) 800-0004; jupiterhotel.com; $$$. The Jupiter Hotel is a restyled motel built in the 1960s, and the hotel evokes that era's Land-of-Tomorrow, modern sensibility. Its 80 rooms are divided into the "quiet" side and the "party" side, which is important information depending on how you view proximity to the adjacent Doug Fir Lounge (one of Portland's hottest night spots). The hotel offers the important amenities, as well as chalkboard doors for doodling, an outdoor fire pit, and Blu Dot furnishings.

NORTH & NORTHEAST PORTLAND

GEORGIAN HOUSE BED & BREAKFAST, 1828 NE Siskiyou St., Portland, OR 97212; (503) 281-2250, (888) 282-2250; thegeorgianhouse.com; $$. This classic, immaculately maintained Georgian colonial home was built in 1922, and it features a winding staircase, stained-glass windows, and antique furnishings. Guest rooms have either a private or shared bath and are furnished with antiques. Children 12 and older are welcome in the Captain Irving Room. The inn has discounts for corporate travelers and for those on extended stays. The surrounding residential neighborhood is near public transit, the Rose Quarter with the Oregon Convention Center, and the Lloyd Center, with its mix of department stores, movie theaters, and restaurants. It's a short drive to downtown, as well.

THE LION AND THE ROSE, 1810 NE 15th Ave., Portland, OR 97212; (503) 287-9245, (800) 955-1647; lionrose.com; $$$. This beautifully restored Victorian in the well-established Northeast Portland Irvington neighborhood is close to the popular shopping and restaurant district along Northeast Broadway, including the Lloyd district. This inn is listed on the National Register of Historic Places, and its decor and atmosphere create a sense of relaxed elegance. Guests have the option of an early continental breakfast or, a bit later, the real thing. Guests are also served an afternoon dessert tea. All rooms have private baths. Children older than 12 are welcome. Occasionally this inn requires a 2-night minimum, especially on weekends and holidays.

⭐ **MCMENAMINS KENNEDY SCHOOL,** 5736 NE 33rd Ave., Portland, OR 97211; (503) 249-3983, (888) 249-3983; mcmenamins.com/ 427-kennedy-school-home; $$. The wonderful Kennedy School is a favorite recommendation for out-of-town guests. This unusual 57-room brewpub and inn inhabits a pretty ex-school (now on the National Register of Historic Places). It's also close to the Alberta neighborhood, with its outstanding restaurants and shopping. And the Kennedy School is far more than a guesthouse. This extensive campus is a destination for much of Portland; it is very popular for meetings, reunion dinners, parties, and all manner of gatherings.

A PAINTED LADY INN, 1927 NE 16th Ave., Portland, OR 97212; (503) 335-0070; apaintedladyinn.com; $$. A Painted Lady Inn is a well-wrought little gem in the Irvington area, well situated to take advantage of shopping, restaurants, and entertainment, with easy access to downtown Portland as well. There are 3 guest rooms, and—a big plus—delicious, seasonal breakfasts served in your room (or the dining room if you wish). The guest rooms are airy and bright, and the common rooms filled with period furniture that complements this pretty house built in 1904. The grounds are lovely and include a back terrace for sunny morning coffee and newspaper-reading—as well as a porch swing.

> ℹ The beautiful Irvington district, home to many of Portland's bed-and-breakfast inns and more than 20 officially designated historic sites, was one of the first planned communities in the area. Its success was due partly to strict building codes and partly to the trolley that transported its banker and lawyer residents downtown.

PORTLAND'S WHITE HOUSE, 1914 NE 22nd Ave., Portland, OR 97214; (503) 287-7131, (800) 272-7131; portlandswhitehouse.com; $$$. Completely restored to the grand splendor of 1911, Portland's White House was built of Honduran mahogany by early Portland timber magnate Robert Lyle. It has 9 elegant guest rooms, all with private baths and featuring period furnishings and decor. With a circular drive, massive classic Greek columns, fountains, a carriage house, and Japanese maples, this inn bears some resemblance to its Washington, DC, namesake. Guests can visit the parlor for sherry or board games. Children are welcome if you arrange it in advance.

TIERRA SOUL URBAN FARMHOUSE, 4614 N. Michigan, Portland, OR 97217; (503) 489-7645; tierrasoulpdx.com; $. They are not kidding: This really is a working urban farm in the heart of the North Portland district. This green oasis is devoted to sustainability, healing, and eco-culture; you won't find doilies or mini bottles of shampoo, but you may find bees, goats, chickens, fruit trees, and a large garden. There are 4 guest rooms, plus a cute vintage trailer that sleeps 3. Tierra Soul is not for everyone. Be sure to read the website so you understand what they are trying to do. If you do, however, then you can be sure of an authentic Portland experience.

VANCOUVER

THE HEATHMAN LODGE, 7801 NE Greenwood Dr., Vancouver, WA 98662; (360) 254-3100, (888) 475-3100; heathmanlodge.com; $$$$. Known for its charming combination of Pacific Northwest lodge decor and modern conveniences, this hotel has a reputation for friendly service and attention. The lobby and other common areas are done in rustic pine, accented by the color and classic designs of Pendleton blankets and pillows; in fact, the 121 oversize guest rooms have Pendleton bedspreads. This hotel is equipped with an enclosed swimming pool, sauna and whirlpool, and complete fitness center. The Heathman's restaurant, Hudson's Bar and Grill, offers excellent cuisine. The Heathman Lodge is 15 minutes from the Portland Airport.

A sculptural bike rack in downtown Portland

Dining

Portland is obsessed with food, and our obsession has gotten the attention of food-lovers the world over. Rather than having a characteristic regional cuisine, Portland's style is defined by its overall approach to food,. This style has a few elements that make it distinctive: access to high-quality ingredients, preferably local and seasonal; respect for techniques derived from every culture; and a value of eclecticism. We have a collaborative community that encourages experimentation and innovation. At the same time, because the barriers to entry are low—think food carts!—there is also a lot of competition that ultimately breeds excellence. The bar is therefore high—the most ordinary-looking neighborhood cafe will serve, say, a salad of gathered greens with a balsamic vinegar reduction, toasted hazelnuts, and artisanal cheese with house-made pickles, and no one bats an eyelash. They would be shocked to find anything less.

Below are some of our favorite restaurants, both classic and new. Portland's destination restaurants and talented chefs are found all over the city; many neighborhood places are also "destinations" for loyal followers and adventuresome people looking for something new. We concentrate on restaurants in Portland, but you should know that there are many superb places in Beaverton and other Metro-area towns, and especially in wine country, so we encourage exploration. By Oregon law restaurants and bars are all non-smoking. One note about brewpubs: As long as a pub is also a restaurant, most of them allow children until 10 p.m. in designated areas.

Price Code

Most restaurants have offerings at a range of prices. The price

Many restaurants offer pleasant outdoor seating when it's warm.

code here reflects the general cost of a single entree, excluding drinks, hors d'oeuvres, side dishes, and tips. As with other Portland purchases, there is no sales tax. Unless noted, all the restaurants listed take the usual credit cards.

$	Less than $10
$$	$10 to $20
$$$	$20 to $30
$$$$	More than $30

ACADIA, 1303 NE Fremont St., Portland, OR 97212; (503) 249-5001; creolapdx.com; Southern; $$$. This handsome New Orleans–style bistro is packed with adventuresome diners who come in search of delicious Creole dishes. Here you will find soft-shell crab, catfish taco, and jambalaya among the appetizers, as well as a delightful array of entrees such as Pork Chop Galatoire—a chop rubbed with ancho chili and honey, grilled, and served with crawfish, corn bread stuffing, and caramelized onion. Acadia also has a full bar. They serve dinner Mon through Sat.

ALAMEDA BREWING CO., 4765 NE Fremont St., Portland, OR 97213; (503) 460-9025; alamedabrewhouse.com; Brewpub; $$. Alameda offers 9 unique regular micros along with 2 or 3 seasonals and their popular homemade root beer. With well-priced 20-ounce pints, it's a great value. The food is more ambitious than standard pub grub. Entrees range from whiskey baby-back ribs to artichoke linguini to smoked chicken ravioli. Sandwiches and burgers are standouts too. A children's menu is also available. The atmosphere—galvanized metal, acid-stained floor, and the white maple/stainless-steel hop-yard theme—·works splendidly, as the brewery itself is located in the dining area.

ALBINA PRESS, 4637 N. Albina Ave., Portland, OR 97217; (503) 282-5214; Coffee; $. Albina Press is not only justly famous for their delicious coffee, but also for their barista expertise: They hire only the best, the kind that place highly in National Barista championships. The attention to the coffee combined with the capacious feeling of the space makes this an irresistible cafe for writing, reading, or just chatting for an hour or two or six.

ANDINA, 1314 NW Glisan St., Portland, OR 97209; (503) 228-9535; andinarestaurant.com; South American; $$$. This stylishly renovated warehouse in the Pearl District is a star in the Portland restaurant scene. Comprising a tapas bar, an aperitif bar, a wine shop, and the capacious dining room, Andina showcases the cuisine of Peru to great effect. Andina has a number of fish cebiches, and they also serve several vegetarian variations on this dish as well. The meat selections are also outstanding, from simple Peruvian rack of lamb with purple potatoes (the ancestor of all potatoes) to more complex dishes involving stir-fried beef and yucca. Andina serves lunch Mon through Sat and dinner every evening.

APIZZA SCHOLLS, 4741 SE Hawthorne Blvd., Portland, OR 97214; (503) 233-1286; apizzascholls.com; Pizza; $$. Serving authentic New York–style pizza, Apizza Scholls is always busy. Luckily, since they don't take reservations, the pizza is worth the wait. Carefully crafted using a very hot oven, slow-rising dough, and local ingredients, these pizzas are so good that even New Yorkers like them. Open for dinner Tues through Sat.

AUTÉNTICA, 5507 NE 30th Ave., Portland, OR 97211; (503) 287-7555; autenticaportland.com; Mexican; $$$. Serving food in the style of the Acapulco region of Mexico, Auténtica may defy your expectations. There is a full bar, from which margaritas and other fine drinks flow. Seafood cocktails are a house specialty, and they range from a refreshing octopus salad to tangy ceviche. The soups are hearty, the flatiron steak is grilled perfectly, and the tostada is beautifully seasoned. The tamales are close to perfect. Because this restaurant is attempting to achieve authenticity, some things might surprise you, such as the saltine crackers served with the seafood cocktails. Just go with it. Dinner served Tues through Sun.

⭐ **AVA GENE'S**, 3377 SE Division St., Portland, OR 97202; (971) 229-0571; avagenes.com; Italian; $$$$. This pretty restaurant opened with much anticipation in 2013; owned by Stumptown Coffee founder Duane Sorenson, Ava Gene's is extremely hip, its waiters in street clothes and half its menu in Italian (they provide a glossary). If you can get past the hipness, you will be rewarded with perfect pastas such as macaroni in a savory cauliflower sauce or fusilli with tripe. Appetizers are also outstanding, including silky cured meats from local sources and beyond. One nice touch is the option of still or housemade fizzy water. The well-edited wine list offers only Italian wines, though the beer list is more diverse and the cocktails downright international.

⭐ **AVIARY**, 1733 NE Alberta St., Portland, OR 97211; (503) 287-2400; aviarypdx.com; Asian Fusion; $$. One of Portland's best restaurants—and that is saying a lot in our food-obsessed city—Aviary focuses on small plates of luscious bites prepared with perfect technique. There are three different chefs, each of whom brings a different style and training but who share a commitment to excellence. Asian flavors tend to be the primary, but not the only, influence. For example, you might find hoisin-glazed short ribs served with corn pudding, or a pork belly braised in dashi broth and served with greens and ginger caramel. The ambience is modernist and cool; the bar has inventive signature cocktails. Aviary serves dinner Mon through Sat.

BAILEY'S TAPROOM, 213 SW Broadway, Portland, OR 97205; (503) 295-1004; baileystaproom.com; Brewpub; $. The handsome, minimalist decor of this pub is the perfect complement to the maximalist beer list: about 20 taps and a long list of bottled beers, all showcasing top-line craft brews, some of them rare indeed, and mostly from Oregon. Bailey's offers excellent samplers, and hosts many events where you can meet and mingle with brewers—notably their festive, if somewhat chaotic, anniversary event at the end of July, featuring potent barrel-aged microbrews from Oregon's finest. While they don't brew their own beer—or make their own food; it's imported from a great Mexican restaurant across the street—Bailey's is a fine introduction to Oregon beer.

BAR AVIGNON, 2138 SE Division St., Portland, OR 97202; (503) 517-0808; baravignon.com; Small Plates; $. Proprietors Randy Goodman and Nancy Hunt will tell you that Bar Avignon is just a bar, but don't believe them. This sleek and organic spot along Southeast Division offers a beautifully edited wine collection and wonderful spirits that frame an outstanding selection of small plates. These include silky cured meats, creamy cheeses served with honey and Marcona almonds, just-harvested salads, the ripest fruit, the crustiest bread from Little T American Baker up the street—in short, everything you need to make a complete meal for the entire family, provided they are all over 21 (though children are in fact welcome).

BARISTA, 539 NW 13th Ave., Portland, OR 97209; (503) 274-1211; barista pdx.com; Coffee; $. Barista was founded by award-winning barista Billy Wilson, and at this urbane shop in Northwest Portland, you can sample different roasts much the way you would sample different wines. This means that local microroasts are served alongside Stumptown, with profiles of each kind listed—because not all espressos are alike. While Barista won't tell you how to drink your coffee, the purity of coffee flavor is the focus, so you may want to save your butterscotch latte for another place. They also have a shop at 1725 NE Alberta St. and one downtown at 529 SW 3rd. Barista is open from 6 a.m. to 6 p.m. on weekdays.

BEAST, 5425 NE 30th Ave., Portland, OR 97211; (503) 841-6968; beast pdx.com; French; $$$$. Beast features communal cooking—cooks and diners all share the same space, all in one large convivial group spread over 2 tables. Menus are set in advance; they consist of 5 or 6 courses (though some of the courses are amuse-bouche size), beginning with soup and ending with dessert, and wine pairings. The star is meat in many varieties—delicious braised dishes in the winter and perhaps a gorgeous lamb chop in the summer. Beast has 2 seatings on Wed through Sat nights, 6 p.m. or 8:45 p.m., 1 seating on Sun night at 7 p.m., and brunch on Sun at 10 a.m. or noon.

BERNIE'S SOUTHERN BISTRO, 2904 NE Alberta St., Portland, OR 97211; (503) 282-9864; berniesbistro.com; Southern; $$. This fine bistro serves Southern dinners with nods to the Northwest in its use of some seasonal and local ingredients—though not only those ingredients, of course. But Bernie's cornmeal-crusted oysters are a nice twist on a local favorite, as are the green tomatoes (the Northwest gardener's yearly problem), here fried and served with smoked tomato coulis, hearty gumbo, fresh corn bread, and green-onion grits cakes. The catfish is plump, and the chicken-fried steak is savory. The appetizers are also notable, especially the hush puppies. Bernie's serves dinner Tues through Sun.

BESAW'S CAFE, 2301 NW Savier St., Portland, OR 97210; (503) 228-2619; besaws.com; Breakfast & Cafes; $$. Besaw's is a neighborhood joint in northern Northwest, and while it serves very good lunches and dinners, we like it especially for breakfast, which is hearty and delicious. They feature all the staples, plus crispy bacon, apple sausages, succulent smoked salmon, and fluffy pancakes. Expect a wait on the weekends. Besaw's has been a restaurant since the Lewis and Clark Exposition in 1905, and its handsome bar dates from that period.

BIJOU CAFE; 132 SW 3rd Ave., Portland, OR 97204; (503) 222-3187; bijoucafepdx.com; Breakfast & Cafes; $$. The Bijou's excellent breakfasts, lunches, and weekend brunches are a staple of the downtown crowd, and for atmosphere, there are few better places than this urbane and crowded spot. The entrees are attentively made using as many local and organic ingredients as possible. The Bijou makes some of the best French toast, pancakes, and egg dishes in Portland. And the oyster omelet with bacon and onions is definitely worth the wait you'll endure at the door. Open Mon through Fri, 7 a.m. to 2 p.m., and on the weekends from 8 a.m. to 2 p.m. Friday evenings they serve delicious dinners while local jazz musicians perform, which is fun.

⭐ **BIWA**, 215 SE 9th Ave., Portland, OR 97214; (503) 239-8830; biwa restaurant.com; Asian; $$$. Chef Gabe Rosen's stylish Japanese restaurant is in the "small plates" style, emphasizing variety in taste and high-quality ingredients. Standout dishes include the vegetable salad, which features cabbage rolls, carrots, and daikon radish in a silky sesame dressing; a savory fried chicken; pork belly; onigiri, little stuffed rice and nori sandwiches; and offerings of two different noodle styles—in particular, the pork ramen is stellar. The dining room offers both booths and counter seats next to the open kitchen. Biwa also has a fine cocktail list, as well as an excellent selection of sake. Biwa is open Mon through Sat.

Rooms with a View

Feasting your eyes can be almost as satisfying as plain old feasting, and two places to do it are the Chart House and the Portland City Grill. **The Chart House** (5700 SW Terwilliger Blvd., Portland, OR 97239; 503-246-6963; chart-house.com) is a beautiful spot to enjoy the visual feast of the city as it stretches to meet the foothills and Mount Hood in the eastern distance. The **Portland City Grill** (111 SW 5th Ave., 30th floor, Portland, OR 97204; 503-450-0030; portlandcitygrill.com) sits atop the US Bank Tower, where it hands out impressive views that stretch far afield and help you put things in perspective. It's perfect for a romantic drink before dinner.

BLUEHOUR, 250 NW 13th Ave., Portland, OR 97209; (503) 226-3394 bluehouronline.com; Mediterranean; $$$$. Bluehour is routinely noted as the place to see and be seen in Portland, and it does provide a good backdrop for the beautiful people, with its dramatic curtains and low lighting. But don't overlook the food. It is always carefully prepared and well balanced, and its cheese flights are outstanding. The dishes are inspired by France and Italy, everything from seared foie gras to osso buco. Everything is prepared handsomely, with a touch of adventure. Bluehour serves dinner every night, lunch Mon through Sat, and brunch on the weekends.

BOKE BOWL, 1028 SE Water Ave., Portland, OR 97214; (503) 719-5698; bokebowl.com; Asian; $$. This chic noodle shop with long communal tables began as a monthly "pop-up" ramen joint. Now settled in the Eastside industrial district, Boke Bowl specializes in ramen noodles in carefully made dashi.

They make all the noodles in house and provide a crowd-pleasing (omnivores, vegans, children) variety of toppings and sides—the pulled pork ramen is a favorite, especially when served with a side of fried pears. They also serve seasonally stuffed steamed buns, and don't overlook the desserts (house-made Twinkie, anyone?). Boke Bowl is a lunchtime favorite, but they serve a great Korean fried chicken dinner on Thursday. They are open 7 days for lunch.

BRIDGEPORT BREWPUB, 1313 NW Marshall St., Portland, OR 97209; (503) 241-3612; bridgeportbrew.com; Brewpubs; $$. Bridgeport began in 1984 as the first microbrewery in town, producing 600 barrels per year. Now this groundbreaking, award-winning brewery produces more than 100,000 barrels each year. House standards such as Coho Pacific and Blue Heron are available, as well as cask-conditioned ales, which are naturally carbonated, unfiltered, and stored in firkins. Bridgeport offers a variety of British-style ales, including India Pale Ale, Extra Special Bitter, Black Strap Stout, and Porter conditioned in a bottle, keg, or firkin cask. The flagship ale is Blue Heron Amber Ale, brewed in honor of Portland's official city bird. Bridgeport also serves great pub fare.

⭐ **BUNK SANDWICHES,** 621 SE Morrison St., Portland, OR 97214; (503) 477-9515; 211 SW 6th Ave., Portland, OR 97219; (503) 972-8100; bunksandwiches.com; Delis & Sandwiches; $. Bunk is routinely compared to East Coast delis, but we think it's distinctively Portland: You can get an incredible meal for about $10 made with superb local ingredients alongside a variety of your Portland neighbors from the suited to the tattooed. But our friends from the East Coast who routinely do business in Portland make a point of eating here. They're looking for savory sausage and cheese breakfast sandwiches on flaky biscuits, stellar tuna melts, the pork belly Cuban sandwich, an outstanding meatball Parmigiano hero, and multiple other creative fillings. Bunk Bar at 1028 SE Water Ave. is a more spacious and alcohol-friendly incarnation.

CAFÉ PALLINO, 3003 SE Division St., Portland, OR 97202; (503) 232-0907; caffepallino.com; Breakfast & Cafes; $. Café Pallino is a beautiful Italian-modern cafe that specializes in coffee, pastries, breakfasts, and panini—and house-made gelato. Café Pallino serves breakfast, lunch, and dinner; it's all delicious, but we especially love their breakfasts, which are served until 2 p.m. House-made granola, "Breakfast in a Bowl"—Yukon Gold potatoes, an egg, sharp cheddar, and bacon—and vegetarian hash are current favorites. They also have a full bar with some signature cocktails, such as the espresso martini (espresso, vodka, Kahlua, and crème de cacao). That's what we call breakfast.

CASSIDY'S, 1331 SW Washington St., Portland, OR 97205; (503) 223-0054; cassidysrestaurant.com; Pacific Northwest Cuisine; $$. Cassidy's reputation as a good late-night bar is so firm that we sometimes forget how good the food is. Premium-cut meats, crispy Willapa Bay oysters with spicy cocktail sauce, creamy pastas—all these go beautifully with the local wines and microbrews that Cassidy's also features. The bar's dark paneling and old-fashioned wooden refrigerators remind us of Boston or New York, but the food and drinks are definitely Portland. Importantly, Cassidy's serves its menu until 2 a.m., unlike most restaurants in town. Keep that in mind.

CASTAGNA, 1752 SE Hawthorne Blvd., Portland, OR 97214; (503) 231-7373; castagnarestaurant.com; Mediterranean; $$$$. Castagna is a sophisticated restaurant with a minimalist ambience. The presentation here is outstanding, and even simple dishes such as a butter lettuce salad, sea scallops, or french fries are beautifully arranged. The seasonal menu—on which you might find grilled sea scallops with oyster mushrooms, little agnolotti pasta stuffed with duck confit, sautéed halibut with mussels and potatoes, or grilled rack of lamb—is Mediterranean influenced, with local ingredients providing the foundation. A less formal, and less expensive, cafe right next door, Café Castagna (1758 SE Hawthorne Blvd.; 503-231-9959), also provides an excellent meal.

CIAO VITO, 2293 NE Alberta St., Portland, OR 97211; (503) 282-5522; ciaovito.net; Italian & Spanish; $$$. Ciao Vito serves honest food beautifully prepared at good value. The superstars of the menus are small plates: they have an extensive tapas menu, as well as beautifully prepared pastas. The grilled octopus, served with chorizo, is chewy and delicious. The braised meatballs are a superb balance of fragrance, smokiness, and salt; the white bean salad tastes fresh and tangy and perfectly textured. Ciao Vito serves dinner Wed through Mon.

⭐ **COCOTTE BAR AND BISTRO**, 2930 NE Killingsworth St., Portland, OR 97211; (503) 227-2669; cocottepdx.com; French; $$$. Cocotte serves perfect French country cuisine with excellent attention to detail. The signature dish, poulet en cocotte, might be the best roast chicken you will ever eat; depending on the season, it might be served with a "risotto" made of faro, a poached egg, and a silky, savory demi-glace. Other dishes have unique twists, such as a fragrant saffron broth-prepared bouillabaisse. The wine list is excellent; the desserts superb. Cocotte serves its happy menu hour all evening on Sunday and Monday; it's open for dinner daily at 5 p.m.

⭐ **COFFEEHOUSE NORTHWEST,** 1951 W. Burnside St., Portland, OR 97209; sterlingcoffeeroasters.com; Coffee; $. The star feature of this attractive space on West Burnside is the espresso. It's drawn from perfectly roasted beans at the perfect time to grind (several days out of the roaster) and it's drawn ristretto-style, which means the first pulse out of the machine. This attention to quality has earned Coffeehouse Northwest loyal customers and many accolades. The location, on trafficky Burnside, is challenging, but the focus on making perfect coffee has allowed them to overcome this challenge. They make amazing hot chocolate as well, and serve excellent pastries, but truly, this is a coffee geek's paradise.

COMMON GROUNDS, 4321 SE Hawthorne Blvd., Portland, OR 97215; (503) 975-7879; Coffee; $. This coffeehouse, on the eastern side of the Hawthorne shopping district, is both a neighborhood draw and a destination point, one of the best places in the city to read and write with your latte. Graduate students, artists, and writers flock to the place. They stock a good selection of periodicals, from the *New York Review of Books to Wired,* the music is always good, and there are plenty of outlets. Common Grounds also serves wonderful food to help fire up the neurons. Great cookies, pastries, and other desserts are made right there, and the panini will keep you going. Open until 10 p.m.

COUNTRY CAT, 7937 SE Stark Ave., Portland, OR 97215; (503) 408-1414; thecountrycat.net; American; $$$. This handsome, family-friendly restaurant in the cute Montavilla neighborhood offers gratifying "American heritage" cuisine: Think crispy and succulent fried chicken, tangy barbecued brisket, a juicy, molasses-coated smoked duck leg, fluffy mashed potatoes—you get the idea. They cure their own hams, make their own beef jerky, and brew their own ketchup. Chef Adam Sappington has been nominated several times for a James Beard award, and he has developed a well-deserved national following. They serve brunch and dinner every day. Country Cat also has an excellent bar, by the way.

⭐ **DESCHUTES BREWERY & PUBLIC HOUSE,** 210 NW 11th Ave., Portland, OR 97209; (503) 296-4906; deschutesbrewery.com; Brewpub; $$. The Deschutes Brewery, originating in Bend, Oregon, is known for its outstanding brews such as Mirror Pond Pale Ale, Obsidian Stout, Black Butte Porter, and the newest, Armory XPA (a pale ale). In this site, Armory XPA is brewed in gorgeous copper vats made in Germany and calibrated with precision. In Portland style, the menu takes the normal pub fare up a notch, with

The Deschutes Brewery highlights great food in addition to its outstanding brews.

local and organic meats and produce in the delicious burgers, pizzas, and fish and chips. Most of the food is made on site, including the cured meats, pickles, and tartar sauce. The good-natured servers will pour beer and serve you lunch or dinner from 11 a. m to midnight every day.

DOVE VIVI, 2727 NE Glisan St., Portland, OR 97232; (503) 239-4444; dovevivipizza.com; Italian; $. Casual and friendly Dove Vivi is renowned for its pizza built upon a delectable cornmeal crust and paired with unusual toppings such as sauerkraut and small-batch corned beef. The local favorite is probably the fresh sweet corn and smoked mozzarella pizza; it's a showstopper. They offer take-out and par-baked pizza, which is also highly convenient. Dove Vivi is open every night from 4 p.m. to 10 p.m.

EL GAUCHO, 319 SW Broadway, Portland, OR 97205; (503) 227-8794; elgaucho.com/El-Gaucho-Portland; Steak; $$$$. El Gaucho celebrates the ambience and service of the old-fashioned steak house. The dining room is

The Food Carts of Portland

In a town that's wild about food, Portland's food carts offer exquisite food for a single-digit price. All over the city, outdoor food carts are revolutionizing how food is prepared, sold, and eaten. Portland's food carts can be found throughout the city in clusters known locally as "pods"—these are private lots that provide a home to a number of carts. You can also find them at farmers' markets or sharing lots with other businesses. Some are roving—you can keep up with them on Twitter and Facebook. The online guide Food Carts Portland (foodcartsportland.com) provides peerless coverage of all things food cart–related (and tours, as well!). Listed below are a few of the major pods, followed by some of our very favorite carts.

Southwest 5th Avenue between Southwest Oak and Southwest Stark Streets: While it has no formal name, this is the mother pod, the one that gave birth to all the rest. Also known as "the lunch carts."

Southwest Alder Street between Southwest 9th and 11th Avenues: This is one of the older pods; it has a very international feel.

Cartopia: Southeast 12th Avenue and Southeast Hawthorne Boulevard. One of the original pods, Cartopia is notable for staying open very late for hungry clubbers on their way home. But you can come early for dinner, too. It has lots of long communal, covered tables.

Good Food Here: 4262 SE Belmont St.; goodfoodherebelmont .com. Some of Portland's most prized and beloved carts are here.

Many food cart pods offer seating for wet Portland weather.

Mississippi Marketplace: North Mississippi Avenue, just south of Skidmore Street. This pod has comfy seating and many (but not solely) vegan carts.

Portland State University: Southwest 4th Avenue and Southwest Hall. Convenient to downtown, there are many carts in this pod devoted to carnivorous delights such as pastrami, simple burgers, and meatballs.

As promised, here are a few of our best-loved carts—only space prevents us from listing more, because there are almost 600:

Aybla Grill: This Mediterranean food cart (one downtown and one at Belmont and 42nd) makes the best lamb gyro in Portland.

Koi Fusion: Koi Fusion (find them on Twitter @KOIfusionpdx) is a mobile cart whose chef, Bo Kwon, has more than 4,000 followers on Twitter—that's how he tells his customers where he'll be.

La Jarochita: How we love a good taco truck! This Mexican cart is in the mother pod on Southwest 5th Avenue at Stark Street, and its mouthwatering tamales, tacos, and burritos are favorites with the throngs of downtown workers who swarm the place at lunchtime.

Nong's Khao Man Gai: We like this cart because they keep it simple by reducing the number of choices you have to make to one: a delightful and succulent Thai chicken dish with rice, prepared in a sauce of garlic, ginger, and soy. Find them downtown at Southwest Alder at Southwest 10th Avenue and at the Portland State University pod.

The People's Pig: The amazingly savory sandwiches here might be the very best in Portland. We can't stop thinking about the mesquite-grilled pork shoulder sandwich on a house-made sourdough bun with caramelized garlic, arugula, lemon, and fennel pollen (which is sprinkled on like celery salt). This fantastic cart is found in the pod at Southwest Alder and 9th.

Potato Champion: A pioneer cart in Southeast Portland, Potato Champion is known for its Belgian-style fries, and in particular for its fresh take on the Quebecois dish poutine, as well as its stellar peanut butter and jelly fries: fries with peanut satay and raspberry chipotle sauce. Find it at Cartopia, Southeast 12th Avenue and Hawthorne.

dusky and serene, with contemporary polished decor. The service is impeccable—both friendly and understated, with a great deal of tableside attention. And the food is equally good. Starters include a good crab cake, short ribs, and Wicked Shrimp—spicy shrimp with a piquant dipping sauce. Steaks include the Gaucho (accompanied by lobster medallions and béarnaise sauce) and a rib steak stuffed with peppers, rosemary, and garlic. And for dessert, there's nothing like a waiter in black tie flambéing bananas Foster at your table to make you feel that civilization has not disappeared altogether.

FLOYD'S COFFEESHOP, 1412 SE Morrison St., Portland, OR 97214; (503) 230-2167; 118 NW Couch St., Portland, OR 97209; (503) 295-7791; floydscoffee.com; Coffee; $. Floyd's knows that delicious coffee is only half the reason coffee shops exist. The other half is so people can hang out—and nowadays this means providing electricity so people can charge their devices while hanging out, online or in the analog way, at a table. Therefore, we like them not only because of the hand-pulled Stumptown shots but also because there are many outlets—one pretty much for every seat—for when your laptop battery is running low. Look for good tunes and comfortable seats for working; you can get a lot of work done here.

FRESH POT, 4001 N. Mississippi Ave., Portland, OR 97227; (503) 284-8928; thefreshpot.com; Coffee; $. Portland does not lack small, locally owned coffeehouses, but there's always room for more of a good thing. The Fresh Pot occupies the historic Rexall Drug building in this neighborhood, where it serves beautifully roasted coffee from Stumptown to neighbors and visitors. The Fresh Pot also runs the coffee bar in the Hawthorne Powell's. The Fresh Pot shops offer Wi-Fi to keep you connected and award-winning baristas to keep you caffeinated.

FULLER'S RESTAURANT, 136 NW 9th Ave., Portland, OR 97209; (503) 222-5608; Breakfast & Cafes; $. Fuller's has been a Pearl District tradition since before it was the Pearl District, and it retains its working-class roots even as the city gentrifies around it. Of course, that's one of its attractions. Fuller's serves egg sandwiches, pancakes, and other traditional breakfast staples all day until 5 p. m on weekdays, 2 p.m. on Sat. It has 28 stools. Don't be surprised to find yourself in conversation with the guy at the next stool; it's part of the routine. Bring cash—they don't take credit cards. Closed Sun.

GENOA AND ACCANTO, 2832 SE Belmont St., Portland, OR 97214; (503) 238-1464; genoarestaurant.com, accantopdx.com; Italian; $$–$$$$.

Genoa was Portland's favorite fancy dinner restaurant for many years, and when it closed, it left a hole in the hearts of patrons across the city. Now it has been gloriously remodeled, reviving its prix-fixe, 5-course menu focused on regional cuisines. This is the place to go when you want to celebrate something. Accanto is the *enoteca* side; it's bright and casual, but no less delicious. Accanto is open for lunch and dinner daily and for brunch on Sat and Sun, in keeping with its role as an attractive and upscale but neighborhood-focused cafe. Genoa is open for dinner Tues through Sun.

HA & VL, 2738 SE 82nd Ave., Portland, OR 97266; (503) 772-0103; Asian; $. People start lining up early for the savory soups at HA & VL, and by early we mean soup for breakfast. They use free-range chicken and other fine ingredients; the noodles are perfectly chewy and the broths divine. Try snail soup with ginger dipping sauce—only available on Thursday. HA & VL is open daily in its unpretentious location in east Portland, but if you wait, the soup will have run out.

HAIR OF THE DOG BREWERY AND TASTING ROOM, 61 SE Yamhill St., Portland, OR 97214; (503) 232-6585; hairofthedog.com; Brewpub; $. Hair of the Dog epitomizes everything unique about the Portland beer scene: homage to the community, clear individuality, a taste for innovation, incredible

You'll find Hair of the Dog Brewery in a vintage Eastside building.

quality, and plenty of bike parking. These award-winning, bottle-conditioned beers are often named for local beer heroes (such as Fred Eckhardt, possibly responsible for reviving the lost art of brewing in the United States) and carry stellar flavor profiles. The food is simple and hearty, like braised short ribs and sausage sandwiches. If you try one brewpub, make it this one. Hair of the Dog is open beginning at 11:30 a.m. Tues through Sun.

HEATHMAN RESTAURANT, 1001 SW Broadway, Portland, OR 97205; (503) 790-7752; heathmanrestaurantandbar.com; Pacific Northwest Cuisine; $$$$. The Heathman remains a premier Portland dining room that brings a French sensibility to local ingredients. Under the leadership of chef Michael Stanton, the menu varies seasonally, but you can expect standards such as Angus rib-eye steak, roast chicken, and crispy sweetbreads. All this kitchen talent is aided by first-rate service and a simple, handsome decor that includes a collection of fine paintings. Because the Heathman Restaurant is part of the Heathman Hotel, it also serves breakfast and lunch, 7 days a week. The breakfasts are exceptional, and if there are power lunches in Portland, you'll find them here.

HEDGE HOUSE, 3412 SE Division St., Portland, OR 97202; (503) 235-2215; lompocbrewing.com; Brewpub; $. Southeast Division has some of Portland's most prestigious restaurants, but sometimes you just want a sandwich

Southeast's Hedge House offers a casual and friendly spot for beer and sandwiches.

and a beer without standing in line for 45 minutes. This unpretentious pub is in a cute yellow house with cozy indoor spaces and a pretty patio. The pleasant atmosphere is underscored by great sandwiches, salads, and similar pub food—and of course, great beer. Our favorite brew is C-note, a wonderfully hoppy India pale ale, but when the weather is hot, few things are tastier than a cold Fool's Golden Ale. Cheap pints can be found on Tues and weekends; growlers also are available.

HIGGINS RESTAURANT, 1239 SW Broadway, Portland, OR 97205; (503) 222-9070; higginsportland.com; Pacific Northwest Cuisine; $$$$. The inventive ways in which Chef Greg Higgins uses seasonal, organic food from nearby farms, forests, and streams have won this influential restaurant the highest marks from critics—as well as from the customers that fill the restaurant every night. Higgins, who won the James Beard Award in 2002, is unparalleled in his combinations of textures and flavors. If salmon is on the menu, order it. The bar menu carries some notable staples, among them a luscious pastrami sandwich (Greg Higgins makes the pastrami himself). Higgins has an excellent wine list and a beer list that features about 150 different brews from the world over.

Farmer-Chef Connection

In a way, Chef Greg Higgins laid the foundation for Portland's status as a food mecca. It was Higgins who first reached out to local farmers in the area to persuade them to grow things he wanted to cook. This gesture eventually led to an annual conference, the Farmer-Chef Connection, that includes people from farms, ranches, fishing companies, small businesses, specialty food purveyors, institutional buyers, grocery stores, and restaurants, all dedicated to sustaining a healthy local food ecosystem that promotes our regional bounty. This meeting of the minds is responsible for many practical innovations that, behind the scenes, have allowed the area's food-related businesses to flourish. Thanks, Greg Higgins!

HOKUSEI SUSHI, 4246 SE Belmont St., Portland, OR 97215; (971) 279-2161; hokuseisushi.com; Japanese; $$$$. Hokusei is an unpretentious but stylish establishment concentrating on impeccable sushi. Chef Kaoru Ishii, from Tokyo, is attempting to combine that city's focus on perfect technique with Portland's obsession with high-quality local ingredients. We highly recommend the tasting menus so you can be blown away by the quality, but the individual sushi dishes are great too. We love the braised saba in hacho miso and the Hamachi, in particular. Hokusei is open from 5 p.m. to 10 p.m.; closed on Tues.

HOPWORKS URBAN BREWERY, 2944 SE Powell Blvd., Portland, OR 97202; (503) 232-4677; hopworksbeer.com; Brewpub; $. This busy pub brews organic, handcrafted beer and serves it in 4 beautiful spaces: an outdoor beer garden, an indoor family space that includes a play area, a mezzanine, and a bike-up bar. It's not just the beer that's organic. Every inch is devoted to sustainable restaurant practice, from the permeable pavers lining the beer garden to the rain barrels and composting system. But what you will notice is the excellence of the beer. You can get sustainable New York–style pizza to go with it. They have a second location in North Portland: Hopworks BikeBar, 3947 N. Williams Ave., Portland, OR 97227; (503) 287-6258.

THE HORSE BRASS PUB, 4534 SE Belmont St., Portland, OR 97215; (503) 232-2202; horsebrass.com; British; $$. Since 1976—more than a decade before most Portlanders had even heard of microbrews—the Horse Brass Pub has been a haven for crafted ales and authentic, home-style British fare. They serve fantastic meat pies, made on site, as well as tasty Scotch eggs, bangers, and sausage rolls. But mostly they are known for their phenomenal beer selection, on draft and in bottles. They have an international reputation and cultish following among beer aficionados, based on the atmosphere of the place as much as on the beer selection.

HUBER'S, 411 SW 3rd Ave. Portland, OR 97204; (503) 228-5686; hubers .com; American; $–$$. Self-described as Portland's oldest restaurant, Huber's opened its doors in 1879 as the Bureau Saloon. In 1884 the bartender, Frank Huber, became a partner and the rest is culinary history. Still known for its "Roast Young Tom Turkey," Huber's attracts a steady clientele who also enjoy the Philippine mahogany paneling, stained-glass skylights, and a big brass cash register. A flaming Spanish Coffee at Huber's is a rite of passage for all would-be Portlanders. Happy hour (6 to 8 p.m.) features inexpensive appetizers with well drinks at the usual price.

J & M CAFE, 537 SE Ash St., Portland, OR 97214; (503) 230-0463; jandmcafepdx.com; Breakfast & Cafes; $$. The J & M Cafe is one of the best places for breakfast and lunch in Portland. The coffee is self-serve, which is a fine thing if you have to wait for your table. The waffles are excellent— crispy on the outside, tender and flaky inside. The eggs are fluffy and savory.

Their signature dish, the J & M plate, is their own variation on eggs Benedict: here, 2 basted eggs on an English muffin, topped with cheese in place of the hollandaise and thick, crispy bacon. The service is first-rate. Cash only. Open daily until 2 p.m.

JAKE'S FAMOUS CRAWFISH, 401 SW 12th Ave., Portland, OR 97205; (503) 226-1419; mccormickandschmicks.com; American; $$$$. Even though Jake's is now owned by McCormick & Schmick's, which technically makes it a chain restaurant (a Portland chain), this restaurant retains its status as a landmark. Founded in 1892 by Jacob (Jake) Lewis Freiman, Jake's Famous Crawfish still has that turn-of-the-last-century ambience, with its maze of booths snug against brick walls, its antique oil paintings, deep wood paneling, beautiful bar, and crisp white linen. Sister restaurant Jake's Grill (611 SW 10th Ave.; 503-220-1850), the house restaurant for the Governor Hotel, is also a favorite, specializing in comfort food.

JUSTA PASTA, 1336 NW 19th Ave., Portland, OR 97209; (503) 243-2249; justapasta.com; Italian; $. Justa Pasta is the major pasta supplier to the region's top-tier restaurants, but it is also a great restaurant in its own right, serving dinner and lunch in its small (30-seat) venue—and one of the best bargains in town. Justa Pasta offers several kinds of pasta and sauces at each meal, accompanied by bread from the Pearl Bakery and well-flavored salads. Some of our favorites include the butternut squash–hazelnut ravioli and the mushroom sauce. But simpler dishes, such as bucatini in marinara sauce, are also truly satisfying. It is the perfect place for a cozy dinner.

Portland Food Adventures

Want to spend an evening chatting with one of Portland's local chefs? Want to have them serve you an amazing meal while you chat? Then you might like Portland Food Adventures, portlandfoodadventures.com. PFA arranges private dinners with local chefs and a few other likeminded folks. You purchase a series ticket for $125, which will get you about 8 different meals with 8 different local chefs—plus other goodies like gift certificates and advice from chefs about where to go for perfect cupcakes and other trivia. This 8-for-the-price-of-1 deal allows you to hobnob with some of Portland's finest, like Vitaly Paley, John Gorham, and Gabriel Rucker. You know you want to.

THE KENNEDY SCHOOL, 5736 NE 33rd Ave., Portland, OR 97211; (503) 249-3983; mcmenamins.com; Brewpub; $$. Local brewers turned real-estate magnates, the McMenamin brothers converted this beautiful old brick school into a wonderful neighborhood hub. The Kennedy School is an inn, a theater, a restaurant, and a brewpub—or rather, several pubs in one glorious space. The Courtyard Restaurant occupies the center of the complex; and the Honors Bar is on the periphery. There's also a wine bar—the Cypress Bar. Beers include McMenamin offerings, plus some guests. Several beers are brewed on site. It's a hotel, so they have a well rounded breakfast menu; the dinner menu include sandwiches, fries, salads, and other appetizery things, with several more substantial entrees as well.

KENNY & ZUKE'S, 1038 SW Stark St., Portland, OR 97205; (503) 222-3354; kennyandzukes.com; Delis & Sandwiches; $$. This Jewish delicatessen fills a void in Portland. Signature dishes include the Reuben sandwich, as well as its variety of pastrami sandwiches on house-made rye bread. The cheese-burger—while not exactly kosher—is the kind of thing you'll be craving after a long day of shopping. They also have two other locations, a bar and deli at 3901 N. Williams Ave., (503) 287-0782, and a much-needed bagel place at 2376 NW Thurman St., (503) 954-1737. Good bagels are very hard to come by in Portland.

KEN'S ARTISAN BAKERY, 326 NW 21st Ave., Portland, OR 97209; (503) 248-2202; kensartisan.com; Bakeries and Desserts; $. Ken Forkish is one of the most important bakers in town, supplying many restaurants with bread that is absolute perfection. His pastries are similarly outstanding—divinely flaky and balanced, never heavy or greasy. Try to go in the morning, when they are freshest. You'll find a line, but the efficient people behind the counter will move you through quickly. The coffee is also very good, and there are many tables so you can read the paper and drink your coffee while you dissect your croissant.

★ **KEN'S ARTISAN PIZZA,** 304 SE 28th Ave., Portland, OR 97214; (503) 517-9951; kensartisan.com; Pizza; $$. Ken's Artisan Pizza was born because owner Ken Forkish kept having to stay late at his bakery in Northwest Portland on Monday nights, when he first served pizza, because the lines were so long. Now he stays late in Southeast Portland, and the lines are even longer. Forkish uses a 700-degree oven, a perfect pizza technique, and keeps the menu simple: pizza, salad, roast vegetables. Pizzas are seasonal—in the fall you might find a squash pizza, while spring may bring roasted asparagus—but you can count on a Margherita with tomato sauce, mozzarella, and basil or even arugula. Ken's serves crusty pizza for dinner nightly.

THE LAURELWOOD, 5115 NE Sandy Blvd., Portland, OR 97213; (503) 282-0622; laurelwoodbrewpub.com; Brewpub; $$. A friendly pub chain, the Laurelwood offers some of the best beer in the city. They were the first in Oregon to brew organic beers, and they have won numerous awards and national attention. The Laurelwood crafts a great line, including an India Pale Ale, a stout, and a robust porter, along with seasonal beers. The menu is simple, with good beer food: onion rings, nachos, house-made pizza, and savory garlic fries. They have several other locations besides the original Northeast enterprise, including a popular outpost in Southeast (6716 SE Milwaukie Ave., 503-894-8267) and—importantly—on Concourses A and E at the Portland International Airport.

⭐ **LE PIGEON,** 738 E. Burnside St., Portland, OR 97214; (503) 546-8796; lepigeon.com; French; $$$. Don't let its humble trappings fool you: Le Pigeon is probably the most innovative restaurant in Portland today. While Chef Gabriel Rucker does use the local, seasonal approach, he uses it in novel ways. Menus change frequently, but there are some standout regulars—for example, the peanut butter and jelly sandwich with foie gras, served as an appetizer. Even simple dishes such as roast chicken display an authoritative touch. When a chef can make the simple things as interesting as the star dishes, you know he is a master. Le Pigeon is open for dinner nightly. Rucker's other restaurant, Little Bird, 219 SW 6th Ave., is also worth a look.

LINCOLN, 3808 N. Williams Ave., Portland, OR 97227; (503) 288-6200; lincolnpdx.com; Pacific Northwest Cuisine; $$$. Lincoln is notable for their harmonious pairing of cutting-edge and classic food, of tradition and innovation, and of high style and down home. Their house-made pastas are just a little different—serving braised pork belly with malloreddus rather than penne, or lamb ragu with sorcetti rather than gnocchi. The space is beautiful, the service is excellent, and their happy hour is fine. Truly fine: Who wouldn't want a frosty cocktail or a beer along with some baked eggs with cream, olives, and herbed breadcrumbs, or some savory fritters, or a savory little patty melt, on the way home from work? Closed Sun.

LOMPOC TAVERN, 1616 NW 23rd Ave., Portland, OR 97210; (503) 225-1855; lompocbrewing.com; Brewpub; $$. Powerful beers brewed with great attention to balance are the hallmark style of Lompoc Brewing. They produce many seasonal brews, but the year-round varieties are also excellent.

We recommend the rich Sockeye Cream Stout and the Proletariat Red, both strong beers that warrant total attention. The Lompoc Tavern has an outstanding menu as well: fresh, modern pub fare such as a tangy soba noodle salad and mole pork soft tacos, and calamari with a succulent aioli, in addition to savory burgers, fries, and other standards.

LUCKY LABRADOR BREWING COMPANY, 915 SE Hawthorne Blvd., Portland, OR 97214; (503) 236-3555; luckylab.com; Brewpub; $. The Lucky Labrador lies on the fringes of Southeast Portland's Industrial District, a sprawling, refurbished warehouse featuring tasty, handcrafted microbrews. The brews are good, especially the robust Black Lab Stout, a slightly malty Konigs Kolsch, and the crispy Top Dog Extra Pale. We also like Hawthorne's Best Bitter, which is an amber-hued, dry-hopped bitter, very characteristic of an English pint. They serve a straightforward, unpretentious menu including deli sandwiches and Bento. There are three other Lucky Lab locations: the Lucky Labrador Public House (7675 SW Capitol Hwy.), the Lucky Labrador Beer Hall (1945 NW Quimby), and the Taproom (1700 N. Killingsworth).

MACTARNAHAN'S TAPROOM, 2730 NW 31st Ave., Portland, OR 97210; (503) 228-5269; portlandbrewing.com; Brewpub; $$. This huge brewery in the Guild's Lake Industrial District at the edge of Northwest Portland shows off its 140-barrel copper brewing vessels by making them a part of its brewpub's interior design. The kettles are from the Sixenbrau Brewery, dating back to the 16th century in Bavaria. As for the brew, the line includes its gold-medal winning Amber Ale—the first amber ale in Oregon—as well as a well-edited collection of porters, Belgian-style ales, and seasonal brews. Great pub fare, including a Kobe beef burger and locally made sausages, rounds out the experience.

MURATA, 200 SW Market St., Portland, OR 97201; (503) 227-0080; Asian; $$$$. Murata serves excellent sushi in a modest downtown building. But don't let appearances fool you. This is the real thing: authentic, traditional, and serious. The tasting menu, which is very expensive, is worth every penny and is the ideal showcase for Murata's talents. The tangy salads and savory noodle soups are as good as the sushi, but it's the latter that you'll be dreaming about later. Open for lunch and dinner Mon through Sat.

⭐ **NED LUDD**, 3925 NE Martin Luther King Jr. Blvd., Portland, OR 97212; (503) 288-6900; nedluddpdx.com; Pacific Northwest Cuisine; $$. Everything in this attractive and remarkable restaurant is cooked in a wood-fired oven, from the vegetables to the pastas to the desserts (wood-fired s'mores, anyone?). Dishes change with the seasons, but you can always find delicious flatbread served Ned Ludd style (with "good olive oil and sea salt"), and you can usually find trout—stuffed, perhaps, or roasted and served with charred leeks. A recent menu we enjoyed featured succulent and smoky roast lamb served with rapini, olives, and anchovy. The menu is highly focused; check it out online before you go so you know what to expect.

NOSTRANA, 1401 SE Morrison St., Portland, OR 97214; (503) 234-2427; nostrana.com; Italian; $$. Nostrana has behind it one of Portland's favorite chefs, Cathy Whims, who brings a deep knowledge of Italian cooking to this attractive eastside restaurant. Pasta dishes feature house-made noodles and sauces; the grilled and rotisseried meats are perfectly done, sharing touches of Tuscany while being, at the same time, all Oregon. On the wine list you'll see a good selection of wines from Italy, though it also has some nice Oregon pinot noirs. Nostrana is open for lunch Mon through Fri from 11:30 a.m. to 2 p.m., and for dinner every night.

NUESTRA COCINA, 2135 SE Division St., Portland, OR 97202; (503) 232-2135; nuestra-cocina.com; Mexican; $$. Nuestra Cocino serves complex and savory dishes from Mexico's central regions As pleasant as the service and dining room are, the food is what, rightly, should draw you. For one thing, the tortillas are *heche a mano*—made by hand using a tortilla press. Salads and other appetizers are fresh and delicious. Other standouts include a great Caesar salad (yes, it is a Mexican dish), ceviche, and savory little tacos made from shredded pork that are not just crowd pleasers but genuine haute cuisine. Nuestra Cocina is closed Sun and Mon, open for dinner Tues through Sat from 5 to 10 p.m.

OLYMPIC PROVISIONS, 107 SE Washington St., Portland, OR 97214; (503) 954-3663; olympicprovisions.com; Salumeria; $$$. This delightful salumeria—amazingly, given all the house-cured meats here, Portland's first—has both a retail side and a restaurant side. On the retail side, you can take home savory Italian, French, and Spanish-style salamis and other cured meats, as well as fresh sausages and pâtés. On the restaurant side, you may want to tarry over beautiful charcuterie, wine, and cheese, as well as sumptuous meat dishes or daily fish specials. The wine list is expansive, and there is also a well-edited hard alcohol selection. Also see their Northwest Portland restaurant at 1632 NW Thurman St.; (503) 894-8136.

ORIGINAL HALIBUT'S, 2525 NE Alberta St., Portland, OR 97211; (503) 803-9600; halibuts.squarespace.com; Seafood; $. A small restaurant in a great

DINING

neighborhood, Original Halibut's serves wonderfully fresh fish and chips that are perfectly textured: crispy outside and tender inside. The chef varies the fish depending on the season and offers several battered delicacies each day. The clam chowder is also excellent.

ORIGINAL PANCAKE HOUSE, 8601 SW 24th Ave., Portland, OR 97219; (503) 246-9007; originalpancakehouse.com; Breakfast & Cafes; $. This Portland classic has been serving fabulous pancakes, omelets, and other breakfast fare since 1953. This is the spot that launched the national chain, and it is justly famous for its apple pancake, an oven-baked confection with Granny Smith apples and a perfect cinnamon glaze; its puffy, lemony Dutch baby; and its house-made corned beef hash. The restaurant has also won—along with Greg Higgins, Philippe Boulot, Andy Ricker, Gabriel Rucker, and other stars—a James Beard award. The Original Pancake House serves breakfast Wed through Sun until 3 p.m.; no reservations. Cash or check only.

OX, 2225 NE Martin Luther King Jr., Blvd., Portland, OR 97212; (503) 284-3366; oxpdx.com; Argentine; $$$. This South American–Portlandia hybrid focuses on grilling meat and fish to perfection and accompanying them with amazing combinations of flavors and textures—a starter of braised octopus and tripe with mint aioli, for example, or a porcini mushroom risotto with mascarpone. The stars—grilled grass-fed Uruguayan beef rib-eye, wild Alaskan halibut, house-made chorizo, for example—are served with tangy and fresh chimichurri. Ox opened in 2012; in 2013, it was the Restaurant of the Year for the *Oregonian*, and the accolades have piled up ever since. Watch out for high corkage fees. Ox is open for dinner beginning at 5 p.m. Wed through Mon.

DINING

The Food Dude

For the most unvarnished restaurant reviews, news, and gossip, check out Food Dude's blog, an Exploration of Portland Food and Drink, at portland foodanddrink.com. Food Dude started his blog as an antidote to reviews that sounded like advertising, in an effort to create a more reality-based picture of the Portland food and wine scene. He and his team review restaurants anonymously and multiple times, relating their experiences in great detail. As a result, he is irresistible reading for Portland foodistas—including Portland chefs, who often lurk here. Sometimes they post, too.

★ **PALEY'S PLACE,** 1204 NW 21st Ave., Portland, OR 97209; (503) 243-2403; paleysplace.net; Pacific Northwest Cuisine; $$$$. Paley's Place is justifiably one of Portland's favorite restaurants: Between chef Vitaly Paley's imagination and talent and Kimberly Paley's gregarious command of the dining rooms, Paley's Place offers one of the best meals in town. Here, the simplest ingredients are turned into Northwest-nuanced, French-inspired dishes prepared by a masterful chef. The menu is always changing, but you might find garlicky mussels prepared with hand-cut fries; a beautiful cut of Kobe beef; maple-glazed chicken with Granny Smith apples, sour cherries, and bacon; or halibut served with lentils, fennel, and fiddlehead ferns. Paley's is open 7 nights a week for dinner only.

PAPA HAYDN, 701 NW 23rd Ave., Portland, OR 97210; (503) 228-7317; papahaydn.com; Bakeries & Desserts; $$. With the onslaught of excellent new patisseries in Portland, it is easy to neglect the stalwarts. In Papa Haydn's case, this would be a mistake. It is still a charming place to go for fancy desserts, with an impressive array of elaborate gateaux, tortes, ice creams, tarts, and cheesecakes. Dishes such as lemon chiffon torte, marjolaine, and black velvet cake draw folks with a sweet tooth from all over the city to the comfortable dining room on Northwest 23rd Avenue. But don't overlook the dependably delicious pastas, salads, and grilled chicken and steak. Papa Haydn has another location in Southeast Portland.

PARK KITCHEN, 422 NW 8th Ave., Portland, OR 97209; (503) 223-7275; parkkitchen.com; Pacific Northwest Cuisine; $$$. Park Kitchen is a small restaurant featuring superlative tavern-style cooking. Chef Scott Dolisch is one of Portland's best, and everything here is tempting, beautifully prepared, and chosen with great care. Entree choices are kept to a minimum but offer excellent variety nonetheless—grilled pork chops, spring lamb, risotto, and two kinds of fish were the stars of one recent menu. Their attention to detail extends to the wine list, as well as the fine selection of bourbons and other liquors in the bar. Park Kitchen serves lunch and dinner. It's closed on Sun and open only for dinner on Sat.

PEARL BAKERY, 102 NW 9th Ave., Portland, OR 97209; (503) 827-0910; pearlbakery.com; Bakeries & Desserts; $. Pearl Bakery is one of several excellent artisanal bakeries in town, featuring rustic Italian breads, as well as breakfast and dessert pastries. But Pearl Bakery also operates a tiny cafe in its retail operation on Northwest 9th. Here, you will find a wonderful array of panini, focaccia, and deli sandwiches. The breads are outstanding—traditional sour-doughs are favorites but so are country-style loaves such as levain with green or kalamata olives. Breakfast pastries include tempting specialties such as apple coffee cake and pear Danish.

PHILADELPHIA'S STEAKS AND HOAGIES, 6410 SE Milwaukie Ave., Portland, OR 97202; (503) 239-8544; phillypdx.com; Brewpub; $. This is Oregon's most micro of all the microbreweries, and not only does it serve frosty ales and stouts, but also really good cheesesteak sandwiches. They offer a variety of sandwich styles, all of which are complemented by the handcrafted beers brewed on site, up to 11 of them on tap at a time. A favorite is the ginger hefeweizen, but all of them are pretty yummy. Also available are Tastykake products—it's the only place in town you can have peanut-butter Kandy Kakes with your IPA.

PIAZZA ITALIA, 1129 NW Johnson St., Portland, OR 97209; (503) 478-0619; piazzaportland.com; Italian; $$. This seductive little cafe serves authen-tic Italian dishes prepared by actual Italians. It is reminiscent of the cafes one finds on the back streets of Rome, with dishes lined up in the case, looking very modest until you bite into them. In this case, you may want to bite into the gnocchi with braised beef or the bucatini with pancetta, or both. Antipasti and salads are perfect as well. Piazza Italia serves lunch and dinner daily.

PIX PATISSERIE, 2225 E. Burnside St., Portland, OR 97214; (971) 271-7166; pixpatisserie.myshopify.com; Desserts; $–$$. Pix specializes in pas-try—cakes, tarts, tortes, petit-fours—and in chocolates. Here you will find a spectacular Carmen Miranda tart, with glossy fruit in artful balance. You'll find the award-winning Amelie, a chocolate mousse confection that embraces a well of orange-vanilla crème brûlée. And you'll find traditional patisserie favorites, such as the Opera, a thin almond cake layered with chocolate ganache and coffee buttercream. Pix supplies many local shops and restaurants, as well as offering a charming retail shop and restaurant. Tapas, wine, beer, and cocktails are also available. Open daily, 2 p.m. to 2 a.m.

PODNAH'S PIT, 1625 NE Killingsworth St., Portland, OR 97211; (503) 281-3700; podnahspit.com; Barbecue; $$. Podnah's serves excellent barbecue and its standard accompaniments in an unpretentious setting. It's one of the few places in town to get an iceberg wedge salad, but it's a salad that goes well with the sliced brisket, lamb spare ribs, and pulled pork. These and other smoky delights are made with local meats and served with refreshing slaws, beans, and other sides. Wine and beer are available, as is an impressive array of sodas. It's open for lunch and dinner Tues through Sun.

POR QUE NO, 3524 N. Mississippi St., Portland, OR 97227; (503) 467-4149; porquenotacos.com; Mexican; $. This is the kind of Mexican restaurant that makes you hungry just by thinking about it. It offers impeccably fresh, well-flavored dishes—the guacamole has nice chunks of avocado, the carne asada is smoky, and the fish tacos are brightly complemented by bits of mango. Tortillas are handmade and delicious. Also see the location at 4635 SE Hawthorne Blvd. There are long, long lines at both places, but the lines move quickly.

☆ Pok Pok and Whiskey Soda Lounge

Inhabiting a teeny hut and a vintage house on Southeast Division, Pok Pok's modest exterior belies its perfect and authentic Thai cooking. Pok Pok serves the cuisine of the northern part of Thailand, in particular the Chiang Mai valley, a mouthwatering balance of crispy and soft; of sweet, salty, and spicy; of yin and yang. Everything here is delicious, but the major draw is the roasted guinea hens, cooked on a special rotisserie that was imported just for this purpose. They have a gorgeous crispy golden skin, and the meat is juicy, infused with lemongrass, garlic, and smoke. Combine this with coconut rice and you may not want to eat anything else ever again.

Chef Andy Ricker, James Beard award winner in 2012, has opened a number of restaurants in Portland (and now in New York). They are all excellent—and they draw interested diners from across the world. This means that getting seated can be challenging, so many patrons head across the street and down half a block to the Whiskey Soda Lounge, which serves excellent cocktails along with the spicy Pok Pok wings and other bar treats, to wait for their table. Visit Pok Pok Mon through Sun. Lunch is served from 11:30 a.m. to 3:30 p.m.; dinner from 4:30 p.m. on. The Whiskey Soda Lounge is open every night starting at 5 p.m. Pok Pok is at 3226 SE Division St., Portland, OR 97202; (503) 232-1387; pokpokpdx.com; Thai; $$.

DINING

RIMSKY KORSAKOFFEE HOUSE, 707 SE 12th Ave., Portland, OR 97214; (503) 232-2640; Desserts; $. Rimsky Korsakoffee House offers a wide range of specialty coffees, desserts, and live classical music. They are noted for desserts like raspberry fool, lemon mousse pie, ginger cake, and pot de crème, which are indeed delicious—but they are also noted for their funky Portland vibe. The restaurant is in an early 20th-century house, with lots of vintage furniture, but it is the bathroom that is renowned. Really—check it out. Open evenings only: 7 p.m. to midnight during the week and 7 p.m. to 1 a.m. on Fri and Sat. Cash only.

RINGSIDE, 2165 W. Burnside St., Portland, OR 97210; (503) 223-1513; ringsidesteakhouse.com/home.html; Steak; $$$$. Since 1944, the RingSide has fed Portlanders prime and choice aged beef, fresh seafood, and excellent wine. If you're a rib connoisseur, try the 10-ounce RingSide Prime Rib served with au jus and creamed horseradish sauce. Also, don't leave without ordering the huge, luscious onion rings. The desserts, such as the chocolate raspberry torte (made locally by JaCiva), an exquisite Swiss-chocolate layer cake with raspberry filling, are a terrific way to finish off your feast. RingSide is open weekdays for lunch and daily for dinner.

RISTRETTO ROASTERS, 2181 NW Nicolai St., Portland, OR 97210; (503) 227-2866; 3808 N. Williams Ave., Portland, OR 97227; (503) 288-8667; 555 NE Couch St., Portland, OR 97232; (503) 284-6767; ristretto roasters.com; Coffee; $. Ristretto serves small-batch-roasted coffee for coffee purists, but even if you are not a purist, you will love this delicious coffee, attentively prepared on an old-fashioned Probat roaster. Good coffee stewards that they are, they will grind whatever kind of coffee bean you would like to try and make perfect, perfect drip coffee out of it. They also serve espresso, of course, and pastries, sandwiches, and other forms of carbohydrates. Free Wi-Fi, too. And you can buy their coffee online.

ROGUE DISTILLERY & PUBLIC HOUSE, 1339 NW Flanders St., Portland, OR 97209; (503) 222-5910; rogue.com; Brewpub; $$. Rogue Ales are full of flavor and variety and brewed specifically to go with food, and the food here is also full of flavor and variety. The star of the menu at this comfortable brewpub is American-raised Kobe beef burgers and dogs from Snake River Farms in Oregon. They also serve fantastic cheeses from Rogue Creamery and other local enterprises. Rogue offers the hard stuff, crafted on site, as well as its excellent beer. The beers served here include Rogue Red, Brutal Bitter, Buckwheat Ale, Porter, Stout, Rogue Smoke, and Maierbock. They also usually offer a cask-conditioned beer.

SABURO'S, 1667 SE Bybee St., Portland, OR 97202; (503) 236-4237; saburos.com; Japanese; $$. Serving good sushi in Portland, Saburo's popularity is evident by the crowds who gather outside in the evening, awaiting beautiful slices of velvety, firm fish and magnificent, fresh rolls. The sake list is also good, as are the tempura, noodles, and other traditional dishes. We order these because we can't help it, and they are good, but the true attraction is the sushi. The lighting is bright and the tables are tiny and crowded. There are always long lines, so we have been known to write our names on the list and then sneak up the street for a cocktail.

★ ST. JACK, 2039 SE Clinton St., Portland, OR 97202; (503) 360-1281; stjackpdx.com; French; $$$. This beautiful restaurant prepares classic Lyonnaise cuisine, which, frankly, is a little unique in Portland. Steak and frites with béarnaise, lamb confit, hearty terrines, moules a la crème—it's all here. If you are lucky, they will have salade Lyonnaise on the menu. The wine list is extensive and the cocktail menu superb, with some unique house-made cocktails such as Le Vieux Bouchon: bacon-infused apple brandy, cynar, maraschino, almond, and bay leaf. They also have a wonderful patisserie that's open from 8 a.m. to 3 p.m.; here you can get fantastic croissants, madeleines, and other amazing French pastry. Dinner is served nightly beginning at 5 p.m.

SCREEN DOOR, 2337 E. Burnside St., Portland, OR 97214; (503) 542-0880; screendoorrestaurant.com; Southern; $$. Screen Door is famous for its brunch. And brunches are excellent, with delicious fried chicken and waffles, biscuits, grits, and other homey deliciousness. But you can also eat dinner at Screen Door and indulge in fried chicken—as well as brisket, pulled pork, grits, and so on—then as well. The lemonade cocktail goes well with either. Brunch is served from 9 a.m. to 2:30 p.m. on Sat and Sun; dinner beginning at 5:30 p.m. daily.

Portland Spirits

In addition to its microbreweries and purveyors of hand-roasted coffee and artisanal wine, Portland is also home to a number of microdistilleries. These include Clear Creek (eau de vie and brandy), Rogue Spirits (gin and rum), New Deal Distillery (vodka), and House Spirits (vodka, aquavit, and gin). But how can you tell whether these homegrown brews are better than, say, bathtub gin? To that end, the Wine & Spirit Archive offers classes in spirit appreciation, where you can train your palate to be more discerning: wineandspiritarchive.com/classes/certification/spirits.html. They offer the only such certification in the country.

SERRATO, 2112 NW Kearney St., Portland, OR 97210; (503) 221-1195; serratto.com; Italian; $$$. Serrato is dedicated to the proposition that eating is meant to be a pleasurable, unhurried event, and the pretty dining room, with its big windows and blond wood, does inspire a bit of lingering over the dessert wine. The Italian-inspired menu is varied, making good use of our region's abundance. Good choices for antipasti might include the tomato and mozzarella salad with olive oil and basil or the potato and spinach tart with arugula and truffle oil. The pastas and risotto are very good; we have had luck with the ravioli in particular, especially when it is stuffed with crab.

SPELLA, 520 SW 5th Ave., Portland, OR 97204; (503) 752-0428; spellacaffe .com; Coffee; $. Spella Caffe is renowned in Portland for its authentic Italian-style espresso and coffee. The fragrant microroasts—hand-roasted by owner Andrea Spella—are sold by well-trained baristas who know how to draw a proper shot with an old-fashioned espresso machine. Such expertise is not uncommon in Portland, where barista is a respectable profession, but rarely are such beautiful shots pulled by people who are so friendly and unpretentious. They also make superb chai and serve possibly the best affogato (espresso poured over ice cream) in Portland. Spella Caffe is open from 7:30 a.m. to 3:30 p.m.

STUMPTOWN COFFEE ROASTERS, 4525 SE Division St., Portland, OR 97206; (503) 230-7702; stumptowncoffee.com; Coffee; $. This first-rate roaster with a cult following has numerous shops of its own as well as a wholesale and distribution outfit. Stumptown also provides an outstanding product to coffee shops all over town—and now has outposts in New York and Seattle. We can't really call them small roasters anymore, but we still like hanging out in their cool shops. The Division shop is like Starbucks's Pike Place store in Seattle: It's Store #1, and for that reason, worth a pilgrimage. It is open from 7 a.m. to 7 p.m. daily, and it retains its new urban industrial charm and nice, nice service.

★ **TASTY N SON'S**, 3808 N. Williams Ave., Portland, OR 97212; (503) 621-1400; tastyntasty.com; Brunch; $$. Tasty n Son's originally opened as a brunch spot featuring a delicious and eclectic variety of hashes, biscuits, eggs, sandwiches, and meats combined in unique ways—for example, polenta with a sausage ragu, topped by an egg. This proved to be a winning formula, and Tasty n Son's became an instant hit and amazingly popular with ridiculous lines in which people are nevertheless content to wait (and inspiring a *Portlandia* episode). Owner John Gorham (of Toro Bravo) decided that adding dinner service might ease the crush, and now they have also added a second location downtown, 580 SW 12th Ave.; (503) 621-9251.

Close-up

Dining at the Cusp: Oregon Culinary Institute

With all the attention to food in Portland, it is only natural that the city has several culinary schools. And it turns out that these schools are excellent places to have lunch or dinner—the students are cooking food, and someone must eat it. Why not you?

The Oregon Culinary Institute has an excellent restaurant for the adventuresome diner. The immediate appeal is the price: for less than the price of an entree in many restaurants, you can have an entire dinner. Oregon Culinary appears to be simply a stylish restaurant with a busy kitchen. But dig a little deeper and you'll find a dedication to focused, hands-on, real-world training of future chefs. The Portland area is ideal for training, given the farm-to-table paradise that is the Northwest. And, as OCI president Eric Stromquist observes, the entire city is like a laboratory for chefs, a unique environment that allows them to experiment and learn from one another. Oregon Culinary Institute also emphasizes the values and ethics behind using local and seasonal ingredients. This emphasis is not just a fashion, but also an important component of the discipline—plus, these ingredients tend to be the best products.

At OCI, the student cooks are under the trained eye of a master instructor; they work the dining room as well, wearing their chef uniforms as they practice balancing trays. They are also trained in restaurant management, labor costs, and other critical aspects of learning how to run a sustainable business. For many students who want to own restaurants some day, this training is as important as knowing how to debone a chicken and concoct the perfect consommé. And customers enjoy—along with truly praiseworthy meals—getting to know the students and following their careers as they become rising stars in the culinary firmament.

Oregon Culinary Institute serves a 3-course prix-fixe lunch for $9 (seating at noon) and a 4-course prix-fixe dinner for $18 (seating at 7 p.m.); beverages not included; and all gratuities benefit the Student Scholarship Fund. To make a reservation, call (503) 961-6200 from 9 a.m. to 6 p.m., Mon through Fri (office hours). You'll find Oregon Culinary Institute at 1701 SW Jefferson St., Portland, OR 97201. The atmosphere is fun and casual. But it is a school, so it's important to manage your expectations.

DINING

★ **TORO BRAVO**, 120 NE Russell St., Portland, OR 97212; (503) 281-4464; torobravopdx.com; Spanish; $$. Toro Bravo is relaxed and sociable, but with outstanding food. It truly is a tapas "bar," and the best approach to take there is to order just a few dishes, hang onto the menu, and then order some more. The kebabs, the paellas, the tortillas: Each of these is prepared as an homage to Spain but with decided Northwest accents. Local favorites include the coppa steak, prepared with spinach and golden raisins; bacon-wrapped dates; scallops; duck rillettes; and grilled chanterelle mushrooms. Plus there are enough dishes to please everyone from vegans to omnivores. Toro Bravo is open for dinner nightly.

TUGBOAT BREWING CO., 711 SW Ankeny St., Portland, OR 97204; (503) 226-2508; d2m.com/tugwebsite; Brewpub; $. This charming little family-owned spot on a downtown side street is in the old tradition of cottage-style, handcrafted brewing—the kind of beer everyone used to drink and that you can only get on-site. Tugboat likes to make powerful British-style beers, and their offerings include a fantastic extra special bitter, a hoppy India pale ale, a medium-bodied hop red, and a really special cask-conditioned stout. You may also wish to try their interesting Czech bitter brewed with imported Saaz hops. The owner also repairs watches—the brewery is housed in a historic watch- and clock-repair shop.

WIDMER BROTHERS GASTHAUS, 929 N. Russell St., Portland, OR 97227; (503) 281-3333; widmer.com; Brewpub; $$. Widmer Brothers Brewing Company is a top-selling craft brewer in the region and produces original European- and Pacific Northwest–style beers. Their flagship ale is America's original hefeweizen. The attractive Gasthaus, in an old refurbished 1890s hotel adjacent to the Widmer brewery, serves a complete menu. Their seasonal beers are delicious, but we also thirst for their IPAs—and the special Brothers' Reserve, fleeting runs of small-batch beer. The menu here is excellent, featuring delicious grilled meats, tasty salads, and sausages from Olympic Provisions—including a sausage fondue, which is probably the best dish ever invented to go with a nice hoppy beer.

VERITABLE QUANDARY, 1220 SW 1st Ave., Portland, OR 97204; (503) 227-7342; veritablequandary.com; American; $$$. The VQ has been a cocktail favorite for years, with its good location at the western edge of the Hawthorne Bridge and its pretty brick patio and its dark, old-fashioned bar. But it has a growing reputation as a destination for American cuisine inspired by Italy—and by the Pacific Northwest. First-rate signature dishes include osso buco, as well as nightly fish specials. Also of note here are the remarkable and rare wines offered by the glass. The VQ also offers an outstanding Sunday brunch.

VICTORY, 3652 SE Division St., Portland, OR 97202; (503) 236-8755; thevictorybar.com; Small Plates; $. In some respects, Victory is the ideal neighborhood restaurant—not because it is perfect, but because it indicates the benchmark quality that Portland restaurants regularly achieve. Here, they specialize in small plates, with a variety of excellent house-cured meats and a savory spaetzle in a delightful cheese sauce as signature dishes. But they also serve fine salads, mussels, a good cheese plate, and other cafe food. Victory has a well-edited wine list and a number of special cocktails. In fact, the owners of other Division Street restaurants appear at their bar with a regularity that is telling. Victory is open for dinner nightly.

Voodoo Doughnut

Security lines at Portland International Airport are full of people carrying large pink boxes that are too precious to check. What's in them? Voodoo Doughnuts, that's what. These treats have become a national phenomenon. Besides the usual cakes and crullers, you'll find innovations such as the Arnold Palmer, frosted with lemonade and tea powder; the Tangfastic, with orange Tang and marshmallows; or the justly famous Maple Bacon Bar. These punk-rock alternatives to cupcakes can be found at 22 SW Third Ave., (503) 241-4704, in Portland's Old Town, 24 hours every day. Cash only! They are also licensed to perform legal marriages, which might be a good option because you will probably wait in line a very long time. A second location is in Northeast Portland, at 1501 NE Davis St., (503) 235-2666, but the lines aren't really any faster there. They are also Tangfastic, just like the doughnut.

SPECIALTY FOOD SHOPS

⭐ **ALMA CHOCOLATE**, 140 NE 28th Ave., Portland, OR 97232; (503) 517-0262; almachocolate.com. Not surprisingly, Portland has a number of chocolatiers and candy-makers, and Alma Chocolate is among the best. Alma is the Spanish word for soul and also the name of proprietor Sarah Hart's grandmother, and we contend that Alma Chocolates do possess heart and soul in equal measure. Among the more unusual items are the gold-encrusted

Close-up

Portland's Microroasters

While many of the coffee shops listed in this chapter serve Stumptown Coffee, a growing number are starting to purchase, roast, and sell their own coffee beans. This trend in "microroasting" is no surprise in some ways: Starbucks and Peet's Coffee were once microroasters—as was (dare we say it) Stumptown. Microroasting fits in perfectly with Portland's indie, DIY business ethos, as well as its focus on the quotidian, daily pleasures that make life worth living no matter the size of your bank account. Plus it fits with the functional aesthetic that is so much a part of the character of Portland—coffee is a necessity. Why not style it up?

Here are some notable microroasters in Portland. Others are listed elsewhere in the chapter—in particular, Spella and Ristretto have led the recent microroaster renaissance. Many microroasters sell their coffee in local grocery stores and gourmet food shops as well as online.

Cellar Door Coffee, 2001 SE 11th Ave., Portland, OR 97214; (503) 234-7155; cellardoorcoffee.com. This husband-and-wife team started, like many DIY roasters, roasting by popcorn popper and progressed to a barbecue before they took it professional.

Coava Roastery, 1300 SE Grand Ave., Portland, OR 97214; coavacoffee.com. One of the top new microroasters, Coava shares its sleek space on Grand Avenue with a firm that features sustainable and Oregon-based bamboo design. They offer coffee flights of their single-origin brews so that you can directly compare different varieties.

Courier Coffee Roasters, 923 SW Oak St., Portland, OR 97205; (503) 545-6444; couriercoffeeroasters.com. This meticulous and customer-friendly roaster is renowned for their bicycle deliveries throughout Portland from their roastery on Hawthorne. They have a tiny shop downtown serving their excellent coffee. Bean varietals change seasonally.

Heart, 2211 E. Burnside St., Portland, OR 97214; (503) 206-6602; heartroasters.com. This ultra-modern roaster is notable for its single-origin espresso beans—yes, like wine—and its gorgeous shop near the Jupiter Hotel.

Public Domain, 603 SW Broadway, Portland, OR 97205; (503) 243-6374; publicdomaincoffee.com. Public Domain is the high-end roastery of the largest coffee roaster in Oregon, Coffee Bean International, which supplies stores such as Target with their house-brand coffee beans. Here, though, you'll find beautifully roasted single-origin varieties and a state-of-the-art Slayer espresso.

Schondecken Roasters, 6720 SE 16th Ave., Portland, OR 97202; (503) 236-8234. Old-school Schondecken roasts and sells their coffee in a cute shop in Westmoreland, where they also sell spices, teas, and herbs. They were here when Stumptown was just a gleam in Duane Sorenson's eye, and they still roast some great coffee.

Water Avenue Coffee, 1028 SE Water Ave., Portland, OR 97205; (503) 808-7084; wateravenuecoffee.com. This stylish microroaster helped to reclaim the Southeast industrial district, recycling old fir and other materials from nearby buildings. Their coffee is available at a number of local grocers.

Water Avenue Coffee's home base in the Eastside Industrial district

chocolate icons from various faith traditions, as beautiful to look at as they are to eat. Barks, caramels, and toffees are superb, as are ice creams. The caramel sauces—sea salt, lavender, and habanero—are heaven itself. Alma is open daily at 11 a.m., except for Sun, when they open at 12 p.m.

BOB'S RED MILL, 5000 SE International Way, Milwaukie, OR 97222; (503) 654-3215; bobsredmill.com. Bob's Red Mill is nationally noted for its excellent whole-grain products. Although Bob's Red Mill is now a giant, it still does things the old-fashioned way. Their huge, 120-year-old millstones still operate 24 hours a day, grinding out every grain under the sun. Bob's Red Mill is also a certified organic processor and carries a vast number of organic whole-grain products. The original plant is in a gorgeous, landscaped setting complete with a duck pond, with an attractive and well-organized on-site retail store for everything from rice, beans, nuts, seeds, milk powders, and pastas to dried fruits, sweeteners, and other related products, in either bulk or small packages.

★ **THE CHEESE BAR,** 6031 SE Belmont St., Portland, OR 97215; (503) 222-6014; cheese-bar.com. This cheese counter and deli has a phenomenal selection of more than 200 cheeses from around the region and the world. They also have excellent charcuterie, bread, chocolate, and other delicious treats. You can get your cheese to go, or you can sit at the nice bar and have a glass of wine with it. Cheese Bar is open from 11 a.m. to 11 p.m.; closed Mon.

FLYING FISH, 2310 SE Hawthorne Blvd., Portland, OR 97214; (971) 258-5212; flyingfishcompany.com. Flying Fish offers sustainably harvested fish and other seafood out of an unpretentious shack on Hawthorne. It is incredibly fresh and delicious, and the low overhead means that the prices are very reasonable. Try to get there before the local chefs grab all the troll-caught tuna and salmon. Flying Fish is open from 9 a.m. to 8 p.m. Mon through Sat, 11 a.m. to 7 p.m. on Sun.

★ **FOSTER AND DOBBS,** 2518 NE 15th Ave., Portland, OR 97212; (503) 284-1157; fosteranddobbs.com. Foster and Dobbs is a shop featuring artisanal cheese and a wide variety of other small-batch and gourmet food. They have an excellent wine and beer collection and often feature wonderful tastings that offer pairings of wine or beer with some delicious pickle or cheese. And they have a deli; you can have them make you a sandwich and pour you a cold one to enjoy on their pretty patio. Foster and Dobbs is open daily.

KOBOS COMPANY, 2355 NW Vaughn St., Portland, OR 97210; (503) 222-2302; kobos.com. Kobos was a pioneer of coffee roasting, setting up retail roasting in 1973 and serving espresso beginning in 1981. This major roaster features specialty coffees, wonderful pastries, and a lot more. Teas, herbs and spices, chocolates and Torani syrups, and cooking utensils from around the world are temptingly displayed at their stores. They also sell gourmet kitchen utensils and supplies. And you can buy their delicious coffee.

⭐ **LITTLE T AMERICAN BAKER**, 2600 SE Clinton St., Portland, OR 97202; (503) 238-3458; littletbaker.com. It is the sign of a true Portland food snob that he can sit at a restaurant and tell if the bread comes from Pearl Bakery, Ken's, Grand Central, or Little T. It is possible that Little T makes the best baguette in Portland, so good that all the Paleo diet fanatics fall off the wagon when they are presented with this bread. It has the most exquisite, chewy texture and fragrant yeasty flavor. Little T also makes excellent pastries and sweets (try the chocolate doughnut!), and they serve breakfast and lunch in their stylish cafe. Little T is open daily, thank goodness.

THE MEADOW, 3731 N. Mississippi Ave., Portland, OR 97227; (503) 288-4633; atthemeadow.com. The Meadow is a shop that focuses mostly on salt. You probably thought you were pretty fancy using kosher salt. Think again: The Meadow carries over 120 different kinds of salt, from fleur de sel to smoked and everything in between. They also carry Himalayan salt blocks for cooking (and hold classes in this intriguing art), as well as accoutrements for storing and serving salt and for curing things with salt. They also sell chocolate, wine, bitters, and flowers—basically, everything you need for a flavorful life.

⭐ **NEW SEASONS**, various locations; newseasonsmarket.com. New Seasons is Portland's answer to Whole Foods. After a locally owned upscale market, Nature's, was sold and resold to big corporations, some of its former employees missed having stores that were integral parts of neighborhood communities and driven by local interests. Thus, they founded New Seasons, which is designed to help bring back the local and seasonal emphasis to organic groceries. New Seasons is a full-service grocery store that features natural and organic foods, with exceptional produce, meats, takeout, and service. Indeed, they have an overt commitment to providing an excellent experience for the customer. You will find them all over the Metro area; more seem to be opening weekly—they are very, very popular.

⭐ **PASTAWORKS,** 3735 SE Hawthorne Blvd., Portland, OR 97214; (503) 232-1010; 735 NW 21st Ave., Portland, OR 97209; (503) 221-3002; pasta works.com. Pastaworks makes fabulous fresh pasta and sauces, from light-as-air fettuccine to superbly flavorful ravioli. You'll find many local and imported specialty items here, including truffled olive oils from Italy and melt-in-your-mouth ginger cookies from Sweden. Wines are also a strong suit of the store; the Hawthorne branch offers tastings, as well as a fine selection of stemware, cookware, and cooking classes—as well as a superb butcher and excellent cheese counter. Open 9:30 a.m. to 7 p.m., except on Sun, when they open at 10 a.m. You'll find another location in City Market, 735 NW 21st Ave., Portland, OR 97209; (503) 221-3002.

SALT & STRAW, 2035 NE Alberta St., Portland, OR 97211; (503) 208-3867; 838 NW 23rd Ave., Portland, OR 97210; (971) 271-8168; 3345 SE Division St., Portland, OR 97202; (503) 208-2054; saltandstraw.com. This insanely popular ice-cream shop offers rich, full-fat ice cream, house-made cones, and unusual flavors such as goat cheese with marionberry and habanero or strawberry with lime cilantro cheesecake or cinnamon snickerdoodle. They will let you try any flavor (which is why the lines are so long—from people trying every flavor) so you know what you're getting into.

SHERIDAN FRUIT CO., 409 SE Martin Luther King Jr. Blvd., Portland, OR 97214; (503) 236-2113; sheridanfruit.com. Sheridan Fruit Co. is another Portland institution, offering many unusual herbs, exotic plants, and vegetables. Sheridan's is known for its produce, but also carries an excellent selection of pasta, wine, and cheese—and it has one of the best meat counters in town. The butchers are absolutely stellar and will cheerfully take custom orders. They make outstanding sausages and marinated products as well. Sheridan's also has a good bulk section. They are open Mon through Sat from 6 a.m. to 8 p.m.

WINE SHOPS

DIVISION WINES, 3564 SE Division St., Portland, OR 97202; (503) 234-7281; divisionwines.com. This delightful shop carries more than 600 wines, most of which are smaller-profile labels. The extremely nice owners will guide you toward the perfect choice based on their vast knowledge of the flavor profiles of all those 600 wines. They have fun tasting events on Wednesday evenings. Open daily, 11 a.m. to 7 p.m., except on Sun and Mon, when they open at 12 p.m.

GREAT WINE BUYS, 1515 NE Broadway, Portland, OR 97232; (503) 287-2897; greatwinebuys.com. This friendly shop has congenial proprietors and more than 700 wines from around the world. They offer classes and group events in addition to great tastings on Friday and Saturday evenings. Open daily at 10:30 a.m., except on Sun, when they open at 12 p.m.

LINER & ELSEN, 2222 NW Quimby St., Portland, OR 97210; (503) 241-9463; linerandelsen.com. Liner & Elsen is regularly touted by the local and national press as one of the nation's best wine shops—and rightly so, for they offer outstanding service, selection, and stemware. They host

Division Wines is a friendly choice for novice wine buyers and experts alike.

many events, and they also have a comprehensive online shop. The brick-and-mortar one is open Mon through Sat from 10 a.m. to 6 p.m.

MT. TABOR FINE WINES, 4316 SE Hawthorne Blvd., Portland, OR 97215; (503) 235-4444; mttaborfinewines.com. This shop was named as one of the best wine shops in America four years running by *Food & Wine* magazine. They have an outstanding selection of Oregon pinot noirs, as well as hard-to-find, hand-crafted gems from around the world. They are open Tues through Sat and have superb tasting events.

PORTLAND WINE MERCHANTS, 1430 SE 35th Ave., Portland, OR 97214; (503) 234-4399; portlandwinemerchants.com. The friendly and knowledgeable folks at this shop specialize in Oregon wines but extend their expertise across the globe as well. They have regular tastings on Friday evenings and all day on Saturday and Sunday.

Entertainment

There is a kind of seasonal rhythm to entertainment in Portland. In the summer, when it stays light well into the evening, we linger outdoors, strolling the boulevards and sitting at sidewalk cafes or patios; we enjoy concerts on the lawn at the Oregon Zoo or at Tom McCall Waterfront Park. In the winter, when it gets dark at 4:30 p.m., we get through the rainy months by amusing ourselves indoors, at the theater, at the symphony, or at a Blazers game. Be sure to look at the Annual Events chapter for more information on seasonal concerts and other evening activities. You will find interesting entertainment venues all across town, so look in your neighborhood, too.

The Arlene Schnitzer Conference Hall— popularly known as "the Schnitz"— hosts musical events of all kinds in its vintage Portland setting.

CLASSICAL MUSIC

★ **CHAMBER MUSIC NORTHWEST,** various locations; (503) 223-3202, (503) 294-6400 (tickets); cmnw.org. Chamber Music Northwest, under the inspired direction of artistic director David Shifrin, promotes the diversity and exquisite beauty of chamber music, old and new. This organization brings renowned soloists and ensembles for a year-round program of music, lectures, films, symposia, master classes, and other events. Their season is divided into a summer concert festival and a fall-winter-spring series, and they are often organized thematically. Guest artists have included such stars as Wu Han, Bill T. Jones, the Orion Quartet, and Anne-Marie McDermott. Chamber Music Northwest also collaborates frequently with other groups in town—Bodyvox, PICA, the Oregon Symphony, for example—for amazing and innovative performance art.

OREGON REPERTORY SINGERS, various venues; (503) 230-0652; or singers.org. The 60-plus voices of the Oregon Repertory Singers present neglected classics as well as contemporary pieces to international acclaim. Directed by versatile conductor Ethan Sperry, the group often joins the Portland Baroque Orchestra to reinterpret work by Handel, Mozart, and Bach. They also have an extremely well-run youth choir program, with 170 children in 6 choirs.

OREGON SYMPHONY, 923 SW Washington St., Portland, OR 97205; (503) 228-1353; orsymphony.org. This ensemble of world-class performers delivers outstanding music. The sensitive and exciting principal conductor of the Oregon Symphony is the European-trained Carlos Kalmar, who also serves at the helm of Chicago's Grant Park Music Festival. He has won the hearts and ears of Oregonians, aided by Pops conductor Jeff Tyzik. The Oregon Symphony keeps it fresh with innovative events such as inviting Steve Martin to play with them, playing a live accompaniment to Alfred Hitchcock's film *Psycho*, or performing ABBA tribute concerts, in addition to playing the works of Schubert, Beethoven, and their brothers and sisters. They perform at the Arlene Schnitzer Concert Hall.

PORTLAND BAROQUE ORCHESTRA, 1020 SW Taylor Ave., Portland, OR 97205; (503) 222-6000; pbo.org. The Portland Baroque Orchestra is devoted to the performance of classical and baroque music on original instruments (or replicas) to provide an authentic experience of the great composers. This excellent 35-member group plays at different venues across the city, concentrating on works written between 1600 and the mid-19th century on these instruments. To enhance this time travel, visiting soloists on violin, cello, and harpsichord join the orchestra to render historical versions of Handel, Haydn, and Mozart.

PORTLAND CHAMBER ORCHESTRA, various venues; (503) 771-3250; portlandchamberorchestra.org. Portland Chamber Orchestra is one of the oldest chamber orchestras in the nation. Music for the chamber orchestra, a group that numbers about 35, is intimate but powerful—the size of the group allows greater flexibility compared with ensembles that are bigger or smaller. And Portland Chamber Orchestra takes full advantage of this in their repertoire; for example, their interpretation of Handel's *Messiah* is stunning. Also, they will often accompany stand-out soloists, such as pianist Mei-Ting Sun. They play city-wide, including at Lewis & Clark College, where they were first incorporated.

ENTERTAINMENT

PORTLAND YOUTH PHILHARMONIC, various venues; (503) 223-5939; portlandyouthphil.org. Portland Youth Philharmonic has a long history as the country's first youth orchestra. In 1912 Oregon's first children's orchestra was christened as the Sagebrush Symphony. This group turned into the Portland Junior Symphony in 1924 and then in 1930 it settled into its current title. The Youth Philharmonic has two full-symphony orchestras, as well as a strong orchestra for younger students. They regularly perform at the Arlene Schnitzer Concert Hall (part of the Portland Center for the Performing Arts) and are worth hearing every time.

DANCE

★ BODYVOX, 1201 NW 17th Ave., Portland, OR 97209; (503) 229-0627; bodyvox.com. Known for their combination of physical prowess and visual wit, Bodyvox offers some of the most innovative and original choreography around. The founders came from Pilobolus, Momix, and other important companies; they used that training to develop amazing shows that bring together music, dance, and film. Their range is impressive and compelling—they work with everyone from Chamber Music Northwest to live bands that play Elvis Costello covers. Bodyvox performs at various venues; they also have a studio and school.

OREGON BALLET THEATRE, 818 SE 6th Ave., Portland, OR 97214; (503) 222-5538 (tickets), (503) 227-0977 (administration); obt.org. The Oregon Ballet Theatre presents classics such as *Giselle* and *The Nutcracker* as well as showcasing the work of new choreographers. Artistic director Kevin Irving joined OBT in 2013 after a long performance career that included working with Alvin Ailey and Twyla Tharp. Although most of the performances are at the Keller Auditorium and the Newmark Theatre (see the Portland Center for the Performing Arts for more information), Oregon Ballet Theatre also takes to smaller stages such as Lincoln Hall at Portland State University as well as touring engagements throughout the United States. Oregon Ballet Theatre also has an outstanding classical ballet school.

WHITE BIRD DANCE, various venues; (503) 245-1600; whitebird.org. White Bird Dance is a presenter that brings elite dance performances to Portland. Most shows are staged at the Arlene Schnitzer Concert Hall, but a few performances require more intimate venues. White Bird Dance has sponsored, among many groups, the Cloud Gate Dance Theater of Taiwan; the Paul Taylor Dance Company; Ballet Hispanico, the nation's leading Hispanic-American dance company; and the Diavolo Dance Company, a group that leaps, spins, and flies through the air. White Bird also collaborates with local dancers to create innovative choreography and sponsors education and outreach programs for the Portland Public Schools and other groups.

DANCING, NIGHTCLUBS & LIVE MUSIC

BACKSPACE, 115 NW 5th Ave., Portland, OR 97209; (503) 248-2900; backspace.bz. Backspace is a great coffee shop and live-music venue that aspires to be a "third place"—a home away from home, where you can hang out, drink coffee (or beer), play pool, do some work, look at cool art, or maybe hear a show. Its Old Town location, near the MAX line, is convenient and central. But one of the biggest attractions is the networked gaming room, which provides 10 terminals where you can settle in with your coffee and play solo or with friends. If you go when there's a band, you'll need to pay the cover.

BLUE MONK, 3341 SE Belmont St., Portland, OR 97214; (503) 595-0575; thebluemonk.com. The Blue Monk started out as a jazz venue but has now expanded into related genres—including swing dancing and belly dancing. Hey, as the Duke said, if it sounds good, it is good. The Blue Monk has a good happy hour, good free pool, and a good cheap cover as well. Upstairs is a fetching contemporary room with an open kitchen, where cooks are busy preparing spaghetti, shrimp scampi, and other mostly Italian dishes. Downstairs, Portland's finest musicians are jamming.

⭐ **CRYSTAL BALLROOM,** 1332 W. Burnside St., Portland, OR 97209; (503) 225-0047; danceonair.com. The Crystal Ballroom is a renovated dance hall with a floating floor on ball bearings and rockers. Back when it opened in 1914 as the Cotillion Hall, Portlanders could be arrested for dancing the tango. Since then it's witnessed the likes of Rudolph Valentino, Jimi Hendrix, and the Grateful Dead. The dance hall closed in 1968 and sat empty for 30 years until the McMenamins tackled a major rehabilitation. Now Portlanders are once again enjoying this dance floor with a capacity of 1,500. Live bands play throughout the week. The dress code ranges from jeans and T-shirt to black cocktail dress or suit and fedora.

DARCELLE XV, 208 NW 3rd Ave., Portland, OR 97209; (503) 222-5338; darcellexv.com. Darcelle is a classic Portland female impersonator who puts on a fun Las Vegas–style cabaret revue Wed through Sat. On Fri and Sat, Men of Paradise, a Chippendale-style male strip show, takes over at midnight. It is said to be the longest-running drag show in the United States, and who are we to argue? Unsurprisingly, Darcelle XV is a big favorite with bachelorette parties, but if you want to bring yours, be sure to call ahead to reserve a seat.

DOUG FIR, 830 E. Burnside St., Portland, OR 97214; (503) 231-9663; dougfirlounge.com. The Doug Fir looks like a mountain lodge that has been given a makeover by Danish modernists. The food is good, and while some might claim that going to the Doug Fir for the food is like reading *Playboy* for the interviews, they might be telling the truth. But the big draw is the club: This space features great bands from all over, and it's a great space to see them because it was designed and built specifically to showcase live music, with a fantastic sound system and stage. The Doug Fir is open 7 nights. It's right by the Jupiter Hotel, which has obvious benefits.

EMBERS AVENUE, 110 NW Broadway, Portland, OR 97209; (503) 222-3082; theembersavenue.com. Embers Avenue—more popularly known as Embers—is a gay dance club that demonstrates tolerance by letting anyone in. With its 3 stages, it's a great place for dancing, and the music is a fun blend of retro, dance-party, and Top 40. Drag shows are a reliable feature of any night at the Embers. The fishtank bar alone is worth a visit.

HOLOCENE, 1001 SE Morrison St., Portland, OR 97214; (503) 239-7639; holocene.org. Holocene is dedicated to the avant-garde of the Portland art and music scene, with an über-modern interior, 2 large rooms, and a huge bar. Excellent dancing can be had here, as well as similar music experiences—secret shows by famous artists, up-and-coming bands that will be famous shortly, veteran and nouveau DJs, house music, shoegaze, modern soul, and other musical attractions keep hipsters crowding the place. The last Friday of the month brings SNAP!, a '90s dance party designed to evoke middle school dances, at least for some of us. The pours at the bar are, thankfully, generous.

MISSISSIPPI STUDIOS, 3939 N. Mississippi Ave., Portland, OR 97227; (503) 753-4473; mississippistudios.com. Part recording studio, part concert venue, Mississippi Studios attracts artists from all over to their excellent space. Here, musicians such as Kristin Hersh, Rickie Lee Jones, John Gorka, and Glen Tillbrook have all recorded or performed or both. The space is small and intimate and absolutely ideal for acoustic music. Yet it can, and does, also host a fantastic dance party. It's a great place to see a show, with a beautiful outdoor garden, bistro, and bar adjacent (called Mississippi Station).

Zoo Concerts

One of the most beloved venues for live music in Portland is the Oregon Zoo (zooconcerts.com). On summer evenings, the zoo stays open late and invites people in to sit on its big lawn and enjoy live music from the likes of Miranda Cosgrove, Taj Mahal, Chris Isaak, and the B-52s. The Oregon Zoo was the first such venue to hold summer concerts, in 1979, and they have been a sweet, sweet Portland tradition since then. It's a classic Portland experience to listen to great music, linger on the lawn with a picnic basket, and watch the sun set and the stars emerge. You can bring in food; wine and beer are available for purchase there, as are other food options. (See the Attractions chapter for more Oregon Zoo info.)

PRESS CLUB, 2621 SE Clinton St., Portland, OR 97202; (503) 233-5656; presclubpdx.com. During the day, this charming shop serves coffee and crepes and provides a huge periodical selection that you can read or purchase. At night, however, along with its dinner menu and wine list, the Press Club serves up expertly prepared live and DJ'd music from local greats and beyond. The Press Club is small and intimate but its high ceilings give it a feeling of spaciousness, a combination that allows the musicians and the audience to bond. They sponsor monthly readings from folks from Mountain Writers, Thursday night jazz sessions, and weekly trivia games (Tues).

PRODUCE ROW CAFÉ, 204 SE Oak St., Portland, OR 97214; (503) 232-8355; producerowcafe.com. For a long time, the Produce Row Café was a little lonely, serving up beer and playing great tunes in the inner Southeast industrial district. But now it looks like a pioneer, since this area is the leading edge of the culinary scene. Produce Row has been refurbished into a handsome bar and the deck has been refreshed, but it still offers an excellent selection of beer and ales, good pub food, genuine friendly service, and a variety of live music offerings ranging from jazz to bluegrass to folk. On the first Saturday of the month, they have a great hip-hop and R&B dance party.

⭐ **SECRET SOCIETY**, 116 NE Russell St., Portland, OR 97212; (503) 493-3600; secretsociety.net. The Secret Society is part speakeasy, part lounge, and part dance floor. Early Saturday evenings, they often play jazz and swing for all ages at no charge; couples swirl and dip in a riot of color and rhythm while kids watch from the seats or even join in. The music is great the rest of the time as well: from pop to more avant-garde and alternative folk. Cocktails are excellent here; this is really their specialty, and they have a long list of classic cocktails and the barware to serve them in.

SPIRIT OF 77, 500 NE Martin Luther King Jr. Blvd., Portland, OR 97232; (503) 232-9977; spiritof77bar.com. This sports bar is very Portland: lots of draft beer, excellent food, servers who know about the beer and the food, an indoor bike rack—oh, and lots of big screen TVs for televising sports events from here and beyond. The 16-foot screen is the main event, but there are others as well, including a couple in a private event space. Electronic basketball is free; there are also foosball and other game tables. It's fun for watching Blazer games.

TEARDROP COCKTAIL LOUNGE, 1015 NW Everett St., Portland, OR 97209; (503) 445-8109; teardroplounge.com. Some of us didn't ever know that the cocktail needed to be revived but we are awfully glad that the Teardrop is here to help out. The Teardrop is where you go when you want to put on some nice clothes and have a swanky cocktail experience. They serve craft cocktails at their finest, paying great attention to the individual ingredients but with the understanding that the whole is more than the sum of its parts. The servers are expert, and the atmosphere sophisticated, at least by Portland standards.

VAULT, 226 NW 12th Ave., Portland, OR 97209; (503) 224-4909; vault martini.com. Signature habanero martinis and other frosty concoctions keep the well-clad patrons of this Pearl District hangout returning. Vault has millions of martinis (okay, 44) to choose from, as well as a long list of other cocktails. The ambience is upscale modern, with the work of local artists festooning the walls, a fireplace, and an 18-foot glass bar. It's also fun for parties—but make sure to arrange them in advance.

VOICEBOX, 2112 NW Hoyt St., Portland, OR 97210; (503) 303-8220; voiceboxpdx.com. Someday we will get beyond our collective Journey obsession, but in the meantime, feel free to belt out the lyrics to "Don't Stop Believin'" or to "Bohemian Rhapsody" or any of your old favorites at this fun box karaoke bar, because you'll be doing it in your own private suite in front of the people that you care about most, or at least those whom you have invited. You make your own playlists too. Persons under 21 are welcome before 9 p.m., but you can't have alcohol in the suite when they're there. Closed Mon.

Portlanders are reputed to be the most movie-going population in the United States. Here are a few of the many excellent theaters in town.

CLINTON STREET THEATER, 2522 SE Clinton St., Portland, OR 97202; (503) 238-8899; clintonsttheater.com. Once exclusively a film theater, this multipurpose rumpus room offers poetry readings, performance art pieces, concerts, and movies of various genres, including science fiction, foreign, classic, and art films, most of which are decidedly not mainstream. Tickets are $6; matinees are $4; and on Tues, all shows are $4. *The Rocky Horror Picture Show* is a regular feature, showing every Saturday night at midnight—since April 1978, in what is undoubtedly the longest run of the cult favorite.

HOLLYWOOD THEATRE, 122 NE Sandy Blvd., Portland, OR 97212; (503) 281-4215; hollywoodtheatre.org. Open since 1926 this grand movie parlor is not only a splendid place to see a movie, but it's also a cultural center with classes, events, and workshops. This theater has been restored to its original glory, and it offers one of the few screens in town devoted to art and foreign films, as well as Hollywood classics, old and new. This is not some creaky old cinema, however (much as we also like those): It sports state-of-the-art digital sound and a 50-foot screen. And, as is typical of Portland's independent film venues, you not only can get coffee but also wine and beer.

LAURELHURST THEATER AND PUB, 2735 E. Burnside St., Portland, OR 97214; (503) 232-5511; laurelhursttheater.com. This classic neighborhood movie house offers pizza, wine, and microbrew beer with first- and second-run films, independent films, and classics at $4 ($3 for shows before 6 p.m.) per show for adults 21 and older. On weekend afternoons, children accompanied by an adult can see the matinee shows; children's tickets are $2. (All shows after 3 p.m. are for ages 21 and older.) Also note the neon swirl out front and along the ceiling.

★ **LIVING ROOM THEATER**, 341 SW 10th Ave., Portland, OR 97205; (971) 222-2010; pdx.livingroomtheaters.com. The Living Room Theater takes the idea of the home theater and reverses it: You get comfortable seating and great food and drinks, but you don't have to make it yourself or vacuum up any stray popcorn. The theater features independent films and shows them in an intimate but cozy setting—and serves you dinner and cocktails as well. You'll want to order dinner half an hour ahead of showtime if you want to eat while

Portlandia

A couple realizes they can pickle anything. A movie theater sells artisanal concessions. A local league holds adult hide and seek games. Is it real? Or is it *Portlandia*?

It's *Portlandia*. a sketch comedy show on the Independent Film Channel (IFC) starring Fred Armisen, Carrie Brownstein, and the city itself. Filmed on site, the show attracts first-rate guest stars, such as Andy Samberg, Chloe Sevigny, Kristin Wiig, and Kyle MacLachlan (in a recurring role as the mayor) because of its strong comedic writing.

Its premise is that Portland is "almost an alternative universe" like the 1990s, a place where you can work at a coffee shop and survive just fine, where people ride bikes and trams, where the tattoo ink never runs dry—in short, where young people go to retire.

A Southeast Portland house used for several episodes of Portlandia

It gently pokes fun at our bike culture, long brunch lines, our obsession with food, our earnestness, our bookstores, and our fashions. One of the funniest sketches is a spoof of the show's own opening credits: With Portland's fascination with artisanal everything, as well as its current obsession with facial hair, the writers assert that Portland is the dream of the '90s—the 1890s.

Portlandia has been polarizing, which is an uncharacteristic Portland feeling. Most people love it or hate it, and it's always an interesting character study to find out people's responses. It's common among hipsters and upscale residents to profess hatred for it; others, however—including some members of our national political delegation—describe the show as documentary masquerading as satire. Some people, however, like it without reservation: It won a 2013 Writers' Guild Award for Outstanding Achievement in Writing Comedy/Variety, beating out *Saturday Night Live*, *The Colbert Report*, and the *Daily Show*.

Portlandia (ifc.com/shows/portlandia) can be seen on the Independent Film Channel (IFC) on Fridays at 10/9 central and on Netflix.

you're actually watching the movie; otherwise, you can just hang out in the lobby cafe, which is worth a visit on its own. Seats can be chosen ahead of time.

NORTHWEST FILM CENTER, 1219 SW Park Ave., Portland, OR 97205; (503) 221-1156; nwfilm.org. The Northwest Film Center sponsors a number of festivals and events. Two of the most important: the Portland International Film Festival and the Northwest Film and Video Festival, featuring work by regional filmmakers, animators, and cinematographers. The Portland International Film Festival is the biggest film event in Oregon. It's 2 weeks of screen madness, with nearly 100 films from 30 countries shown at theaters all over town. The Northwest Film and Video Festival, while not so large, is in some ways more interesting. It showcases local talent and also brings in important independent filmmakers, such as Todd Haynes, Gus Van Sant, and Matt Groening.

PERFORMANCE VENUES

⭐ ALADDIN THEATER, 3017 SE Milwaukie Ave., Portland, OR 97202; (503) 234-9694 aladdin-theater.com. We love the Aladdin Theater—it presents great national, international, and occasionally local acts in a theater with about 600 seats, with great sound and sightlines. It feels quite intimate, and the performers seem to like it as much as the fans. The lineup is eclectic, and superb. Expect to see outstanding acoustic performers such as Rufus Wainwright and Norah Jones as well as more rocking artists. Advance tickets are available daily at the box office out front from 11 a.m. to 6 p.m. and just before the show, as well as through Ticketmaster.

COMMUNITY MUSIC CENTER, 3350 SE Francis St., Portland, OR 97202; (503) 823-3177; portlandonline.com/parks.community. Music Center was built in 1912 and served the neighborhood as a fire station until it was abandoned mid-century. Now beautifully renovated, it's a training center for hundreds of music students in the Portland area who present their recitals at the center. Many students go on to play with the Metropolitan Youth Symphony and Portland Youth Philharmonic. The center, a member of the National Guild of Community Schools of the Arts, is also a recipient of Chamber Music Program grants from the Amateur Chamber Music Players Foundation. The Community Music Center also hosts concerts in its acoustically sophisticated performance space.

THE PORTLAND CENTER FOR THE PERFORMING ARTS, 1111 SW Broadway, Portland, OR 97205; (503) 248-4335 (box office); pcpa.com. The Portland Center for the Performing Arts hosts more than 900 events annually, entertaining more than one million ticketholders. It comprises a number of buildings and theaters within buildings, with the main box office at 1111 SW Broadway. The Arlene Schnitzer Concert Hall, just to the north, is the home of the Oregon Symphony and host to other entertainment. Just south of the Schnitzer are the large Newmark Theatre and the Dolores Winningstad Theatre, a black-box theater with 292 seats. Keller Auditorium on Southwest 3rd Avenue between Market and Clay Streets is the venue for traveling Broadway shows.

ROSELAND THEATRE, 8 NW 6th Ave., Portland, OR 97209; (503) 224-2038; roselandpdx.com/roseland-theater. Housed in an old church, the Roseland Theatre is a somewhat chaotic all-ages concert pavilion with a bar and roomy balcony upstairs for those over 21. This is a popular venue that features national acts as well as local music. It fits about 1,400 people at a time—standing up; there are only a few seats, and they are in the bar—but sometimes the security makes it seem like there are three times that many. Still, the Roseland has great sound and good stage visibility. Expect to see anyone from Bob Dylan to Adam Ant to Sara Bareilles to Neko Case.

SPECTATOR SPORTS

Auto Racing

PORTLAND INTERNATIONAL RACEWAY, West Delta Park, 1940 N. Victory Blvd., Portland, OR 97217; (503) 823-7223; portlandraceway.com. Portland International Raceway is situated in a big park at the north end of the city, with Mount Hood providing an appropriate background to the drama on the field. The racetrack is to the west of I-5 at exit 306-B. This is where sportscars and motorcycles do their stuff. The raceway also hosts bicycle races, motocross, and other less revved competitions. Admission fees and starting times vary according to the event. The season at PIR is July through Nov, with most races held on weekend nights.

WOODBURN DRAGSTRIP, 7730 SR 219, Woodburn, OR 97071 (I-5, exit 271); (503) 982-4461; woodburndragstrip.com. Half an hour's drive south of town, the Woodburn Dragstrip showcases motorcycle, dragster, and funny car events from May through Sept. Classes include pro stock cars, alcohol-run dragsters and funny cars, jet cars, sport compacts, and street-legal drags with mandatory mufflers. Woodburn also sponsors events for junior racers (8 to 17 years). They even have track-side camping spaces available for those folks who don't want to miss a thing. Admission fees and starting times vary according to the event.

Basketball

THE PORTLAND TRAILBLAZERS, The Moda Center, 1 Center Court, Portland, OR 97227; (503) 234-9291, (503) 321-3211 (events); nba.com/blazers. The Portland Trailblazers—who play in the Western Division of the National Basketball Association—are beloved by Portlanders: They get us through the long rainy months of winter and give us plenty of thrills and lots of misery. The Moda Center, with seats going from $10 (bring your own oxygen) to more than $150, is one of the best places to be a spectator. It's a great show, with the BlazerDancers swooshing about and many events for the audience. Tickets are available from the Rose Garden box office and from Ticketmaster, (503) 224-4400.

Hockey

PORTLAND WINTER HAWKS, Western Hockey League, Portland Memorial Coliseum & Moda Center, 1 Center Court, Portland, OR 97227; (503) 238-6366; winterhawks.com. The Hawks have been favorites since they started playing here in 1976. This is a strong, fast-playing team that is a perennial contender for their league's championship. Success on the ice in Portland means a trip to the "big show," the National Hockey League (NHL), for players. The team consistently draws a good crowd, and there are lots of special fan events. The season is from late Sept through Feb; games start at 7 p.m., except on Sun, when they start at 5 p.m. Single tickets range from about $15 to $50.

Horseracing

PORTLAND MEADOWS, 1001 N. Schmeer Rd., Portland, OR 97217; (503) 285-9144; portlandmeadows.com. Racing has been a tradition in Portland for more than a century, and Portland Meadows has been here since 1946. Recently, they have been making an effort to cultivate a new generation of devotees, so in addition to actual races, there are resources to help you sort out how to wager and what it means if the morning line has got your horse figured at 5 to 9. It seems to be working—the opportunity to wear hats and drink craft cocktails while watching fast horses is pretty irresistible. Admission is free and so is parking.

Soccer in Portland

The Portland Timbers became a Major League Soccer franchise beginning with the 2011 season, and Portland has not been the same since. At each game, beautiful Jeld-Wen Field fills with highly enthusiastic but friendly fans—known as the Timbers Army—with unique traditions that include smoke bombs and singing. Sit with them in the general-admission area, and be prepared for the storied rivalries with the Seattle Sounders and the Vancouver Whitecaps. If you want a no less enthusiastic but less boisterous experience, sit in the family area. There's a long wait list for season tickets, but individual tickets are available, including from Stub-Hub (which is often your best bet).

The Portland Thorns are the affiliated National Women's Soccer League team, established in 2013, and they are also very popular. They are the only team in their league with a formal affiliation with a Major League Soccer team, and that's great for them and for fans, since they are backed by strong infrastructure. Portland Timbers and Portland Thorns, 1844 SW Morrison St., Portland, OR 97205; (503) 553-5400; portlandtimbers.com.

Other Spectator Sports

Most of the area's colleges and universities—Portland State University, University of Portland, Lewis & Clark College, and Reed College, among others—have sports programs that may include football, basketball, soccer, and baseball teams. The University of Portland has consistently produced decent men's and women's basketball teams, as well as championship women's soccer teams. PSU's Vikings (goviks.com) play football at Jeld-Wen Field (1844 SW Morrison St., Portland, OR 97205; jeld-wenfield.com), and their men's and women's basketball teams are fun to watch (some years are more fun than others). PSU's women's softball team, which competes in the Pacific Coast Softball Conference, offers free admission. The smaller schools, such as Reed and Lewis & Clark, may not have men's and women's teams that are contenders in all sports, but they play good college ball and attract some excellent track-and-field athletes, rowers, and lacrosse players. And local high-school teams are always fun to watch in any sport.

⭐ **ARTISTS REPERTORY THEATRE**, 1515 SW Morrison St., Portland, OR 97205; (503) 241-1278; artistsrep.org. An intimate black-box theater is home to this company, known for taut performances of new plays and classics. A good example is *Metamorphoses* by Mary Zimmerman—a recipient of the MacArthur "genius" fellowship. ART's beautiful space has 2 separate theaters; both are intimate and actor-focused—the ideal environment for its cutting edge performances that include many West Coast and world premieres.

DO JUMP!, Echo Theater, 1515 SE 37th Ave., Portland, OR 97214; (503) 231-1232; dojump.org. This one-of-a-kind physical theater and dance troupe has been celebrated since its beginning in 1977 for its distinctive choreography, which also features aerial acrobatics and live music. Do Jump! tours the nation, but its home is still the unpretentious Echo Theater just off Hawthorne Boulevard. That's also the home of its wonderful camps and classes that teach stilt walking, trapeze flying, aerobatics, and other gravity-defying tricks to children and adults. Do Jump! has become a classic Portland experience.

The Gerding Theater is home to the Portland Center Stage theater company.

IMAGO THEATRE, 17 SE 8th Ave., Portland, OR 97214; (503) 231-9581; imagotheatre.com. Imago Theatre blends physical comedy, acrobatics, and pathos, and somehow brings all of these characteristics together to perform award-winning shows that have traveled as far as Broadway. This boundary-blurring company performs new works as well as adaptations of classics. They are best known for their comedy. Portland's most avant-garde theater ensemble, Imago tackles edgy drama and comedy that slice across theatrical history from Japanese Noh to Sartre's *No Exit* to contemporary works by emerging playwrights. When Imago is not touring the globe, Portlanders line up to see their newest, strangely captivating performances.

MIRACLE THEATRE GROUP, 425 SE 6th Ave., Portland, OR 97214; (503) 236-7253; milagro.org. Comprising Miracle Mainstage and Teatro Milagro, this Portland-based operation is the largest Hispanic arts and cultural organization in the Pacific Northwest. Since it started in 1985, Miracle Theatre has offered Hispanic theater, arts, and cultural experiences throughout the region, particularly to low- and moderate-income Spanish-speaking audiences and those in rural settings who often don't get to see quality drama. Mainstage presents 4 English-language plays by Hispanic playwrights and 2 festivals each season on the Portland stage. Teatro Milagro is the group's touring theatrical company that journeys to rural communities in the West, where it invites local amateur actors and youth-at-risk to join the troupers onstage.

★PORTLAND CENTER STAGE, 128 NW 11th Ave., Portland, OR 97209; (503) 445-3700; pcs.org. Portland Center Stage, our city's only fully professional resident theater company, presents its dramas and comedies in the Gerding Theatre, a beautiful LEED-certified (Leadership in Energy and Environmental Design) building in the Pearl District. Recent productions have included *Fiddler on the Roof*, *The Fantasticks*, *Grey Gardens*, *Othello*, and a wonderful adaptation of Ken Kesey's novel *Sometimes a Great Notion*. PCS also shows compelling Christmas presentations such as *The Santaland Diaries* and *A Christmas Carol*. Ticket prices depend on seating and day of the week. PCS sponsors an intensive playwrights' festival each summer, JAW (for Just Add Water), which is free and open to the public.

PORTLAND OPERA, Keller Auditorium, 222 SW Clay St., Portland, OR 97201; (503) 241-1802; portlandopera.org. Since the early '60s, the Portland Opera has been presenting operas that have earned the group a ranking in the top 15 opera companies in the United States. As well as presenting classic operas such as *Aida*, *Carmina Burana*, and *The Mikado*, Portland Opera became the first opera company in the world to sponsor a subscription series to national touring Broadway musicals. This "Best of Broadway Series" has brought *The Sound of Music*, *Sunset Boulevard*, *Les Miserables*, *Mamma Mia*, *Wicked*, and many more crowd-pleasers to the Keller Auditorium. Tickets are available from them directly or via Ticketmaster, and they have excellent deals for senior citizens and students.

TEARS OF JOY THEATRE, Imago Theatre, 17 SE 8th Ave., Portland, OR 97214; (503) 248-0557; totj.org. Award-winning Tears of Joy Theatre is an amazing puppet theater troupe that has been delighting kids and adults for years with its mythologically driven dramas, life-size puppets, and wondrous costumes. As well as performing in Portland and touring through the United States, Tears of Joy also has a Puppet Camp where children ages 7 to 12 get to join the puppeteers in creating their own puppet plays. But don't think that this company is for children only—it's sophisticated theater in every regard.

Shopping

No sales tax in Oregon. What else do you need to know? All right, we'll tell you more. Portland is a great town for shopping. Here you will not only find the usual suspects—department stores, like Nordstrom and Macy's, chain stores such as H&M and Pottery Barn, and so on—but also many interesting, chic, and independent shops. And Portland also has other unusual shopping opportunities such as Portland Saturday Market, which takes place every weekend under the Burnside Bridge from Feb through Dec. (See the Annual Events chapter for more about Saturday Market.)

SHOPPING DISTRICTS

The soul of Portland shopping can be found in its shopping districts. Because the city organizes itself around its neighborhoods, the shopping and business districts play a vital role in creating neighborhood identity and atmosphere. These districts are clustered throughout the city, and we list some of our favorites here. We encourage you to stroll whatever neighborhood you're in—unless you do a little fieldwork on your own, who knows what fine harvests are in store?

Southwest Portland

Downtown
Downtown Portland retail is undergoing a bit of a renaissance. Department stores, luxury boutiques, emerging independent stores, and Pioneer Place, a pedestrian mall with high-end retail, are the traditional highlights of downtown shopping (no sales tax!). But the edges of the downtown core are seeing interesting new stores. Check out Southwest Morrison between 3rd and 10th and Southwest 10th between Burnside and Yamhill; these areas have some excellent shops, including new clothing boutiques established by local designers attracted to the downtown area.

Multnomah Village
Multnomah really does feel like a village—it is a tight-knit community in addition to its identity as a retail, coffee-shop, and hang-out mecca. Adding to the cohesive feel are the wonderful Multnomah Arts Center, 7688 Capitol Hwy., a popular Portland Arts and Recreation facility. You will find wonderful bookstores, gift shops, housewares, and an excellent yarn shop, among other things.

Northwest Portland

Northwest 23rd District

This upscale neighborhood includes a number of shops on 21st, but is known to Portlanders simply as Northwest 23rd. Filled with lovely Victorian homes and countless trees, this neighborhood is one of the prettier balances of the domestic and commercial in Portland, and it's a great walking neighborhood—the pedestrian traffic here is at times so uppity that it stops the automotive traffic. In addition to locally owned dress shops and high-end housewares, you'll find chains such as the Gap, Urban Outfitters, and Pottery Barn.

> **i** Many downtown merchants will validate your Smart Park parking slips if you spend $25 or more at their shops. It never hurts to ask.

Pearl District

Colonized by starving artists, then domesticated by hipsters, the Pearl District is now becoming the home of the haute bourgeoisie. Evidence of all three classes is readily apparent here, in the Soho of Portland. Not only are there dozens of art galleries (and a gallery walk the first Thurs night of each month) and an art school (the Pacific Northwest College of Art, 1241 NW Johnson), but the housewares, art supplies, furniture, clothing, hardware, and even light fixtures for sale in the area have a distinctly aesthetic quality to them. Powell's is here, as are chains such as Anthropologie, Lululemon, adidas, and Lucy.

Southeast Portland

Hawthorne District

A local favorite, the busy Hawthorne District is Portland's left-coast hip shopping area, where granola meets granita. You'll find excellent gift shops, some of the best clothing and shoe boutiques in town, great housewares, and a plethora of music shops. Powell's on Hawthorne, 3723 SE Hawthorne, and Powell's Books for Cooks, 3747 SE Hawthorne, are the eastside siblings of the City of Books, and these are smaller and less overwhelming but still feature a fantastic selection and major literary events. Hawthorne is the earthier alternative to the slick Northwest 23rd: You're more likely to get a whiff of patchouli than Chanel No. 5, although the Perfume House, 3328 SE Hawthorne, can supply either one.

LoBu

On the east side of the Willamette River, Lower Burnside, or "LoBu," has a number of terrific restaurants and shops, especially in the area between Martin Luther King Jr. Blvd. and Southeast 10th. New shops are opening all the time. Look for good vintage shops—including the remarkable Hippo Hardware (see the listing on p. 113)—and design-focused businesses. In particular, the shops at 811 E. Burnside, across from the Doug Fir Lounge and Le Pigeon, are standouts: it's a mini-mall for Portland's cool designers.

Sellwood District

Sellwood, one of Portland's most distinctive and historic neighborhoods, is brimming with charming antiques stores, particularly in the area along Southeast 13th Avenue, which is known as Antique Row. Because the shopping area is so condensed, you can park your car and then get around on foot. Laced in between the dozen blocks of antiques and collectibles stores, you'll find numerous delightful espresso shops and cafes.

Many shopkeepers hang signs on their buildings explaining their original use and date of construction, but our sources say that Sellwood has been known as Portland's antiques district since the 1950s. The adjacent Westmoreland district near Southeast 16th and Bybee, also has excellent shopping.

NORTH & NORTHEAST PORTLAND

Alberta Street

Northeast Alberta Street is a festive district that has been the focus of much redevelopment over the years. Community banks, city government, and neighborhood groups have converged to make this area one of the most vital places in the city. This gentrification is not without controversy, and not every citizen thinks that opening a new Starbucks counts as progress. The source of this renaissance is the distinctive homegrown businesses, ranging from restaurants and art galleries to clothing designers and gift shops, most of which are clustered along Alberta Street between Martin Luther King Jr. Boulevard and Northeast 33rd Avenue. This is some of the best shopping in Portland.

Broadway District

Northeast Broadway is a lively east-west stretch of shops, cafes, and offices; its bike- and foot-friendly design has helped to make it one of the most enjoyable shopping districts in the city. The anchor of all this glittery commerce is the Lloyd Center, Oregon's historic indoor mall.

North Mississippi

In some ways the soul of Portland retail, this charming street has some of the best new shops in town, selling everything from gourmet salts to locally designed dresses to vintage home decor. There are interesting great restaurants and coffee shops as well to sustain you during your hunt.

Where Are the Malls?

Sometimes only a big shopping mall will do. The following are the major shopping malls in the area.

Southeast Portland
Clackamas Town Center, 12000 SE 82nd Ave., Happy Valley, OR 97086; (503) 653-6913; clackamastowncenter.com
Mall 205, 9900 SE Washington St., Portland, OR 97216; (503) 255-5805

North & Northeast Portland
Jantzen Beach Shopping Center, 1405 Jantzen Beach Center, Portland, OR 97217; I-5 at exit 308; (503) 247-1327
Lloyd Center, 2201 Lloyd Center, Portland, OR 97232; (503) 282-2511; lloydcenter.com

Southwest Portland
Pioneer Place, 700 SW 5th Ave., Portland, OR 97204; (503) 228-5800; pioneerplace.com.

Vancouver
Westfield Shoppingtown–Vancouver, 8700 NE Vancouver Mall Dr., Vancouver, WA 98662; (360) 892-6255; westfield.com/vancouver

Outlying Areas
Bridgeport Village, 7455 SW Bridgeport Rd., Tigard, OR 97224; (503) 968-8940; bridgeport-village.com
Columbia Gorge Premium Outlets, 450 NW 257th Ave., Troutdale, OR 97060; (503) 669-8060; premiumoutlets.com
Washington Square and Square Too, 9585 SW Washington Square Rd., Portland, OR 97223; (503) 639-8860; shopwashingtonsquare.com
Woodburn Company Stores, 1001 N. Arney Rd., Woodburn, OR 97071; (503) 981-1900; premiumoutlets.com

ANTIQUES AND VINTAGE SHOPS

HAWTHORNE VINTAGE, 4722 SE Hawthorne Blvd., Portland, OR 97214; (503) 230-2620; hawthornevintagepdx.com. Purported to be rapper Macklemore's favorite thrift shop ever, Hawthorne Vintage has acres of modern and vintage furniture, home accessories, lamps, dishware, and every other thing you could need to stock your house. Lots of vintage leather jackets, dresses, and other clothing items are plentiful as well.

LOUNGE LIZARD, 1310 SE Hawthorne Blvd., Portland, OR 97214; (503) 232-7575. Filled with retro furniture and home decor accessories, Lounge Lizard is just the spot for the newly antique. They aim to please—the prices are affordable and the service is friendly. Plus, they have a large selection of great, basic vintage furniture, as well as odd but wonderful other pieces. The lighting selection is excellent. If you never before thought of putting Eames knockoffs in your 1908 Craftsman, you might start thinking about it now.

One of the many booths at the Portland Saturday Market

⭐ MONTICELLO ANTIQUE MARKETPLACE, 8600 SE Stark Street, Portland, OR 97216; (503) 256-8600; monticelloantiques.blogspot.com. This stunning collection of dealers—more than 100—is replete with inventive displays and gorgeously styled rooms in a range of vintage and antiques styles, from French country to modernist industrial and every aesthetic in between. Especially notable is the exquisite garden salvage room. A sweet cafe and a library will allow you to rest between eras. Monticello is open from 10 to 6 Monday through Saturday and from 10 to 5 on Sunday.

THE SELLWOOD ANTIQUE MALL, 7875 SE 13th Ave., Portland, OR 97202; (503) 232-3755; sellwoodantiquemall.com. The Sellwood Antique Mall is perfect for either the serious or frivolous collector. It has more than 100 different dealers, so the inventory changes constantly. The mall is one of the largest of its kind in the city, carrying a wide range of items from furniture to dishes to lighting fixtures. It also carries nostalgia items from the 1950s.

⭐ STARS, 7030 SE Milwaukie Ave., Portland, OR 97202; (503) 235-5990; starsantique.com. Two hundred dealers of antique and collectible furniture, linens, books, clothes, jewelry, dishes, and tchotchkes are here for the perusal of the antiques hunter. Because there are so many different dealers, the Stars empire cannot be comprehensively characterized, but you're more likely to find a country primitive sideboard than a federal one, although you never know. The managers are very good about display—this is one of the most attractive antiques malls around.

BOOKS & PERIODICALS

Portland is a city of readers. We have the largest bookstore in the nation, Powell's City of Books, which is made even larger by the fact that it has a number of branches. However, Powell's can sometimes overshadow the other fine independent bookstores in the area, including interesting book selections at places like the Oregon Historical Society, Portland State University, or the Audubon Society of Portland. We also have the usual national chain bookstores here in town.

ANNIE BLOOM'S BOOKS, 7834 SW Capitol Hwy., Portland, OR 97219; (503) 246-0053; annieblooms.com. Tucked into the retail center of the Multnomah neighborhood, this store attracts loyal readers from throughout the area who appreciate the selection, the suggestions, and assistance of the well-read staff, as well as the cozy armchairs. The store is also well known beyond

Portland proper for its Children's Corner, with books and a play area, and for its collection of titles on Judaism and Judaic culture and art. Annie Bloom's is frequently mentioned as a contender for Portland's favorite bookstore.

BARNES & NOBLE, 1317 Lloyd Center, Portland, OR 97232; (503) 249-0800; barnesandnoble.com. This store in the Lloyd Center provides a terrific respite from the mall shoppers, and besides all the great books and Nooks, there are author events and a Starbucks. There are 4 other stores in the area as well: Clackamas Town Center, 12000 SE 82nd Ave., Portland, OR 97086, (503) 786-3464; 7227 SW Bridgeport Rd., Tigard, OR 97224, (503) 431-7575; 18300 NW Evergreen Pkwy, Beaverton, OR 97006, (503) 645-3046; and 7700 NE Fourth Plain Blvd., Vancouver, WA 98662, (360) 253-9007.

BROADWAY BOOKS, 1714 NE Broadway, Portland, OR 97232; (503) 284-1726; broadwaybooks.net. This charming shop in the Lloyd District has a thoughtful collection of diverse literaria. In addition to stocking a good selection of literary works, it sponsors poetry readings and author book-signing events. The owners and their employees are friendly, knowledgeable, and articulate, and the well-chosen selection here reflects their expertise; they have crafted one of the best bookstores in town.

CAMERON'S BOOKS AND MAGAZINES, 336 SW 3rd Ave., Portland, OR 97204; (503) 228-2391; cameronsbooks.com. Before there was Powell's—before there was any other bookstore in Portland—there was Cameron's. Tucked into a downtown storefront, Cameron's features windows filled with well-cared-for copies of *Life, Time, Look, Saturday Evening Post, Colliers,* and other publications from the era of the general-interest magazine. They also have back issues of *Sports Illustrated* and *Playboy* as well as a massive collection of comic books. Cameron's claims to have 100,000 magazines, mass-market paperbacks, and comics in stock and to be the home of the birthday magazine gift.

DAEDALUS BOOKS, 2074 NW Flanders St., Portland, OR 97209; (503) 274-7742; abebooks.com/home/daedalus. Daedalus Books carries many kinds of books, but they specialize in the scholarly ones that are harder to find in other bookstores. For example, their philosophy inventory goes far beyond *Zen and the Art of Motorcycle Maintenance.* They are an exceptional resource for history and literature, as well as classics and linguistics. They carry both new and used books, and there is nothing quite like Daedalus in town.

IN OTHER WORDS, 14 NE Killingsworth St., Portland, OR 97211; inotherwords.org. Once inside this cheerful, cozy outlet for women's books and resources, you'll find a bounty of magazines, videos, cards, gifts, and new and used books. Open 7 days a week, the store also sponsors readings and workshops.

LAUGHING HORSE BOOKS, 12 NE 10th Ave. Portland, OR 97232; (503) 236-2893. This unabashedly progressive and vibrant bookstore advertises itself as a resource for social change. Inside are new and used books devoted to political issues, a bulletin board listing meetings and workshops held by local political-action groups, and a gathering space where poets and authors read from their works and actors perform.

LONGFELLOW'S BOOKS AND MUSIC, 1401 SE Division St., Portland, OR 97202; (503) 239-5222; longfellowspdx.com. Longfellow's is a much-accoladed family-run store near the Ladd's Addition neighborhood of Portland—and a destination for its many fans, who regularly cite this friendly shop as their favorite. Their specialties include rare books and magazines, but with more than 7,500 titles, there is a robust general reading section as well. They're open Mon through Sat from 1 to 5 p.m.—as well as having a great online store.

⭐ **POWELL'S CITY OF BOOKS**, 1005 W. Burnside St., Portland, OR 97209; (503) 228-4651; powells.com. With more than a million books in a store covering several levels in a building filling an entire city block, Powell's is the largest bookstore in the country. It even has its own (small) parking garage. Powell's has become an attraction in its own right and really does deserve a visit . . . or two . . . or three.

You'll find both used and new books and a separate rare book room. There are books in other languages besides English, and a small selection of reading glasses. Powell's also has an excellent children's section, as well as a selection of cards, blank journals, and other papery things. The cafe, with its coffee, tea, and snacks, would be a good place to look through potential purchases if one weren't always getting distracted by the interesting people wandering in and out of the room. The frequent literary readings are a big draw. Powell's is open every day of the year and is usually busy, if not downright crowded. There are other sites too: at the airport; in Beaverton, 8725 SW Cascade; Powell's Books for Cooks and Gardeners, 3747 SE Hawthorne Blvd., which is devoted to cooking, gardening, and lifestyle books; and Powell's Bookstore on Hawthorne, 3723 SE Hawthorne Blvd., a general-interest bookstore.

Powell's City of Books attracts readers and writers from across the US.

Powell's online service is incredibly well organized and useful. Don't tell them, but a lot of people look up the books that interest them before they get to the store. It helps make the experience less overwhelming.

READING FRENZY, 3628 N. Mississippi Ave., Portland, OR 97227; (503) 274-1449; readingfrenzy.com. Reading Frenzy, which specializes in publications by independent presses, sells things that you can't find anywhere else in Portland, and sometimes, anywhere else in the world. In addition to a fine selection of smart magazines, this shop carries locally and nationally published 'zines, literary quarterlies, and attractively published essays by academics such as Noam Chomksy. Reading Frenzy also serves as a meeting and distribution place for all kinds of alternative causes.

TITLE WAVE, 216 NE Knott St., Portland, OR 97212; (503) 988-5021; multcolib.org/library-location/title-wave-used-bookstore. The bookstore for discards from the Multnomah County Library is so good that we don't even really want to tell you about it. Prices for paperbacks start at about $1 and go up from there. For hardbacks—which include both contemporary and older fiction, poetry, mysteries, cookbooks, and anything else you might want—look for prices to begin at $2. You will also find a great selection of books on tape and CD, music CDs, and LPs. Back copies of many magazines are also available, and the videos and DVDs are also worth perusing.

WALLACE BOOKS, 7241 SE Milwaukie Blvd., Portland, OR 97202; (503) 235-7350. Just a couple of blocks south of the Moreland business district antiques malls and small shops, Wallace Books is an old house with bookshelves in every room. It's fun to browse upstairs and down to find the words you want to snuggle with later as the day winds down. The store has the newest releases as well as lots of new and used genre paperbacks.

CLOTHING

Portland has a history of supplying the nation with stylish, well-made clothing, and you've probably heard of Pendleton, Hanna Andersson, Jantzen, Columbia Sportswear, and Nike. But Portland's fashion scene also embodies its experimental and innovative edge, attracting young designers from elsewhere and growing some of our own. You may have even seen local star Michelle Lesniak Franklin win Season 11 of *Project Runway* (the fourth Portlander to do so).

ANIMAL TRAFFIC, 429 SW 10th Ave., Portland, OR 97205; (503) 241-5427; 4000 N. Mississippi Ave., Portland, OR 97227; (503) 249-4000. Animal Traffic purveys high-end vintage clothing and Western wear. Both locations are rich sources for vintage Pendletons—shirts, jackets, and other—as well as handmade White's Boots, Smith and Wesson watches, and other handsome accessories.

BLAKE, 26 NW 23rd Place, Portland, OR 97210; (503) 222-4848; loveblake .tumblr.com. Blake is the go-to source for denim—both for the variety and for the help in choosing the perfect fit. They have extensive jeans collections for men and women, as well as chic jackets, sweaters, accessories, and so on.

DUCHESS, 2505 SE 11th Ave., Portland, OR 97202; (503) 281-6648; duchessclothier.com. Duchess has evolved from a fun shop with Western-inspired clothes, reproductions of 20th-century classic silk slips, and petticoats to a purveyor of handsome custom men's suits in a range of historically inspired styles. The suits are also available in a range of prices. But these made-to-measure suits are all beautifully made, affordable, and will be well worth the effort.

THE ENGLISH DEPT., 1124 SW Alder Ave., Portland, OR 97205; (503) 224-0724; theenglishdept.com. Co-owner Elizabeth Dye sells her own work here, as well as that of others. And what is this work? Why, beautiful and feminine clothes inspired by Jay Gatsby's yellow shirts and other literary fashions. Wedding and special occasion dresses are the stars, but you will find other pretty dresses, jewelry, skirts, and tops. You can walk in 11 a.m.–6 p.m. Tuesday–Friday; on Saturday, it's open by appointment only.

FYBERWORKS, 4300 SE Hawthorne Blvd., Portland, OR 97215; (503) 232-7659; fyberworks.com. Street clothes, beautiful accessories, and workout wear are the specialties here. We go for gorgeous hand-knit scarves, for silk shawls, for natural-fiber jackets, dresses, and tunics, and for the wonderful variety of locally made designs. Fyberworks often carries cute vintage and Portland-made home design objects in its friendly shop.

★ **GILT**, 720 NW 23rd Ave., Portland, OR 97210; (503) 226-0629; giltjewelry.com. We love affordable jewelry, and the hallmark of this shop is its immense collection of shiny things from ages past, including vintage engagement and wedding rings. This shop features locally made artisan jewelry in addition to its lovely collection of rings, pendants, and other estate pieces.

HANNA ANDERSSON, 327 NW 10th Ave., Portland, OR 97209; (503) 321-5275; hannaandersson.com. Portland is headquarters for this nationally successful shop featuring Swedish-style, high-quality clothing for kids and their moms. Designs are often, but not exclusively, made with cotton jersey. The underwear and pajamas are especially cozy and comfortable; and the clothes wear very well, through at least two children, and so are a good value. The store is clean, light, and wholesome. This civic-minded company passes along gently used Hannas to needy children—isn't that a good reason to shop here?

JOHN HELMER HABERDASHER, 969 SW Broadway, Portland, OR 97205; (503) 223-4976; johnhelmer.com. One day in 1966, American men stopped wearing proper hats. They revived the habit in 2008. All the time in between, John Helmer has been keeping the flame alive, selling fedoras, bowlers, Panamas, and every other variety of chapeau. They also carry beautiful hats for women; these have made a comeback since the latest royal wedding. John Helmer offers other handsome menswear as well.

LANGLITZ LEATHERS, 2443 SE Division St., Portland, OR 97202; (503) 235-0959; langlitz.com. Since 1947, Langlitz Leathers has forged a world-wide reputation for crafting the highest-quality leather garments. Their shop is small—less than 3,000 square feet—and crowded. Langlitz creates only about 6 garments per day. Half are custom built, and the others are built to stock pattern sizes for walk-in customers. Because their prices are relatively low for custom work (between $500 and $1,000 per garment), their services are in constant demand. They have different products, but the Columbia was the first jacket that store founder Ross Langlitz designed—in the mid-1940s—and it remains the flagship of the jacket line, reflecting the traditional look of motorcycling.

LENA MEDOYEFF, 710 NW 23rd Ave. Portland, OR 97210; (503) 227-0011; lenadress.com. Well-cut, elegant bridal and special occasion dresses in stunning fabrics—this is the hallmark of Lynn Solmonson, the designer behind the name Lena Medoyeff. These dresses are truly alluring, and they'll make you so as well. You'll see a lot of embroidery, some of it by local artisans. They specialize in silks with simple designs that allow the beauty of the fabric to stand out.

⭐ **MARIO'S**, 833 SW Broadway, Portland, OR 97205; (503) 227-3477; marios.com. Mario's is the best source in town for urbane designer clothing, shoes, and accessories from Armani to Prada. Some readers may be familiar with the clean, spare luxury of the Mario's in Seattle, but this one is the original; it was one of the first residents of the Galleria and therefore may be regarded as a chief contributor to the beautification of downtown—and its residents. The store now inhabits a beautiful space in the Fox Tower.

⭐ **MINK**, 3418 SE Hawthorne Blvd., Portland, OR 97214; (503) 232-3500; shopmink.com. Gorgeous dresses that will help you unleash your inner Daisy Miller: That is what Mink will provide you with—as well as great tees by Velvet and jeans by Citizens of Humanity, and all the accessories to go with them. Mink also carries well-selected pieces from local designers. English majors and accountants alike will find something beautiful here.

⭐ **PORTLAND PENDLETON SHOP**, 900 SW 5th Ave., Portland, OR 97204; (503) 242-0037; pendleton-usa.com. On the east side of the Standard

Insurance Building, this store offers the most complete collection of Pendleton clothing for men and women in all of Oregon. Pendleton has always offered classic styles for men and women and excellent value, and they are enjoying a revival. They've updated their clothing lines with a more contemporary look while retaining their well-known fabrics and colors. In addition to clothing, the store carries an excellent selection of blankets and pillows with dramatic designs and colors based on Western and Native American art and symbols.

RED LIGHT, 3590 SE Hawthorne Blvd., Portland, OR 97214; (503) 963-8888; redlightclothingexchange.com. Some of the best vintage clothing in Portland is found in this large, trendy shop, in addition to resale modern clothes from BCBG, Betsy Johnson, Urban Outfitters, and Bébé. The vintage selection is comprehensive and reasonably priced, with everything from slips to coats. Men and women alike will find wonderful old leather jackets, eveningwear, sweaters, and, well, everything you could imagine.

TIME BOMB VINTAGE, 3540 SE Division St., Portland, OR 97202; (503) 922-9745; etsy.com/shop/timebombvintage. This shop is right in the middle of Southeast Division's burgeoning restaurant district, exuding indie charm. We love Time Bomb's collection of '70s and '80s vintage wear. Classic Gunne Sax dresses, wide-leg trousers, high-waisted shorts, and pristine vintage leather are some of their specialties.

Portland's vintage shops are a key element in its DIY spirit.

★TUMBLEWEED, 1812 NE Alberta St., Portland, OR 97211; (503) 335-3100; tumbleweedboutique.com. Tumbleweed is the home base of designer Kara Larson and her Kara-Line brand of clothing. Her simple skirts and dresses are charming without being the least bit fussy; they are made of pretty prints in cottons and rayons. We also love the fact that you can talk to the woman who made them. Beautiful vintage cowboy and other boots, pantaloons, sweaters, and other fabric delights (including a fun basket of remnants) round out the selection.

UNA, 2802 SE Ankeny St., Portland, OR 97214; (503) 235-2326; una negozio.com. A tiny, beautiful shop in LoBu, Una is renowned for its well-edited collection of locally designed, cool clothes from New York and Los Angeles, and vintage offerings. Look for Portland designers such as Jess Beebe and Sarah Weick, as well as small labels from, well, all over. Una features accessories as well—including some home decor items, so you'll feel like you belong in your new outfit.

UNION ROSE, 7909 SE Stark, Portland, OR 97215; (503) 287-4242; unionrosepdx.com. This delightful store in the cute Montavilla neighborhood showcases women's clothing by local designers. One of the best places to explore the range of talent in our design community, Una Rose also carries jewelry and accessories, gifts, and some children's wear.

★XTABAY, 2515 SE Clinton St., Portland, OR 97202; (503) 230-2899; xtabayvintage.blogspot.com. Xtabay is the destination for the most luscious high-end vintage in the city. The window always displays some beautifully lit, lovely confection of a dress. It is here that you will find taffeta dancing dresses and silk cocktail dresses, floor-length jersey gowns, and fabulous clothing from every 20th century era and the accessories to go with them. Xtabay supplies wedding dresses, prom dresses, and red-carpet wear for Portland talent when they attend the Oscars.

CRAFTS

BOLT, 2136 NE Alberta St., Portland, OR 97211; (503) 287-2658; boltfabric boutique.com. Bolt is a beautiful fabric shop in the Alberta neighborhood with the feel of a boutique rather than a warehouse. The shop features luscious fabrics in contemporary designs, as well as the hippest patterns available. They also offer workshops and advice for beginner, intermediate, and expert sewers.

COLLAGE ART MATERIALS AND WORKROOM, 1639 NE Alberta St., Portland, OR 97211; (503) 249-2190; collagepdx.com. These delightful spaces in the Alberta and Sellwood (7907 SE 13th Ave.; 503-777-2189) neighborhoods carry an outstanding and thoughtful selection of craft supplies. They have an excellent selection of papers and bookbinding supplies, as well as great bonding agents, cutters, and other basics. The expert staff really knows their stuff and can make great recommendations for tricky crafting problems. In addition, they provide a great workspace and classes.

★ **HAND-EYE SUPPLY**, 23 NW 4th Ave., Portland, OR 97209; (503) 575-9769; hand-eyesupply.com. This a garden of Eden in a DIY paradise: Hand-Eye Supply offers beautiful pens and paper but also welding supplies and leather aprons and handsaws. They specialize in high-quality tools and other things you need to style the food cart you are building in the driveway.

★ **JOSEPHINE'S DRY GOODS**, 521 SW 5th Ave., Portland, OR 97204; josephinesdrygoods.com. Fabric shopping at large warehouse stores can be overwhelming. This lovely shop solves that problem by offering a well-edited selection of gorgeous fabrics, including those from national and international designers.

KNIT PURL, 1101 SW Alder, Portland, OR 97204; (503) 227-2999; knit-purl.com. A beautiful downtown yarn shop, Knit Purl carries gorgeous yarns, aesthetically pleasing needles and other tools, and a wide, wide range of patterns and books. The staff is very wise and will help you read your confusing pattern in the nicest way possible. They also provide fabulous classes and open knitting circles—as well as knitting celebrity events.

★ **YARN GARDEN**, 1413 SE Hawthorne Blvd., Portland, OR 97214; (503) 239-7950; yarngarden.net. We should all honor our work by using the best materials available, and if knitting is your work, Yarn Garden is the place for the best tools. Luscious yarns in every weight, color, and texture; needles; patterns—all your knitting needs are served here. The staff is so knowledgeable and helpful for beginners and experienced knitters alike that you'll find half the afternoon has passed before you know it. They are open on Wed evening until 8 p.m.; that's when they hold knitting circles at which you can solicit and receive advice, trade ideas, or meet other knitters. Yarn Garden also has a good selection of books.

HOME DECOR

CARGO, 380 NW 13th Ave., Portland, OR 97209; (503) 209-8349; cargo inc.com. Those pictures in *Elle Decor* of lofts decorated with tansu chests and Indian saris have always looked appealing, but where do you get the saris and tansu chests with which to decorate? In Portland, you get them at Cargo, which is a kind of upscale Cost Plus with many beautiful imports, mainly from India and Asia. High-quality silk pillows, baskets, wooden tea chests, bamboo blinds, and so on are all here, as well as sake sets and chopsticks. Cargo is also an excellent place for gifts.

★ **HIPPO HARDWARE AND TRADING COMPANY,** 1040 E. Burnside St., Portland, OR 97214; (503) 231-1444; hippohardware.com. Hippo Hardware, a Portland establishment for many years, carries a wonderfully eclectic assortment of plumbing fixtures, doors, lighting fixtures, and salvaged items for older homes. It takes a long time to search through all the offerings, so plan accordingly. They will also custom-build lighting fixtures. Don't forget to bring your old fixtures in here for a swap. It is a trading company, after all.

KITCHEN KABOODLE, 404 NW 23rd Ave., Portland, OR 97209; (503) 241-4040; kitchenkaboodle.com. Their motto is "We make your house a home," and they've been doing just that since 1975. Kitchen Kaboodle sells functional, unique house accoutrements, providing not only every possible gadget you might use someday, but also the storage unit to put it in. This Portland institution has stores all over town; and whether you need an electric egg cooker, a potato ricer, an enameled French casserole, or a maple sideboard, you can find it here. The staff is very knowledgeable and friendly—make use of them. That's what they're paid for. A second central location is at 1520 NE Broadway (503-288-1500).

THE REBUILDING CENTER, 3625 N. Mississippi Ave., Portland, OR 972; (503) 331-1877; rebuildingcenter.org. A nonprofit salvage outlet, the Rebuilding Center sells reclaimed hardware, windows, doors, plumbing fixtures, moldings, and lumber. This is the retail outlet of a firm that disassembles houses and other buildings; what is not immediately reused in other projects is sold here. For the recycling-conscious do-it-yourselfer, this place is heaven.

★ **REJUVENATION,** 1100 SE Grand Ave., Portland, OR 97214; (503) 238-1900; rejuvenation.com. Another Portland landmark, Rejuvenation is well known nationally for its period lighting fixtures, but it also carries new and salvaged plumbing, doors, windows, moldings, and lumber. You'll also find handsome furniture and garden ornaments. A knowledgeable staff provides useful information and referral lists of competent home rehabilitation specialists. There's a tiny nook for children to play in while their parents browse; the Daily Cafe, inside the store, is a good place for eating lunch while you figure out what to do with the salvaged staircase you've just bought. Rejuvenation also sells their seconds, which can be a fine source for well-priced lighting fixtures and other things.

THE WHOLE 9 YARDS, 1820 E. Burnside St., Portland, OR 97214; (503) 223-2880; w9yards.com. Specializing in interior fabrics and trim, the Whole 9 Yards has developed a national reputation for its gorgeous fabrics, inventive combinations, and original style. Their chenilles, jacquards, and velvets are renowned, but they carry everything from dupioni silk to cotton. They'll help you put together your drapes and upholstery, as well as providing you with general expertise, curtain rods and trim, and their own line of freshly designed, competitively priced furniture. The shop also offers brilliant classes in fashioning slipcovers, curtains, and pillows.

MUSIC

ARTICHOKE MUSIC, 3130 SE Hawthorne Blvd., Portland, OR 97214; (503) 232-8845; artichokemusic.com. This friendly Hawthorne shop specializes in guitars, banjos, mandolins, dulcimers, harps, accordions, and unusual folk instruments. They also buy and sell all kinds of musical instruments and are extremely knowledgeable about the local music scene. Not only do they carry a wide selection of high-quality musical instruments, but they also feature live performances, music lessons, and cool events—among them open-mike sessions so you can show off your best bluegrass licks.

JACKPOT RECORDS, 209 SW 9th Ave., Portland, OR 97204; (503) 222-0990; jackpotrecords.com. In an iPod era, fabulous Jackpot Records is better than ever, with an outstanding catalog of new and used CDs and vinyl, as well as an online store and MySpace page. This great shop not only has excellent finds in indie music—as well as electronica, jazz, hip-hop, metal, blues, and more—but it also has amazing in-store events featuring bands such as the Decemberists, Sleater-Kinney, and Franz Ferdinand. A second location is at 3574 SE Hawthorne (503-239-7561).

★ **MUSIC MILLENNIUM**, 3158 E. Burnside St., Portland, OR 97214; (503) 231-8926; musicmillennium.com. Music Millennium, a Portland institution since 1969, carries the latest releases from national, international, and local acts in every variety of music, from blues to spoken word and everything in between. The knowledgeable and friendly staff can help you find whatever you're looking for, as well as tell you about exciting in-store performances on the schedule. They also offer the widest selection of classical CDs in the entire city.

2ND AVENUE RECORDS, 400 SW 2nd Ave.; Portland, OR 97204; (503) 222-3783. A voluminous outlet for all musical genres, 2nd Avenue has the biggest selection of hip-hop in town. You can also track down obscure performers on independent labels. Indie, metal, reggae, postpunk, and more are yours for the buying.

SHOES

HALO SHOES, 938 NW Everett St., Portland, OR 97209; (503) 331-0366; haloshoes.com. Halo features high-end shoes for fashionistas and their brothers. This cultured boutique specializes in beautiful and chic shoes from Corso Como, Fiorentini & Baker, CYDWOC, Costume National, and hard-to-find lines from around the world. Halo also carries sleek bags and other good accessories. Many of these beautiful shoes are handmade. An outstanding shoe shop, from service to selection.

★ **IMELDA'S AND LOUIE'S SHOES**, 3426 SE Hawthorne Blvd., Portland, OR 97214; (503) 233-7476; imeldasandlouies.com. Alluring shoes at reasonable prices—that's why stylish Portlanders seek out Imelda's and Louie's. Kenneth Cole, Frye, Franco Sarto, Born, and Secs are some of the lines that Imelda's and Louie's carries; but also look for special handmade shoes from New York, groovy handbags, and really pretty jewelry. Everybody buys shoes here, because the collection is perfectly edited for Portland. A second location is at 935 NW Everett St. (503-595-4970).

JOHNNY SOLE, 815 SW Alder St., Portland, OR 97205; (503) 225-1241; johnnysoleshoes.com. Johnny Sole can satisfy almost any shoe craving, from Seventh-Avenue high-fashion diva to Portland-style alternative-culture goth. Favorite lines include Diba, Giraudon, and Kenneth Cole. It's got a stand-out selection of cool yet weather- and walking-appropriate boots. This light, spacious boutique in the heart of downtown features men's and women's lines.

Attractions

This chapter emphasizes the local and regional attractions—natural, historical, and contemporary—that define and characterize our area. Portland is an attractive city with a friendly skyline in a beautiful region of the country. In some ways, the entire Portland Metro area is an attraction, full of interesting things to watch, do, hear, and taste. Here, we list some of the most popular attractions—and a few of the less famous features that give Portland its unique ambience.

Most of the features listed here are concentrated within the city center. Downtown Portland is agreeable for walking, and even if the weather is not entirely cooperative, the distances are relatively short. Visitors to attractions in outlying areas, such as Fort Vancouver, will depend more on cars. You can still take public transportation, but it requires more planning and commitment. We have made every effort to report the most current and accurate hours and addresses. However, given the rate of change in the area, you may want to call or check websites before you visit to make sure the information is up to date. If you're traveling with kids, you may want to check out the children's museums and amusement parks in the Kids chapter.

Price Code

Prices reflect the cost of 1 adult admission. Most attractions have discounts for children, students, and seniors, so bring your ID.

$	Less than $8
$$	$8 to $16
$$$	More than $16

IN PORTLAND

CRYSTAL SPRINGS RHODODENDRON GARDEN, Southeast 28th Avenue and Southeast Woodstock Boulevard, Portland, OR 97202; (503) 771-8386; rhodies.org; $. Long periods of gray days create a great appreciation for color in many Oregonians. Beginning in April they flock to the 7-acre Crystal Springs Rhododendron Garden to savor the brilliant colors of the garden's 2,500 rhododendrons, azaleas, and other plants. In the fall, the Japanese maples and sourwood trees burst into flame, a defiant gesture against the coming monotones of winter. Even when the seasons' colors have peaked, the garden attracts visitors looking for solitude and a temporary respite from urban life. An admission fee of $4 is charged from Thurs through Mon, March 1 through Labor Day, but is waived the rest of the year. Children under 12 are always free. The park is open from dawn to dusk. (For further information see the Parks chapter.)

HOYT ARBORETUM, 4000 SW Fairview Blvd., Portland, OR 97221; (503) 865-8733 (visitor center); hoytarboretum.org; free. Hoyt Arboretum, which is part of Washington Park, provides 183 acres and 10 miles of trails with striking views of the city, Mount Hood, and Mount St. Helens. Nine hundred tree species keep the arboretum fragrant in the spring, cool in the summer, and flushed with color during the fall. For those of us who weren't paying attention during Outdoor School, most species are labeled, and for those who want to learn more, tours are offered. A 1-mile section of the Bristlecone Trail is paved for wheelchair access. The grounds are open from 6 a.m. to 10 p.m. The lovely visitor center is open from 9 a.m. until 4 p.m. and until 3 p.m. on Sat and Sun; it's closed on holidays.

⭐ **INTERNATIONAL ROSE TEST GARDEN,** 400 SW Kingston, Portland, OR 97201; (503) 823-3636; rosegardenstore.org/international-rose-test-garden.cfm; free. With its spectacular views of the city and the Cascades,

The International Rose Test Garden invites exploring for locals and tourists alike.

the International Rose Test Garden in Washington Park is a popular stop for visitors. These appealing gardens beckon you to linger awhile, offering many summer concerts, plays, and other outdoor events in addition to lovely views. This site has been a public rose garden since 1917—it's the oldest public rose test garden in the nation. The 5-acre gardens offer visitors the sight and scent of 8,000 plants representing some 500 varieties of roses, from those producing fragile miniatures to some with blossoms nearly 8 inches broad. The roses begin to bloom in May and usually reach their peak sometime in June, depending on the weather. But there will be flowers on the bushes until October.

IRA KELLER MEMORIAL FOUNTAIN, Southwest 3rd Avenue and Southwest Clay Street, Portland, OR 97201; free. Named after Ira C. Keller, a self-made millionaire with a well-developed social conscience, this water sculpture is across from the Keller Auditorium in downtown Portland. Designed by noted landscape artist Lawrence Halprin, this space is an irresistible gathering spot. In spring and summer, downtown workers eat lunch, nap, talk with friends, read, and sun themselves to the soothing sounds of water cascading down the structure's various levels. Children splash in the cooling waters and delight in the fountain's different waterfalls, pools, concrete and metal islands and terraces, and the design's overall human scale. Ada Louise Huxtable, the *New York Times*'s respected architecture critic, described the fountain as

The Ira Keller Memorial Fountain is an inviting spot on a hot summer's day.

"perhaps the greatest open space since the Renaissance"—no faint praise for a work of public art, especially in a city with many public spaces.

⭐ **JAPANESE GARDENS,** 611 SW Kingston Ave., Portland, OR 97205; (503) 223-1321; japanesegarden.com; $$. Established in 1963, the Japanese Gardens were designed by Takuma Tono, a distinguished landscape and garden designer. His achievement is remarkable, compressing 5 different garden spaces—the Flat Garden, the Strolling Pond Garden, a Tea Garden with a chashitsu (a ceremonial tea house), the Natural Garden, and the Zen-inspired Sand and Stone Garden—into little more than 5 acres. The trees and plants, water, and rocks here change with the season, offering visitors different perspectives of color, texture, shape, shadow, and sound throughout the year. The gardens are open daily, except on Thanksgiving, Christmas Day, and New Year's Day. Hours vary according to the season, but visitors can be assured of admission between 10 a.m. and 4 p.m.—later in the spring and summer—except on Mon, when the garden opens at noon.

ℹ The Equitable Life building, designed by renowned Portland architect Pietro Belluschi and completed in 1948, was one of the first modern glass towers, and it was a major trendsetter. It was the first building to be clad in aluminum, the first to use double-glazed windows—and the first to be completely air-conditioned. You can find it at the intersection of Southwest Stark and Southwest Washington Streets.

KIDD'S TOY MUSEUM, 1301 SE Grand Ave., Portland, OR 97214; (503) 233-7807; kiddstoymuseum.com; free. This unique collection of toys was inspired by Frank Kidd's automotive business, beginning with toy cars and other transportation vehicles such as toy trains and planes. Eventually, however, Kidd's joy in toy collecting extended to other areas, including a stellar collection of mechanical banks. To preserve the collection, the owner created a museum that is open to the public free of charge. The Kidd's Toy Museum is open Mon through Thurs from noon until 6 p.m., and on Fri from 1 until 6 p.m. Weekend visits can be arranged by appointment.

ATTRACTIONS

LEACH BOTANICAL GARDEN, 6704 SE 122nd Ave., Portland, OR 97236; (503) 823-9503; leachgarden.org; free. Beginning in the 1930s, Lila and John Leach, two amateur botanists, started their 5-acre garden along Southeast Portland's Johnson Creek. Credited with discovering 11 new species of Northwest plants, the Leaches eventually grew their garden to include some 14 acres. More than 1,500 species of native ferns, wildflowers, shrubs, and irises contentedly grow in the garden. Rock gardens, bog gardens, and an experimental recycling and composting center are features, as well as classes, summer camps, and events (it's popular for weddings, for example). Cool trails allow you to ramble through the woods, and a fairytale stone hut adds a note of fantasy to this lovely spot. The garden is open Sun from 1 until 4 p.m. and Tues through Sat from 9 a.m. until 4 p.m. (Also see the entry in the Parks chapter.)

LINCOLN STREET KAYAK & CANOE MUSEUM, 5340 SE Lincoln St., Portland, OR 97215; (503) 234-0264; traditionalkayaks.com; free. This small museum features an impressive collection of traditional—that is, hand-made—kayaks and other human-powered craft. Most of the specimens are crafted by the proprietor, Harvey Golden, who completed these replicas as part of his research into kayaks and their incredible, but underappreciated, role in human culture. You will also find some original crafts from across the world as well. This museum is a labor of love, so its hours are limited, but you can visit from 5 to 7 p.m. on Wed evenings, by appointment, and—as we have discovered—some spontaneous weekend hours.

MULTNOMAH COUNTY LIBRARY CENTRAL BRANCH, 801 SW 10th Ave., Portland, OR 97205; (503) 988-5123; multcolib.org; free. The Multnomah County Library is the oldest public library building west of the Mississippi. Some, but only some, of the highlights include the Henry Failing Art and Music Library, which contains one of the most significant sheet music collections in the nation, and the John Wilson Room, housing rare books and paper-type artifacts, such as the Nuremburg Chronicle (dating from 1493). The library is open every day: Mon through Sat, from 10 a.m. to 6 p.m., except on Tues and Wed, when it's open until 8 p.m.; Sun, the library is open from noon until 5 p.m. Portland citizens don't like to be far from coffee, so Starbucks operates a small store, and the coffee scenting the air on the main floor adds a piquant Portland touch.

OAKS AMUSEMENT PARK, 7805 SE Oaks Park Way, Portland, OR 97202; (503) 233-5777; oakspark.com; $$. Originally opened in 1905 for the Lewis & Clark Exposition, Oaks Park is an old-fashioned amusement park that has never lost its appeal. Kids still love the rides such as the roller coaster, the Screaming Eagle, and the Tilt-a-Whirl, as well as gentler teacups and merry-go-rounds. The park's roller-skating rink is very popular. It is one of the oldest continuously operating roller rinks in the country and the only one with a live Wurlitzer organ. (Skate rentals are available.) The park is open throughout the year; high season is during the summer. It also sponsors Fourth of July fireworks, weather permitting. For more information, see the Kids chapter. Gate admission is free except for major events, but rides, games, and roller-skating carry fees.

Don't Miss the Murals

The Oregon Historical Society building displays two 8-story-high trompe l'oeil murals by Richard Haas. These illustrate symbols of Oregon's past. The West Mural, at Southwest Park Avenue and Madison Street, captures in larger-than-life scale the key members of the Lewis and Clark Expedition, including Sacagawea, and her child, Baptiste; Clark's slave, York; and Seaman, the dog. The East Mural, visible from Broadway and Jefferson Streets, symbolically depicts early Oregon characters, among them Native Americans, trappers, and settlers.

★ **OREGON HISTORICAL SOCIETY MUSEUM,** 1200 SW Park Ave., Portland, OR 97201; (503) 222-1741; ohs.org; $$. The Oregon Historical Society Museum is a fine place to begin a visit to Portland; it covers the history of Oregon from the earliest Indian civilizations through the saga of the Oregon Trail to contemporary times. Part museum, part research facility, it's a leading and influential force in the city and state, sponsoring seminars, workshops, festivals, and celebrations, in addition to its extensive library and its own publications. An afternoon spent here will illuminate Pacific Northwest history in surprising and engaging ways. The Oregon Historical Society Museum is open Tues through Sat from 10 a.m. to 5 p.m. On Sun, the museum is open from noon to 5 p.m. The research library is open Thurs through Sat from 1 to 5 p.m. Multnomah County residents can visit free with proof of address.

OREGON JEWISH MUSEUM, 1953 NW Kearney St., Portland, OR 97209; (503) 226-3600; ojm.org; $. The Oregon Jewish Museum is the only institution in the Pacific Northwest devoted to Jewish history and culture; it features an archival library with papers and oral histories about the history of Jews in Oregon, permanent exhibits, and changing exhibits of Jewish history both in Oregon and throughout the world. They also host lectures and special events. The museum is open Tues through Thurs from 10:30 a.m. to 4 p.m., on Fri from 10:30 a.m. to 3 p.m., and on Sat and Sun from 12 to 4 p.m.

OREGON MARITIME CENTER AND MUSEUM, at the foot of Southwest Pine Street between the Morrison and Burnside Bridges, Portland, OR 97204; (503) 224-7724; oregonmaritimemuseum.org; $. This small museum, housed in the charming stern-wheeler steam tug *Portland*, is filled with artifacts, models, historic paintings, and a collection of navigational instruments recounting Oregon's seagoing history. One room details the regional shipbuilding industry during World War II, and many of the exhibits feature military craft launched in Oregon's waters. Restorations have brought this craft back to life, and now it is the last operating steam-powered stern-wheel tug in the United States in addition to being a museum. The museum includes a small gift shop with a selection of nautical items and books. Hours are 11 a.m. to 4 p.m., Wed, Fri, and Sat. Closed Sun, Mon, Tues, and Thurs.

OREGON MUSEUM OF SCIENCE AND INDUSTRY (OMSI), 1945 SE Water Ave., Portland, OR 97214; (503) 797-4000; omsi.edu; $$. One of the most popular attractions in Oregon, OMSI is a thoroughly engaging museum where visitors are encouraged to touch things, try experiments, and question why things happen. In addition to its permanent exhibits, OMSI offers an exciting array of temporary exhibits, rotating features in the Empirical 3-D theater, and a planetarium. The USS *Blueback* is also on site; it was the US Navy's last diesel-powered submarine The *Blueback* tour lasts 40 minutes. OMSI is closed Mon except when a public school holiday falls on a Mon. During the school year it is open Tues through Sun 9:30 a.m. until 5:30 p.m. Summer hours are Mon through Sun 9:30 a.m. to 7 p.m. OMSI also offers camps, classes, field trips, and special programs. Parking is $4.

OREGON RAIL HERITAGE CENTER, 2250 SE Water Ave., Portland, OR 97214; (503) 233-1156; orhf.org; free. The Oregon Rail Heritage Center opened in 2012, sited at the confluence of railroad, light-rail, and streetcar lines and poised to serve as the cultural hub for the rail industry in Portland. The center is built around three historic steam locomotives originally donated in 1958. These are for display only, but there are other train-related things to do and see, as well as interesting docent-led tours. The Oregon Rail Heritage Center is very close to OMSI, so it makes a good stop on the way to or from. You can experience the locomotives in action during December weekends, when they tour up and down the Willamette, blaring their mournful whistles; tickets for these limited train rides are sold separately and go quickly. Hours for the Center are Thur through Sun, 1 to 5 p.m.

★ **OREGON ZOO**, 4001 SW Canyon Rd., Portland, OR 97221; (503) 226-1561; oregonzoo.org; $$. The Oregon Zoo was originally established in 1887 with the gift to the city of an animal collection and has evolved into a world-class research facility, offering a constantly changing mix of exhibits and amusements. It's an internationally respected center for breeding Asian elephants, and it is a leader in recreating natural habitat. The Zoo Railway is a narrow-gauge railroad taking visitors to Washington Park and the Rose Gardens. The Oregon Zoo is open every day except Christmas Day. Hours are seasonal; it opens each day at 9 a.m. (10 a.m. in the winter) and closes essentially an hour past sunset. Summers bring popular concert series in the evenings. There is a $4 fee for parking. See more about the Oregon Zoo in the Kids chapter.

The Oregon Zoo is the largest attraction in the state.

PIONEER COURTHOUSE, 700 SW 6th Ave., Portland, OR 97204; (503) 833-5305; pioneercourthouse.org; free. Pioneer Courthouse, the second-oldest federal building west of the Mississippi, was Portland's first restoration project back in the 1970s. Built in the late 1860s of beautiful Bellingham sandstone, the Italianate building survived ill-considered plans that would have had it demolished for a mundane office building in the 1930s, for a parking lot in the 1940s, and for a new federal office building in the 1960s. It now houses the US Court of Appeals for the Ninth Circuit. You can climb to the cupola of Pioneer Courthouse for a rarely seen view of the city: Hanging between the cupola's 8 windows is a series of restored photos of the city in 1877 by a local photographer, A. H. Wulzen. Many of the photos were taken from the cupola and offer the viewer an unusual "before and after" scene.

★ **PIONEER COURTHOUSE SQUARE,** between Broadway and Southwest 6th Avenue at Southwest Yamhill and Southwest Morrison Streets, Portland, OR 97204; thesquarepdx.org; free. Pioneer Courthouse Square has been many things during its long life. The site was home to the city's first public schoolhouse; then home to the Portland Hotel, an impressive building that was torn down, to much local dismay, to make way for a parking lot. Now it is known as "Portland's living room" for its warm blend of red brick, park benches, flowers, sculpture, and coffee—as well as the more than 300 entertaining events each year. The Portland Oregon Visitor Association and TriMet both have major offices here, and you can board the Big Pink Trolley for sightseeing tours (see Welcome to Portland). Expect to see musicians, jugglers, pierced and tattooed teenagers, tourists, students, and city office workers strolling about. It's the heart and soul of downtown Portland.

> **i** Director Park, just up the street from Pioneer Courthouse Square, is another favorite gathering spot. This handsome urban piazza features glass and granite arranged to invite lingering, although it is technically designed for cultural events. You'll find those—as well as cafes, a fountain, and a "big" chess set—at 815 SW Park Ave., Portland, OR 97205; directorpark.org.

The Pittock Mansion provides historical perspective on the city, as well as great views.

PITTOCK MANSION, 3229 NW Pittock Dr., Portland, OR 97210; (503) 823-3623; pittockmansion.org; $. Henry Pittock, founder of the *Oregonian*, the city's daily newspaper and the largest paper in the state, built a 22-room, 16,000-square-foot château 1,000 feet above the city, where he could keep an eye on things. It stayed in the family until 1964, when it was sold to the city of Portland. Guided tours are offered each afternoon, and visitors can wander through the gardens of roses, azaleas, and rhododendrons. The Pittock Mansion is open for public viewing 7 days a week from 11 a.m. to 4 p.m., except in July and Aug, when it opens at 10 a.m. and stays open until 5 p.m. It is closed on major holidays, for a few days in late Nov when holiday decorations are being put up, and during Jan for annual maintenance.

POLICE HISTORICAL MUSEUM JUSTICE CENTER, 1111 SW 2nd Ave., Portland, OR 97204; (503) 823-0019; portlandpolicemuseum.com. This small museum highlights the fascinating history of crime and punishment. The museum displays early arrest records, a working traffic signal, and a collection of badges, uniforms, weapons, handcuffs, and other tools of the trade representing both sides of the cops-and-robbers paradigm. There is also a great collection of historical photos. Current and retired Portland police officers make up the volunteer staff, so mind your manners. Entry to the museum is free, though donations are welcome. The museum is open Tues through Fri, from 10 a.m. to 3 p.m.; you should call ahead. There's also a gift shop. If you're over 18 you'll need some photo ID since it is, actually, in the building that houses the city jail.

⭐ **PORTLAND ART MUSEUM,** 1219 SW Park Ave., Portland, OR 97205; (503) 226-2811; portlandartmuseum.org; $$. The Portland Art Museum, the oldest museum in the Pacific Northwest, is an attraction with dimensions that extend beyond the allure of the Pietro Belluschi–designed building and the art within it. The museum now has multiple galleries, educational facilities, a multimedia room, an appealing public sculpture garden, and a cafe. This wealth of space allows the museum to feature its important collections in Northwest and Native American art and in European painting, as well as creating space for recent acquisitions. Hours are Tues, Wed, and Sat, 10 a.m. to 5 p.m.; Sun from noon to 5 p.m.; Thurs and Fri the museum is open until 8 p.m. Reduced ticket prices are available for children and seniors, and the fourth Fri each month, admission is free between 5 p.m. and 8 p.m.

The Portland Art Museum is noted for its outdoor sculpture mall.

PORTLAND AUDUBON SOCIETY SANCTUARY, 5151 NW Cornell Rd., Portland, OR 97210; (503) 292-6855; audubonportland.org; free. The Portland Audubon Society, a nonprofit group with a long and established concern about Oregon's ecology and wildlife, has worked closely with government agencies to further protect Oregon's natural beauty. A leading example is the Audubon Sanctuary, a 160-acre tract surrounded by Forest Park, a 5,000-acre municipal park, and linked to that park's Wildwood and Macleary Trails. The society also provides a Wildlife Care Center where injured owls, hawks, herons, cranes, and other birds and waterfowl are cared for until they can be returned to the wild. Hours for the sanctuary and gift shop are 10 a.m. to 6 p.m. Mon through Sat and 10 a.m. to 5 p.m. on Sun. Trails are open daily dawn to dusk. Pets should remain at home.

PORTLAND BUILDING, 1120 Southwest 5th Ave., Portland, OR 97204; free. Opened in 1982, this wonderful, controversial, 15-story building still evokes potent reactions from local, regional, and national architects, designers, critics, local politicians making some point about public spending and public art, and almost everyone who views it. Designed by Michael Graves as the first public building in a postmodern style in the United States, the colorful Portland Building houses an administrative wing of Portland city government, next door to Portland City Hall, so between 8 a.m. and 5 p.m. you can walk around the lobby and other public areas where local artists' works are on display. The building is also the home of the original *Portlandia*—not the television show but the statue. This 25-foot-tall hammered-copper statue represents Lady Commerce, the classic female figure on the city of Portland's official seal.

PORTLAND CITY HALL, 1221 SW 4th Ave., Portland, OR 97204; free. Portland City Hall is a sandstone Italianate building completed in 1895. Controversial at the time it was built, it endured many insults, both spiritual and physical, right up until it was placed on the National Register of Historic Places in 1974. Among these were complaints about its design; the failure to actually complete the design; terrible renovations that covered up its elegant skylights, woodwork, and copper plating; and even, in 1970, a bomb attack. Now, however, it has been gracefully restored. In true Portland style, the exterior features an organic vegetable garden—as well as an ecoroof. The interior provides a beautiful backdrop for Portland's growing public art collection, some of which can be found on display here. Especially of note is an ever-present but constantly changing exhibit called *A Visual Chronicle of Portland* on the main floor.

⭐ **PORTLAND CLASSICAL CHINESE GARDEN,** 239 NW Everett St., Portland, OR 97209; (503) 228-8131; portlandchinesegarden.org; $. The exquisite Portland Classical Chinese Garden, more formally known as the "Garden of Awakening Orchids," is a double-walled oasis built in a traditional Chinese style with extensive help from Portland's Chinese sister city Suzhou. Once you enter this well-designed garden, it is difficult to remember you are in a city at all, let alone in Portland. There are also classes in everything from horticulture to movement arts such as qigong. The garden is open daily, from 10 a.m. to 5 p.m., Nov through Mar, and from 10 a.m. to 6 p.m., Apr through Oct. Public tours are offered at noon and 1 p.m., and private tours can be arranged. The garden is wheelchair accessible.

Tom McCall Waterfront Park

Southwest Naito Parkway and the Willamette River from Steel Bridge South
to River Place

If Pioneer Courthouse Square is Portland's living room, then the Tom
McCall Waterfront Park is the city's front yard. The park starts at the Broadway Bridge, stretches south for about 2 miles, and then converts into a portion of the Greenway, a path continuing south to Willamette Park, a total
distance of 3.25 miles. Once an ugly freeway cut off the downtown from the
Willamette River. Led by Governor Tom McCall, planners came up with the
Downtown Plan of 1972, which included the removal of the freeway and
the creation of open space that would reunite the city and river. Portlanders
have adopted the park with such fervor that it is in danger of being loved to
death by an unending series of events, including the Rose Festival Fun Center, the Bite, Brewers' Festival, Cinco de Mayo, Blues Festival, Fourth of July
fireworks, and the Race for the Cure (see the Festivals and Annual Events
chapter for more).

Center stage for Waterfront Park is the Salmon Street Springs Fountain
at the foot of Southwest Salmon Street. In hot weather, this fountain, with its
spurting jets of water, attracts crowds of adults and children who splash in the
streams of water and the shallow pool. The dock for the *Portland Spirit*, an
excursion boat offering cruises on the Willamette, is nearby.

The park contains bicycle paths, walkways, open grassy fields, and a
number of monuments and memorials. The Founders' Stone memorializes
Asa Lovejoy and William Pettygrove, who tossed the fateful coin that gave
Portland its name. Another memorial is the Japanese American Historical
Plaza, sometimes referred to as the Garden of Stones. This solemn memorial is best walked from south to north. Along the formal plaza are stones,
some broken, some cut, some shattered, to represent the disrupted lives of
110,000 Japanese Americans interned in camps throughout the western
United States during World War II. Farther north, near the Steel Bridge, is
the Friendship Circle. This sculpture emits the sounds of a Japanese flute
and drum and honors the Sister City relationship between Portland and
Sapporo, Japan.

Across from the Oregon Maritime Museum is the battleship USS *Oregon* monument. The *Oregon,* known as "McKinley's Bull-dog" because of its role in the Spanish-American War, was a turn-of-the-20th-century battleship launched in 1893. Between the two world wars, the Oregon was tied up along the sea wall at the foot of Southwest Jefferson Street as a memorial and museum, but in 1942, as a patriotic gesture, the ship was returned to the US Navy. One of the ship's masts was removed before she was reclaimed by the navy, and it is that battleship-gray mast from which the American and Oregon flags fly along the river.

Waterfront Park has received numerous accolades over the years as an exemplar of freeway removal and urban renewal. In 2012, the American Planning Association designated it as one of the top 10 greatest public spaces in the United States, alongside New Orleans's Jackson Square and Chicago's Union Station. The thousands of daily visitors apparently agree.

The Morrison Bridge opens in anticipation of the Portland Spirit *as it leaves its berth along the Willamette.*

VIETNAM VETERANS MEMORIAL, 4000 SW Canyon Rd., Portland, OR 97205; (503) 823-7529; portlandoregon.gov/parks; free. Oregon's tribute to its Vietnam veterans sits on 11 acres of land in the southwest corner of Hoyt Arboretum, above the World Forestry Center. The Vietnam Veterans Memorial honors the 57,000 Oregonians who served in Southeast Asia, listing by name and date of death the state's nearly 800 known dead and still missing. The memorial puts those deaths in a historical context by including references to state, national, and international events occurring at the same time. As at the national memorial in Washington, DC, visitors often find personal remembrances—military insignia, campaign ribbons and medals, faded pictures, flowers, toys, candles, photos of sons and daughters, grandsons and granddaughters—left near a name. Each Memorial Day, an honor guard of ROTC cadets from the University of Portland stands a silent 24-hour guard at the memorial.

★ **WASHINGTON PARK,** 611 SW Kingston, Portland, OR 97205; (503) 823-7529; portlandoregon.gov/parks; free. Washington Park, which features some of Portland's most important attractions, is set on 546 acres on the city's West Hills, where it overlooks downtown Portland and east beyond into the mountains. It is the home of the Oregon Zoo, the World Forestry Center, the Japanese Garden, the Children's Museum, and the Rose Gardens. All these attractions are within walking distance of one another, if you're a sturdy walker. The Zoo, Forestry Center, and Children's Museum are right off the MAX stop, and the Japanese and Rose Gardens are about a mile away along the roads or trails of Washington Park. You can also take the zoo train, which has a station at the Rose Gardens, or the TriMet #63 buses that traverse the park and back to town. See the Parks chapter for more on this wonderful park.

WORLD FORESTRY CENTER MUSEUM, 4033 SW Canyon Rd., Portland, OR 97221; (503) 228-1367; worldforestry.org; $. Before Oregon's Silicon Forest, there were real forests where giant trees were felled by handsaws and axes, hauled or floated to mills, and then cut and finished to build the nation's houses and factories. Built by a consortium of timber and related industries, the World Forestry Center Museum offers informative and entertaining hands-on exhibits on how the forests of the Pacific Northwest and elsewhere shape our experience and history. The museum holds special art and photography exhibitions in addition to its permanent exhibits, and there are also adventure rides—a white-water "rafting" trip and a 45-foot lift up into the tree canopy, for example. The World Forestry Center Museum is open daily from 10 a.m. to 5 p.m. On Wed, admission is discounted to $3 per person. Parking costs $4 per car, payable with admission.

The World Forestry Center is right next to the Oregon Zoo.

IN OUTLYING AREAS

⭐ **BONNEVILLE DAM,** Off I-84 (exit 40), Cascade Locks, OR 97014; (541) 374-8820; nwp.usace.army.mil/Locations/ColumbiaRiver/Bonneville .aspx; free. A half-hour of scenic driving through the Columbia River Gorge will take you to the Bonneville Dam, which has an attractive visitor center with interactive exhibits, short films, and displays that illustrate the history and culture of local and regional Native American tribes. You can watch steelhead and Chinook salmon climbing the fish ladders and boats passing through the locks. There are no restaurants here, but this is a popular picnic stop for

Fort Vancouver National Historic Site

Fort Vancouver was originally built by the British not only as a fur-trading center, but also as an attempt to solidify Britain's claim to the entire Northwest Territory. One of 34 such forts that the Hudson's Bay Company built, Fort Vancouver became an American outpost in 1846 when a treaty between the United States and Britain established the 49th parallel as Canada's southern border. Now restored and administered by the National Park Service, Fort Vancouver offers a look at frontier life through a range of restored buildings, exhibits and displays, and re-creations.

Adjacent to Fort Vancouver National Historic Site sits Vancouver Barracks, the first military post in the Oregon Territory. From this base, Americans explored Alaska, provided security to settlers, and developed an early network of roads, dams, and locks. From May 1849 to the present, Vancouver Barracks has been an active military post.

To the north of the Fort Vancouver National Historic Site and just across a vast green is Officers Row, an immaculately restored and rare collection of 21 Victorian-era homes built between 1850 and 1906 by the federal

schoolchildren on field trips or families exploring nearby trails, so there are lots of picnic tables, some of them covered. Hours are 9 a.m. to 5 p.m. for the visitor center; other areas may be open later.

CLARK COUNTY HISTORICAL SOCIETY AND MUSEUM, 1511 Main St., Vancouver, WA 98660; (360) 993-5679; cchmuseum.org; $. A good starting place for a visit to Vancouver, the museum displays a range of historical artifacts relating to the founding and growth of the area. Additional displays and exhibits document the original Native American residents of the region. There is also an exhibit detailing how the expansion of the railroads across the country and along the Pacific Coast changed the area's economy, population, and contact with the rest of the nation. The museum is open all year (except on major holidays) Tues through Sat from 11 a.m. until 4 p.m.

government. The houses were the residences for the military officers and other government officials and their families assigned to Fort Vancouver, Vancouver Barracks, and the army's Department of the Columbia. Homes such as these were once common on American military bases, but this is the only entire Officers Row preserved in the nation. Among the army officers who lived on Officers Row were Generals Phillip Sheridan, Benjamin Bonneville, and Omar Bradley. Guests at Officers Row included three US presidents: Ulysses S. Grant, Rutherford B. Hayes, and Franklin Delano Roosevelt.

At 1301 Officers Row you will find the George C. Marshall House. Built in 1886, it was originally the home for the commanding officer of Vancouver Barracks. General Marshall, who was awarded the Nobel Peace Prize in 1953, served as Vancouver Barracks' commanding officer from 1936 to 1938 and lived in the house during that period. In 1937 Marshall opened his home to the three Russian fliers who landed at Pearson Airfield after their transpolar flight. The building was later renamed to honor his service to the nation as the US Army's Chief of Staff during World War II and later as Secretary of Defense and Secretary of State. The George C. Marshall House is open 7 days a week, except for major holidays, from 9 a.m. to 4 p.m. There is no charge.

This site is truly compelling for history buffs—and everyone else. It is open from 9 a.m. to 5 p.m., 10 a.m. to 5 p.m. on Sun, but hours are seasonal, so be sure to check the website or call. Find it at 1501 E. Evergreen Blvd., Vancouver, WA 98661; (360) 816-6200; nps.gov/fova; $.

★ **VISTA HOUSE AT CROWN POINT**, 40700 E. Columbia River Historic Hwy., Corbett, OR 97019; vistahouse.com; free. We inevitably take visitors to beautiful Vista House to show off the dramatic beauty of the Columbia Gorge from its vantage point 733 feet above the river. Designated a Natural Landmark of national significance, Vista House is also listed on the National Register of Historic Places. Visitors are impressed by the sweeping views of the Columbia River, the Cascades, and the Columbia Gorge. The Vista House is open spring through fall from 9 a.m. to 6 p.m. daily, and on winter weekends from 10 a.m. to 4 p.m., weather permitting; you will find a gift shop and espresso bar as well. It can be reached by taking the Historic Columbia River Highway (SR 30) off I-84 at Corbett (exit 22), 15 miles east of Portland— about a 20-minute drive east from the airport.

Kids

"If a place has a reputation as being great for children," one of our friends once observed, "it's probably no good for adults." Fortunately, he wasn't referring to his native city. Portland is a great place both for children and for the adults who live with them. Many of the area's major attractions—Washington Park, the Chinese Garden, the Oregon History Center—interest persons both small and large, and many of the attractions designed just for children hold a kind of giddy appeal for their guardians. Here are some of our favorite places to go with children in the Portland Metro area and a little beyond. Just a note: Many of these are cross-listed in other chapters as well.

Price Code

The following price codes reflect the price of a single admission ticket. Designations marked "Free" mean there is no entrance fee; however, there may be additional costs for some activities.

$	Less than $8
$$	$8 to $15
$$$	More than $15

ATTRACTIONS & MUSEUMS

ALPENROSE DAIRY, 6149 SW Shattuck Rd., Portland, OR 97221; (503) 244-1133, (503) 246-0330 (Velodrome), (503) 246-2826 (Quarter-Midget Racing); alpenrose.com; free. Alpenrose Dairy is a rich blend of past and present. The dairy has been in operation since 1891, though the cows have moved to other Willamette Valley farms. Now the site includes a wide range of family activities: Dairyville, a little frontier town, faithfully reproduces the pioneer atmosphere; the Alpenrose Stadium hosts Little League games, including the Little League World Series; and there are several racing arenas, including a rare and beautiful Olympic-style velodrome. Alpenrose hosts multiple events throughout the year. For information on the bike races at the velodrome, check the Oregon Bicycle Racing Association's web page: obra.org/track.

JEFF MORRIS FIRE MUSEUM, Belmont Firehouse, 900 SE 35th Ave., Portland, OR 97214; (503) 823-3615; jeffmorrisfoundation.org; free. This museum occupies a historic firehouse, and here you will find a collection of antique fire equipment that helps children learn about the history of fire fighting. There's also a modern fire engine that helps you learn what it's like to fight fires today. This little museum is the legacy of Jeff Morris, a firefighter who established the safety-education program at the Portland Fire Bureau and who died of cancer in the 1970s. Admission is free; donations are welcome. You should call ahead and plan your visit, since hours are sporadic. Check the website for the Saturday open houses held throughout the year.

★ **OAKS AMUSEMENT PARK,** at the east end of the Sellwood Bridge on the Willamette River, 7805 SE Oaks Park Way, Portland, OR 97202; (503) 233-5777; oakspark.com; $$. An appealing and old-fashioned amusement park, Oaks Park features rides, games, and a roller-skating rink. (It's also the home of the Multnomah County Fair.) The park offers more than two dozen rides, including a Ferris wheel, a carousel, a miniature train, and bumper cars for smaller children and the Frog Hopper and Screamin' Eagle for their big sisters and brothers. Go-karts and miniature golf are popular draws, as is the roller-skating. Oaks Park is also an irresistible birthday party venue. Concessions are available, but picnics are welcome.

★ **OREGON MUSEUM OF SCIENCE AND INDUSTRY (OMSI),** 1945 SE Water Ave., Portland, OR 97214; (503) 797-4000; omsi.edu; $$. OMSI is home to engaging science exhibitions; it's a preferred destination for wiggly preschoolers on rainy afternoons, as well as for older children on field trips. OMSI has the gift of making science interesting without reducing it to mindless entertainment, and children really love this place. The museum has standout permanent exhibits, such as a computer station that allows you to see what your face will look like as you age. They also regularly feature traveling exhibits, such as Bodyworlds. Children also love other parts of OMSI: the submarine USS *Blueback*, the planetarium, and the Empirical 3-D theater. OMSI also has great education programs and camps.

★ **OREGON ZOO,** 4001 SW Canyon Rd., Portland, OR 97221; (503) 226-1561; oregonzoo.org; $$. One of Oregon's most popular attractions, the Oregon Zoo features extensive and compelling exhibits that make it a great place for families. Exhibits try to be faithful to the natural habitat of the animals. Many allow you surprising proximity to the zoo's creatures: There's nothing like the feeling of being mistaken by a butterfly for a flower or being separated by a mere inch of glass from a fierce Amur leopard. The zoo also has many events. During the summer, concerts (many are free with admission)

A young giraffe gazes back at zoo visitors.

entice families to spend the afternoon at the zoo and then sit down with a picnic dinner in the warm summer twilight.

PORTLAND ART MUSEUM, 1219 SW Park Ave., Portland, OR 97205; (503) 226-2811; portlandartmuseum.org; $$. The Portland Art Museum has a number of programs designed to educate—and entertain—children and their families. Even babies. Among these programs, Museum Family Sundays help children explore the artistic process, inspired by the displays in the museum. Family Sundays feature special tours, story times, and art-making activities. Hours are Tues through Sat 10 a.m. to 5 p.m., except on Thurs and Fri, when the museum is open 10 a.m. to 8 p.m.; Sun from noon to 5 p.m. Family programs can fill up fast, so plan ahead. (For more information see the Attractions chapter.)

⭐ **PORTLAND CHILDREN'S MUSEUM,** 4015 SW Canyon Rd., Portland, OR 97221; (503) 223-6500; portlandcm.org; $$. The Portland Children's Museum is popular with preschoolers who adore the high-quality and varied play spaces, ranging from a child-size grocery store and restaurant to a pet hospital to an ingenious waterworks room. Their older siblings love it too, especially for its arts workshops—for example, the clay room allows children to pound, roll, and shape real clay. The museum has many popular events, classes, camps, and other programs, and it's a favorite for birthday parties. The Children's Museum is adjacent to the Oregon Zoo and the World Forestry Center.

WORLD FORESTRY CENTER MUSEUM, 4033 SW Canyon Rd., Portland, OR 97221; (503) 228-1367; worldforestry.org; $. This museum is dedicated to educating us about the roles that forests have played in culture and in nature. Its permanent collections feature a number of interesting exhibitions, including one on the history of tropical rain forests. These life-size dioramas were developed in collaboration with the Smithsonian, and they tell the story of three different forest families and their struggles in the changing tropical woods. The Forest Discovery Lab offers hands-on activities, and galleries feature rotating exhibits of photography and other art. The World Forestry Center Museum is open daily from 10 a.m. to 5 p.m. On Wed, admission is discounted to $2 per person. Parking is $4.

Outlying Areas

⭐ **A. C. GILBERT'S DISCOVERY VILLAGE,** 116 Marion St. Northeast, Salem, OR 97301; (503) 371-3631, (800) 208-9514; acgilbert.org; $. A. C. Gilbert, a Salem native, was a toy inventor who gave us the Erector Set and American Flyer trains and this museum. It's made up of 3 Victorian houses that are filled with interactive exhibitions. It's hard to say which you'll like best. Is it the Frozen Shadow room, which captures your shadow on the wall? Is it the bubble room, where you can inhabit a giant bubble? Perhaps it's the Earth's Fury room, which allows you to build buildings and towns and then wipe them out with floods and earthquakes. You'll find many wonderful exhibitions, special events, and a spectacular outdoor play area.

BONNEVILLE DAM, Off I-84 (exit 40), Cascade Locks, OR 97014; (541) 374-8820; nwp.usace.army.mil/Locations/ColumbiaRiver/Bonneville.aspx; free. Take a beautiful half-hour drive through the Columbia River Gorge to the Bonneville Dam and Fish Hatchery. Watching large boats pass through the dam's locks is compelling, as are the dam's huge generators inside the powerhouse. Little ones are entranced by the sight of sturgeon, trout, and salmon stubbornly climbing the fish ladders, though sometimes older siblings grumble about dam breaching and fisheries policy. At the Hatchery, be sure to visit popular Herman the Surgeon, a 10-foot-long fish estimated to be more than 70 years old. No restaurants are nearby, so you may want to bring food.

ENCHANTED FOREST, 8462 Enchanted Way Southeast, Turner, OR 97392; (503) 371-4242; enchantedforest.com; $$$. We were grateful to

> ### Slappy Cakes
>
> We don't really believe in children's restaurants in Portland—we just take the kids with us, whether it's to the carts or somewhere nicer—but we do love Slappy Cakes. While not technically a kids' restaurant, this casual and bright diner is a good destination for them because of its chief novelty: You make your own pancakes at the table. Order a pint of batter and then order pancake add-ins like chocolate chips or bacon and then flip away. They also have food that you don't have to cook yourselves. Slappy Cakes, 4246 SE Belmont St., Portland, OR 97214; (503) 477-4805; slappycakes.com.

finally have children so that we could have an excuse to visit the Enchanted Forest. One of the nicest things about this place is the balance between thrilling rides and gentler activities. A half-timbered English Village and a replicated Old West town are fun to poke around, while a bobsled-inspired roller coaster and a scary haunted house provide more adrenaline-inducing entertainment. And the Big Timber Log Ride and bumper boats are fun ways to cool off on a hot summer day. Take I-5 south from Portland to exit 248 (Sunnyside-Turner) to get there.

FARMS

It is a habit of many Portland children to mark the seasons by what's going on at area farms. Summer is berry- and peach-picking season, fall means it's time for the pumpkin patch, winter brings Christmas trees, and spring means tulips. Many local farms have made the most of their naturally interesting happenings and have become attractions in their own right. For a complete guide to local farms, seasonal bounty, and agriculture activities for kids, check Oregon Agri-Business's consumer website, oregonfresh.net. In the meantime, here are some of our favorites.

★ **FIR POINT FARMS**, 14601 Arndt Rd., Aurora, OR 97002; (503) 678-2455; firpointfarms.com; free. Less than 30 miles from downtown Portland, Fir Point Farms offers flowers, produce, rides, games, and ice cream. In the fall, they host swarms of pumpkin-picking schoolchildren, and weekends in October feel more like a farm exhibit in Central Park than a farm in Oregon, but between the excellent homemade doughnuts and the hay-wagon rides, it's not easy to resist the charm of Fir Point Farms. You can feed most of the animals;

the owners have capitalized on the attraction of this activity for city folks by charging 25 cents per handful of chow. Fir Point Farms is open from 9 a.m. to 6 p.m. every day.

FLOWER FARMER, 2512 N. Holly, Canby, OR 97013; (503) 266-3581; flowerfarmer.com; $. A principal attraction of the Flower Farmer, south and east of Portland in Canby, is the 15-inch narrow-gauge train that winds through flowerbeds and fields. The train makes its circular journey through tunnels and past fun displays, making a stop at a petting zoo with chickens, turkeys, and a miniature donkey. Another stop brings you to a pumpkin patch, with a colossal hay pyramid that kids love and parents hate. The final stop is the gift shop. The Flower Farmer is open daily; the train runs on the weekends. The hours may vary. Many events are scheduled throughout the year, especially at Halloween and Christmas.

⭐ **THE PUMPKIN PATCH**, 16511 NW Gillihan Rd., Sauvie Island, Portland, OR 97231; (503) 621-3874; thepumpkinpatch.com; $. The Pumpkin Patch on beautiful Sauvie Island swarms with schoolchildren on field trips in the fall, but it's open as early as June. Its classic red barn is home to rabbits, pigs, and other animals. The u-pick fields are filled with luscious berries as well as apricots, nectarines, tomatoes, flowers, and, of course, pumpkins. During the harvest festival, wagon and pony rides keep the little ones busy. An elaborate, scary, dark, and beloved corn maze attracts older kids and adults, especially on crisp fall nights. (Be forewarned: It is very muddy, even when the weather is dry, and it gets cold.)

RASMUSSEN FRUIT AND FLOWER FARM, 3020 Thomsen Rd., Hood River, OR 97031; (541) 386-4622, (800) 548-2243; rasmussenfarms.com; $. Rasmussen Farms—an hour's drive east from Portland in the scenic Hood River area—is a destination throughout the year because of its varied harvests of cherries (July), pears and apples (Sept), and pumpkins (Oct). Rasmussen's Halloween celebrations make it one of the most popular pumpkin patches around. At the foot of Mount Hood, the beautiful setting of this farm would be enticing with or without the pumpkins. Rasmussen is open from April until just before Thanksgiving, 9 a.m. to 6 p.m. daily. (Rasmussen also has a good online store.)

SLEIGHBELLS, 23870 SW 195th Place, Sherwood, OR 97140; (503) 625-6052, (866) 857-0975; sleighbells.biz; free. Oregon produces more Christmas trees than any other state in the union, and during December, you can't drive

2 miles in the countryside without running into 3 tree farms. Many families begin their holiday season with a trip to Sleighbells on the weekend after Thanksgiving, where they pick out their tree and sip hot cocoa. Sleighbells is more than a tree farm, however; it's a holiday extravaganza. The gift shop features a variety of collectible ornaments (that is to say, breakable things). You can choose between precut trees or hacking one down yourself. Sleighbells is open from 10 a.m. to 6 p.m. daily.

PLANES, TRAINS & AUTOMOBILES

CANBY FERRY, South end of Mountain Road, Wilsonville; north end of Holly Street, Canby, OR 97013; (503) 650-3030; clackamas.us/roads/ferry .html; $. The Canby Ferry is an echo of the past, when the Willamette was not festooned with bridges. If you follow Holly Road north from the Flower Farmer (see separate entry in this chapter) to the end, you'll reach the ferry, in operation since 1914. The friendly operator will take you and your car across the river on a platform ferry that holds 9 vehicles and takes about 5 minutes. After you cross, you can take Mountain Road north; it will turn into Stafford Road and take you to I-205. The Canby Ferry runs from 6:45 a.m. to 9:15 p.m. daily.

COLUMBIA GORGE STERNWHEELER, Cascade Locks, OR 97014; (503) 224-3900, (800) 224-3901; portlandspirit.com; $$$. The Columbia Gorge Sternwheeler, as it chugs down and back through part of the Columbia Gorge National Scenic Area, is a fine way to learn about Lewis and Clark, the Oregon Trail, Bridge of the Gods, and the river routes that were the area's first freeways. Boarding begins at Marine Park in Cascade Locks (take I-84 east from Portland to exit 44). The cruise takes about 2 hours. Summer is the best time to go, for you can sit out on the deck and watch the windsurfers race you. It's a good idea either to purchase tickets ahead of time (on their website) or to call ahead, especially during the summer.

EVERGREEN AVIATION & SPACE MUSEUM, SR 18, 1 mile east of McMinnville, 500 NE Captain Michael King Smith Way, McMinnville, OR 97128; (503) 434-4180; evergreenmuseum.org; $$$. This museum is not only the home of the giant *Spruce Goose*—the Hughes Air H-4 Hercules, which is actually made out of birch—but it also houses myriad aircraft from US aviation history in its 121,000-square-foot facility, including the Apollo Lunar Module. The museum is open daily from 9 a.m. to 5 p.m. except Thanksgiving, Christmas, and New Year's. Children 5 and younger are admitted free of charge, and special discounts are available for students, seniors, and military folk, past and present. There is also an associated waterpark, because why not?

⭐ **PHOENIX AND HOLLY RAILROAD**, Flower Farmer, 2512 N. Holly, Canby, OR 97013; (503) 266-3581; flowerfarmer.com; $. This 15-inch, narrow-gauge train pulls hordes of schoolchildren through the fields of the Flower Farmer. If your children are fans of trains, they will love this one. (See the entry for the Flower Farmer in this chapter.)

SHADY DELL PACIFIC RAILROAD, Pacific Northwest Live Steamers, 31083 S. Shady Dell Dr., Molalla, OR 97038; (503) 829-6866; pnls.org; free. Something about the Molalla area inspires train building. Pacific Northwest Live Steamers, which dates from the 1950s, was one of the first hobby trains in the area. This beautiful, 4-acre private park is devoted to a small-scale railroad featuring handcrafted steam-, electric-, and gas-powered locomotives that wend their way around a 3,800-foot, 7.5-inch-gauge track. The park is open from May to Oct on Sun and holidays from noon to 5 p.m. Admission is free, but (tax-deductible) donations are welcome.

THE WESTERN ANTIQUE AEROPLANE & AUTOMOBILE MUSEUM, Ken Jernstedt Airfield 4S2, 1600 Museum Rd., Hood River, OR 97031; (541) 308-1600; waaamuseum.org; $$. The Western Antique Aeroplane & Automobile Museum, in beautiful Hood River, features not only beautifully restored old planes and cars, but also planes and cars that actually still work. Here you will find Model T's and Studebakers, as well as a very large collection of operating antique planes—among them a rare Curtiss Jenny. The museum also has an extensive restoration program, and they hold numerous events throughout the year where they take the planes up in an inspiring homage to human endeavor.

RECREATION

Portland is a city full of outdoor enthusiasts, and they seem pretty much born that way, but their inclinations are abetted by facilities all over the city. Words can hardly do justice to the extensive, well-run, and popular programs run by the Portland Parks and Recreation Department. They offer the greatest variety of sports and other athletic activities in the city, including dancing, swimming, even snowshoeing. They offer class sessions continually and also sponsor team sports such as soccer and basketball. Call them at (503) 823-PLAY. You can also find out about organized team sports by contacting your child's school.

Playgrounds

In general, Portland's parks, sports programs, and trails are filled with children. The city has many parks with excellent playground equipment, and much of that equipment has undergone a renaissance in the past few years. Exceptional playgrounds include Washington Park, where the substantial, bright red, blue, and yellow equipment near the Rose Garden is designed to keep preschoolers and their big brothers and sisters occupied for hours; Dickinson Park, with its massive climbing structures; Fields Park, with ropes for climbing and modernist play structures; Laurelhurst Park, which has a series of bridges that are good for playing tag; Gabriel Park, with its bright green grassy hills that look like they're straight out of Teletubbies; Sellwood Park and its wonderful tall fir trees; and Mount Tabor Park, which has views of Mount St. Helens in addition to its climbing structure and swings. Many school grounds are adjacent to parks and have good equipment, as well. Places that inspire bursts of running in children include Waterfront Park, Pioneer Courthouse Square, the Eastbank Esplanade, the plaza in front of OMSI, and the big lawn at the Oregon Zoo. Ventura Park has an incredible dirt bike track. The Hoyt Arboretum draws families who love to hike, and Powell Butte, just east of town, offers a network of easy trails so that children can explore the vestiges of the old farm it once was.

The children's playground at Fields Park in the Pearl District

Ice-Skating

⭐ **LLOYD CENTER ICE RINK**, 953 Lloyd Center, Portland, OR 97232; (503) 288-6073; lloydcenterice.com; $$. This popular ice-skating rink, at the Lloyd Center shopping mall, brings people of all ages to glide their way around the ice. Shoppers stand about, sipping coffee, watching beginners lurch past orange cones and pairs of ice dancers whoosh elegantly by. Besides offering ice-skating and hockey lessons, this is a favorite place for birthday parties and other festive occasions. The Ice Chalet also offers a summer camp for youngsters who are serious about wanting to learn to skate. Ice skates are available to rent.

MOUNTAIN VIEW ICE ARENA, 14313 SE Mill Plain Blvd., Vancouver, WA 98684; (360) 896-8700; mtviewice.com; $$. Whether you are looking for hockey, lessons, birthday parties, or just a place to wear out the children, the Mountain View Ice Arena is there for you. Public skating times are Mon through Fri, 10 a.m. to noon and 2 to about 5 p.m. and Sat and Sun from 1 to 4 p.m., as well as Fri and Sat nights from 7:40 to 9:40 p.m. Skates are available to rent.

WINTERHAWKS SKATING CENTER, 9250 Beaverton Hillsdale Hwy., Beaverton, OR 97005; (503) 297-2521; winterhawksskatingcenter.com; $$. This is the beautiful practice facility for the Portland Winterhawks hockey team, and they offer hockey lessons, figure skating, a skating school, and public skating. Open skating times are numerous; they vary depending on what else is going on, but their online calendar will keep you up to date.

Miniature Golf

Miniature golf is the ideal way to keep those grade-schoolers busy when summer starts to get boring. Miniature golf can be found at the **Family Fun Center** (listed under Games in this chapter, p. 146) and the **Mount Hood Summer Action Park** (listed under Summer Activities in this chapter, p. 143). Our favorite is **Tualatin Island Greens** (20400 SW Cipole Rd., Tualatin, OR 97062; 503-691-8400; tualatinislandgreens.com). The putting course on this public range consists of 18 famous golf holes reduced to scale, so it will be extra fun for anyone with a serious interest in golf. For the not-so-serious golfers, try **Glowing Greens** (509 SW Taylor St., Portland, OR 97204; 503-222-5554), which features indoor glow-in-the-dark pirate miniature golf. They are open daily from noon to 10 p.m. (midnight on Fri and Sat).

Rock Climbing

THE CIRCUIT BOULDERING GYM, 6050 SW Macadam Ave., Portland, OR 97239; (503) 246 5111; 410 NE 17th Ave., Portland, OR 97232; (503) 719-7041; thecircuitgym.com; $$. These bouldering facilities are a great introduction to climbing since they don't required a lot of training or special equipment—and kids as young as 5 can enjoy scrambling around the rocks. The Macadam location claims to be one of the largest such gyms in the world. Open daily.

THE PLAYGROUND GYM, 505 NE Grand Ave., Portland, OR 97232; (503) 235-7529; theplaygroundgym.com; $$. This clean and bright play space features many activities that let children blow off steam, and one of them is a climbing wall. Lots of space for birthday parties and games as well. Open daily, though the schedule for the climbing wall varies due to parties and classes.

★**PORTLAND ROCK GYM,** 21 NE 12th Ave., Portland, OR 97232; (503) 232-8310; portlandrockgym.com; $$. Are your kids climbing the walls? Why not let them do it in a place with a 38-foot rope and bouldering courses? This fun climbing gym also has lots of classes and camps for children—and is a popular spot for birthday parties. The instructors are patient and friendly. The Portland Rock Gym is open Mon, Wed, and Fri from 11 a.m. to 11 p.m.; Tues and Thurs from 7 a.m. to 11 p.m.; Sat from 9 a.m. to 7 p.m.; and Sun from 9 a.m. to 6 p.m.

Roller-Skating

Roller-skating is available at several rinks in the area. You can rent skates or bring your own provided they don't have black brakes. **Oaks Park** (listed under Attractions and Museums in this chapter, p. 135) is one of the largest and best rinks in the area, and it has a Wurlitzer theater organ besides. **The Mount Scott Community Center** (5530 SE 72nd Ave., Portland, OR 97206; 503-823-3183) is the cheapest, a great place for birthday parties. **Skate World** (1220 NE Kelly, Gresham, OR 97080; 503-667-6543; and at 4395 SE Witch Hazel Rd., Hillsboro, OR 97123; 503-640-1333) has some good family programs that allow parents in street shoes to help their beskated preschoolers around the rink.

Skateboarding

Portland is a skateboard mecca. It even has designated skateboard paths downtown. Resources for skateboarders include **Cal's Pharmacy Skateboards and Snowboards** (1400 E. Burnside St., Portland, OR 97214; 503-233-1237;

Jamison Square is one of the most inviting family parks in the city.

calspharmacy.com) where they will attentively help even clueless parents. **Cal Skate Skateboards** (210 NW 6th; 503-248-0495; calsk8.com) also has a fantastic selection. An essential resource is the website **skateoregon.com,** featuring a comprehensive guide to all the skate parks in Oregon. And because there are nearly 100, there's probably one near you, or one being built near you. For more information about Portland skateboarding, visit **skateportland.org,** where the state of the skate—including topics such as the Master Skateboard Plan (yes, there is one)—is under debate.

BURNSIDE SKATEPARK, under the Burnside Bridge on the east side of the Willamette River; free. This legendary skate park was built by hand by ambitious skateboarders—illegally. But then the city realized that public concrete everywhere would be better served by allowing a place for skateboarders to go, and they sanctioned it. And thus a revolution was born, for the builders of the Burnside Skatepark inspired a national movement. It's still one of the best. There are no fees and few rules here, but if your kids are inexperienced, try to go at off-peak times (early in the day).

CHEHALEM SKATEPARK, 1210 Blaine St., Newberg, OR 97132; (503) 538-7454; free This is a landmark facility worth a special trip. Skate Oregon calls this the best skatepark on Earth, with 29,000 square feet of skatable surface. It was designed and executed with the help of actual skateboarders. There's also a BMX track at the same site, so BMXers are not competing for space. Helmets are required.

Games

ELECTRIC CASTLES WUNDERLAND, 3451 SE Belmont St., Portland, OR 97214; (503) 238-1617; wunderlandgames.com. Your kids will finally have something to do with the nickels they collect for bottle deposits. Wunderland carries all the hottest video and pinball games, including test games. New games arrive all the time. Wunderland is also a very popular spot for birthday parties. There's a small admission fee; everything else runs on nickels. The Avalon (Belmont) and Milwaukie (11011 SE Main, Milwaukie, OR 97222; 503-653-2222) Wunderland locations also show family-friendly, first-run movies at very good prices. Additional locations are at 10306 NE Halsey St. (503-255-7333); 10 NW Burnside, Gresham, OR 97030 (503-328-8496); and 4070 Cedar Hills Blvd., Beaverton, OR 97005 (503-626-1665).

FAMILY FUN CENTER AND BULLWINKLE'S RESTAURANT, 29111 SW Town Center Loop West, Wilsonville, OR 97070; (503) 685-5000; funcenter.com; $$$. The Family Fun Center offers a double-story game arcade, batting cages, go-karts, and bumper boats. Miniature golf helps kids work on their hand-eye coordination, while a flight simulator provides some high-tech fun. Laser tag is featured as well. The restaurant, Bullwinkle's, specializes in kid-friendly cuisine such as pizza and burgers. A destination birthday spot.

⭐ **GROUND KONTROL CLASSIC ARCADE,** 511 NW Couch St., Portland, OR 97209; (503) 796-9364; groundkontrol.com; $. Ground Kontrol features 90 old-school arcade games, providing you the opportunity to teach your kids about Pac-Man and Mortal Kombat, as well as perennial favorites like Dance Dance Revolution. It's open at 12 p.m., and until 5 p.m., you can take the kids; after that, it's 21 and over. Most video and pinball games cost 1 or 2 quarters.

ULTRAZONE, Holly Farm Shopping Center, 16074 SE McLoughlin Blvd., Milwaukie, OR 97267; (503) 652-1122; ultrazoneportland.com; $$$. The big attraction here: high-tech interactive, laser-tag games. The futuristic atmosphere, with mazes, strobe lights, and special sound effects, adds to the enjoyment. Ultrazone is recommended for kids older than 5. Adults like to play too, and corporations will sometimes sponsor team-building events here, so don't be surprised if you spy Joe from accounting.

Performing Arts

BILLINGS DANCE CENTER, 10160 SW Nimbus Ave., Suite F6, Portland, OR 97223; (503) 670-7008; billingsdance.com. This popular west-side dance studio offers a range of dance classes and activities, from "princess ballet" for preschoolers through a serious performance company. Hip-hop, tap, jazz, contemporary, ballet, and other forms are taught, as well as special classes—musical theater, for example. Recitals are held at the Newmark Theater, downtown.

HOLLYWOOD DANCE, 4419 NE Sandy Blvd., Portland, OR 97213; (503) 249-0534; hollywooddancepdx.com. This family-friendly studio, named for the district in Portland, offers classes in preballet and pretap all the way through advanced ballet, contemporary, and jazz. And they have adult classes for those of you who always wanted to try hip-hop or tap but suffered through a deprived childhood. Hollywood also has an outstanding performance company that showcases fabulous original productions that are truly worth seeing.

METRO ARTS KIDS AT PORTLAND CENTER FOR PERFORMING ARTS, 9003 SE Stark St., Portland, OR 97216; (503) 408-0604; pdxmetro arts.org. Professional educators, visual artists, and performers from the Oregon Symphony, Oregon Ballet Theatre, and various theater companies help students create their own works of art, sing, play instruments, paint, dance, and act in live performances. Some classes charge by the hour, so be sure to call ahead for rates.

★NORTHWEST CHILDREN'S THEATER AND SCHOOL, 1819 NW Everett St., Portland, OR 97209; (503) 222-4480 (tickets), (503) 222-2190 (information); nwcts.org. An outstanding operation, Northwest Children's Theater produces frequent and imaginative shows with children in starring roles. Their classes and camps are first-rate, and they have been responsible for many budding Portland stars. Shows range from interpretations of classic fairy tales such as Sleeping Beauty to adaptations of works such as *Alexander and the Terrible, Horrible, No Good, Very Bad Day* to musicals from *Annie* to *Hamlet* to original works, all performed with incredible professionalism.

OREGON CHILDREN'S THEATRE, 1939 NE Sandy Blvd., Portland, OR 97232; (503) 228-9571; octc.org. This professional theater company takes props, makeup, and sets to Portland-area schools to ignite the magic of drama in classroom workshops and assemblies. And then, at Keller Auditorium, this marvelous outfit turns it around by bringing local kids onstage to help present plays and musicals. They adapt great children's classics such as *Charlotte's Web*,

The Giver, and *Lily's Purple Plastic Purse* into accessible and exciting theater. They also have excellent classes. There are tuition costs for the classes, but discounts and scholarships are available.

TEARS OF JOY THEATRE, Imago Theatre, 17 SE 8th Ave., Portland, OR 97214; (503) 248-0557; tpjt.org. This excellent theater company utilizes puppetry in remarkable ways to bring their stories to life. And what stories they are: everything from classics such as *Pinocchio* (naturally) to modern tales such as *A Ride on a Red Mare's Back* by Portland author Ursula LeGuin.

Summer Activities

Portland has so many parks and playgrounds and is so close to both the mountains and the ocean that summer is never boring. The chapter on Portland's Parks gives comprehensive and plentiful accounts of the Parks and Rec activities and programs. The Festivals and Annual Events chapter surveys the best of the seasonal events. There are also lots of summer camps in the area, with focuses on equestrian pursuits, sports (golf, baseball, soccer, basketball, and roller hockey), arts, theater, science, African arts, music, computers, cooking, fashion design, eco-awareness, politics—all in addition, of course, to plain old sleep-away camps with singing around the campfire. (Nostalgic parents don't have to be left out, either: Camp Westwind, on the Oregon coast, organizes a few sessions each summer for parents and children.) OMSI and the Oregon Zoo both offer popular summer camps. The free monthly papers *Metro Parent* and *Portland Family* provide comprehensive lists of camps each year. You can pick them up at any local library, most schools, and many children's stores.

⭐ **SUMMER FREE FOR ALL**, citywide; portlandoregon.gov/parks. Summer Free for All is Portland Parks & Recreation's gift to the city, consisting of free movies and concerts in parks throughout Portland, as well as free access to the outdoor swimming pools, free lunches and activities at playgrounds, and numerous other activities. You will find something to visit, watch, or listen to every day or evening, all summer long.

SUMMER READING, Children's Library at Central Multnomah County Library, 801 SW 10th Ave., Portland, OR 97205; (503) 988-5123; multcolib .org; free. The library has one activity that should keep kids busy during the summer: the summer reading program, which is theme-based and offers prizes for keeping track of your reading. This popular activity is carried out at library branches citywide, but the Central Library, with its very large children's section, is worth a pilgrimage. Once you enter the Central Library, take a right turn and visit the bronze tree, with a hollow trunk for play and storytelling inside. The Central Branch also offers story times and author events.

> **i** What better way to spend a summer evening than watching a movie with the family at the drive-in? The 99W Drive-In is happy to oblige every weekend spring through fall. You can find it at SR 99W and Springbrook Road in Newberg (503-538-2738; 99w.com).

SAND IN THE CITY, Pioneer Courthouse Square; sandinthecitypdx.org; free (donations accepted). Held in early July, this benefit for the Kids on the Block Awareness Program transforms Pioneer Square into a beach when more than 250 tons of sand are hauled in for sand castle competitions. Master sand sculptors give demonstrations, and children can create their own works of art in a kids' sandbox. Food and craft booths are plentiful, too, as well as live music.

MOUNT HOOD ADVENTURE PARK, Mount Hood Skibowl, 87000 E. US Hwy 26, Government Camp, OR 97028; (503) 272-3206, ext. 1107; ski bowl.com/summer; $$$. The clever people at Mount Hood Skibowl maintain the Adventure Park, which offers more than 20 attractions, including a half-mile dual Alpine slide, as well as Indy Karts, miniature golf, bungee jumping, adventure river rides, rock climbing, batting cages, ziplining, Malibu Grand Prix racing cars, and horse and pony rides. All-day passes, about $70, include unlimited rides down the Alpine slide; the á la carte menu can add up quickly.

Swimming Pools & Water Parks

★ The City of Portland Parks and Recreation Department. The City of Portland offers aquatics programs that are exceptionally popular; the outdoor swimming lessons are a cherished summertime ritual from toddlers on up (adults too!). Young swimmers can get advanced lifeguard certification, take diving lessons, or just come to splash at open swim time. Classes are offered at every pool listed here. The pools at the Southwest Community Center, the Eastside Community Center, and at Mount Scott are beautiful facilities with water toys, water slides, current channels, and other enticements. In the summer, the outdoor pools are a big draw, especially the pretty pools at Creston, Grant, and Sellwood Parks. In addition to open swim times and lessons, the outdoor pools sponsor fun events like "Dive-in Movies," which feature a water-themed, evening movie projected onto a big screen erected above the pool. Indoor pools are open year-round; outdoor pools from early June through Labor Day. Check out the Portland Parks website at portlandoregon.gov/parks or call the park nearest you for specific information and rates. (See the Parks chapter for more information.)

Indoor Pools

Buckman Swimming Pool, 320 SE 16th Ave., Portland, OR 97214; (503) 823-3668; $

Columbia Swimming Pool, 7701 N. Chautauqua Blvd., Portland, OR 97217; (503) 823-3669; $

Matt Dishman Pool, 77 NE Knott St., Portland, OR 97212; (503) 823-3673; $

MLC Pool, 2033 NW Glisan St., Portland, OR 97209; (503) 823-3671; $

Mount Scott Swimming Pool, 5530 SE 72nd Ave., Portland, OR 97206; (503) 823-3813; $

Southwest Community Center, 6820 SW 45th Ave., Portland, OR 97219; (503) 823-2840; $

Outdoor Pools

Creston Swimming Pool, 4454 SE Powell Blvd., Portland, OR 97202; (503) 823-3672; $

Grant Swimming Pool, 2300 NE 33rd Ave., Portland, OR 97232; (503) 823-3674; $

Montavilla Swimming Pool, 8219 NE Glisan St., Portland, OR 97230; (503) 823-4101; $

Peninsula Park Swimming Pool, 700 N. Rosa Parks Way, Portland, OR 97217; (503) 823-3677; $

Pier Swimming Pool, 9341 N. St. Johns St., Portland, OR 97203; (503) 823-3678; $

Sellwood Swimming Pool, 7951 SE 7th Ave., Portland, OR 97202; (503) 823-3679; $

Wilson Pool, 1151 SW Vermont St., Portland, OR 97219; (503) 823-3680; $

Outlying

North Clackamas Aquatic Park, 7300 SE Harmony Rd., Milwaukie, OR 97222; (503) 557-7873; ncprd.com/aquatic-park; $. This pool is a wonderfully wet place for the kids to cool off during the long hot days of July and August. With wave pools, wading pools, diving pools, 3 water slides, and a whirlpool, you can bet the little ones will return home all tuckered out.

SHOPPING FOR TOYS, BOOKS & MORE

⭐ **PORTLAND SATURDAY MARKET,** Southwest Ankeny and Southwest Naito Parkway, just south of the Burnside Bridge, Portland, OR 97204; (503) 222-6072; portlandsaturdaymarket.com. The Portland Saturday Market, which also runs on Sun, is a characteristic Portland experience that should be on every family's to-do list. There are blocks and blocks of vendors selling art, hand-blown glass, clothing, jewelry, pottery, and most anything else locally crafted that you can imagine. You'll also find great music and entertainment. The food is delicious, and the eye candy is even better. Saturday Market takes place from the first weekend in March to Christmas Eve. On Sat the market opens at 10 a.m. and closes at 5 p.m.; Sun hours are 11 a.m. to 4:30 p.m.

Books

BARNES & NOBLE BOOKSTORE, Lloyd Center, 1317 Lloyd Ave., Portland, OR 97232; (503) 249-0800; barnesandnoble.com. Area Barnes & Noble bookstores offer books and story times and author events for preschoolers through teens. The Lloyd Center location along with the Bridgeport store (7227 SW Bridgeport Rd., Tigard, OR 97224; 503-431-7575) are two of our favorites, but there are five in the area, all of which typically offer a weekend morning storytime and a Saturday event as well. To see what's on deck, click on the store locator tab on the website listed above. Both the Lloyd Center and Bridgeport stores also have toys and games in addition to books. Barnes & Noble stores are spacious and comfortable; most have an in-house Starbucks and free Wi-Fi. Maybe you'll get to browse a little too.

A CHILDREN'S PLACE, 4807 NE Fremont St., Portland, OR 97213; (503) 284-8294; achildrensplacebookstore.com. A Children's Place is a wonderful independent store in the Beaumont neighborhood with an impressive selection of books and music for children of all ages. And they have the expertise that comes with focusing on young readers, so they make wise recommendations if you need advice. They also carry educational toys and puzzles here, as well as games to stimulate those fertile imaginations, a good stock of art supplies, and musical instruments, and they work with teachers and local schools to keep them supplied as well. A Children's Place also hosts many events—including book events for adults—with their Thursday morning storytelling a community favorite.

⭐ **COSMIC MONKEY COMICS,** 5335 NE Sandy Blvd., Portland, OR 97213; (503) 517-9050; cosmicmonkeycomics.com. A fine, large comic store with a wall of Manga and every variety of comic books. Cosmic Monkey is open daily from 7 p.m. They are very kid-friendly and offer summer workshops on how to create your own comics.

EXCALIBUR COMICS, 2444 SE Hawthorne Blvd., Portland, OR 97214; (503) 231-7351; excaliburcomics.net. A premier outlet for comics in the Portland area, Excalibur carries collector's items, books, and alternative comics in addition to their mainstream offerings. Not everything is G-rated, but they do have an impressive selection of children's comics, as well as good service. And you can rent anime flicks and other DVDs from Excalibur.

⭐ **POWELL'S CITY OF BOOKS,** 1005 W. Burnside St., Portland, OR 97209; (503) 228-4651; powells.com. While Powell's City of Books is fully covered in the Shopping chapter, it is worth noting that the children's resources at Powell's are phenomenal. They carry current favorites, but they have vast holdings of used books, classics, collector's items, and, most important, a knowledgeable staff to help you find the perfect book for your child. Furthermore, they carry excellent educational materials; whether you are a home-schooling parent, a teacher, or simply an interested adult, you will be astonished at the wealth here. The Hawthorne branch also has a good, though smaller, children's section.

Toys

CHILD'S PLAY, 2305 NW Kearney St., Portland, OR 97210; (503) 224-5586; childsplayportland.com. A fine neighborhood shop in the Northwest Portland district, Child's Play features well-made, inventive toys. You'll find a decent selection of seasonal toys and dress-up clothes as well as lines like Playmobil, Lego, and Brio. The wide array of Breyer horses and accoutrements is another big draw. The store also carries books. It's useful to note that the shop has a parking lot (a rarity in the area) and they will wrap your gifts for free.

⭐ **FINNEGAN'S,** 820 SW Washington St., Portland, OR 97205; (503) 221-0306; finneganstoys.com. At Finnegan's you'll find whole cities of dolls, lots of building blocks, sidewalk chalk, ant farms, flower presses, boomerangs, dump trucks—in short, every kind of toy a child could imagine. Though it is large, it never has that frantic feeling that so many of the big chain toy stores cultivate; even during the holidays when it's really busy, Finnegan's manages to exude serenity. Classic toys like Color Forms and Brio as well as modern lines like Melissa and Doug can all be found here.

Kids in Portland receive regular inoculations of civic pride even in their toys.

⭐ **KIDS AT HEART**, 3435 SE Hawthorne Blvd., Portland, OR 97214; (503) 231-2954; kidsathearttoys.com. Kids at Heart is a sweet neighborhood store in the Hawthorne shopping district; it keeps area residents supplied with birthday presents, art supplies, Playmobil sets, and Brio trains, but it's worth a trip for nonresidents too. Kids at Heart has a fine collection of dress-up clothes, games, and science-oriented toys—kits turning children into spies and explorers have been recent hits at parties. You won't find Barbie, but you will find Groovy Girls and their sisters, in addition to a whole wall of trains and building toys.

Clothes and Gear

BLACK WAGON, 3964 N. Mississippi Ave., Portland, OR 97227; (503) 916-0000, (866) 916-0004; blackwagon.com. Black Wagon is a charming store in the Mississippi neighborhood that offers beautiful children's shoes and clothing (from birth to age 12), much of it handmade, organic or recycled fiber, and very chic. In addition to the great clothes, however, they also offer a stylish collection of bedding, decor and furniture, toys, books, and music. Their online store is excellent as well, so you can still shop there after you've gone home.

The parks of Portland offer ample and beautiful outdoor spaces for playing and growing.

⭐ **GRASSHOPPER,** 1816 NE Alberta St., Portland, OR 97211; (503) 335-3131; grasshopperstore.com. Grasshopper offers wonderful clothes for children, many of them handmade right there (or down the street at the "mother" store, Tumbleweed). Brands include the store's own Wild Carrots, Kate Quinn Organics, and Picaflor, among many others. There is also a large selection of well-made, lead-free toys. The beautiful space is a pleasure to shop in, and your children will also enjoy themselves, possibly almost as much as you. Grasshopper is open daily from 10 a.m. to 6 p.m. (5 p.m. on Sun and Mon). They have a cool blog, too.

HANNA ANDERSSON, 327 NW 10th Ave., Portland, OR 97209; (503) 321-5275; hannaandersson.com. Beautiful, well-made cotton clothes that look good and feel good are the specialty of this amazing Portland store, and it has acquired an international following through its catalog sales since its founding here in 1983. These clothes last a long time—even the tights. The clothes are meant to last for more than one child, so the company has a program to pass on gently used Hannas to needy children. Hanna Andersson is open Mon through Fri 10 a.m. to 6 p.m. and on Sat from 10 a.m. to 5 p.m. (See the Shopping chapter for more details.)

POLLIWOG, 234 NE 28th Ave., Portland, OR 97232; (503) 236-3903; polliwogportland.com. Beautiful, beautiful children's clothes for newborns and their siblings up to age 6 are the specialty of this pretty store in Southeast Portland—though they also sell diaper bags, gifts, wooden toys, and accessories as well. Shoes from Kaboogies are best-sellers, as well as wonderful baby T-shirts by Glug. Polliwog also carries dresses by Mister Judy, handmade in Portland.

POSH BABY, 916 NW 10th Ave., Portland, OR 97209; (503) 478-7674; 12345 Horizon Blvd. #53, Beaverton, OR 97007; (503) 747-3539; posh-baby.com. Posh is for the 5-and-under crowd. Chic modern nursery furniture, European strollers, cute lunch boxes for day care or preschool, gifts, and clothing are all part of the package. Posh Baby will accessorize your little accessory in an Instagram-worthy manner.

★ **PRESENTS OF MIND**, 3633 SE Hawthorne Blvd., Portland, OR 97214; (503) 230-7740; presentsofmind.tv. It is often difficult to find high-quality baby clothing and gifts that are gender-neutral, but Presents of Mind not only has baby and toddler clothing that is in other colors besides pink and blue, it also has baby and toddler clothing that is made by local Portland artisans. Here you'll find soft baby hats made out of recycled cashmere sweaters, cute organic-cotton onesies, and sweet hand-smocked dresses, among many other inventive things. See the listing in the Shopping chapter for more information on this wonderful shop.

KIDS

Festivals & Annual Events

One thing we never say in Portland is, "We have nothing to do!" So much is going on every month that instead we ask ourselves how we can possibly fit it all in. You can find something happening every weekend, somewhere. In a culture of mass marketing, mass media, and mass consumption, our local celebrations help define and distinguish our area, preserving an awareness of local identity and history and creating a sense of place.

Here, we feature a number of selected annual events organized chronologically by month. One note: This is Oregon. Outdoor events are rarely canceled because of weather, though it may occasionally cause changes in schedules and performances. In general, though, the show goes on. Dress accordingly.

JANUARY

FERTILE GROUND, various locations; fertilegroundpdx.org. Fertile Ground is a fringe festival with a very Portland twist: All the works produced are by local writers, on the theory that this will keep the artistic and financial benefits here in the city. Part of the reason this works is that this festival of new works is put together collaboratively, with just about every theater arts organization participating in the readings, workshops, interviews, and world-premiere full productions. It's held during the end of January and beginning of February. You can buy a season pass for $50, a "discount" button for $5 (to get reduced prices at some events), and see many events for free. Full productions will cost more, of course.

★**ROSE CITY CLASSIC ALL BREED DOG SHOW,** Portland Expo Center, 2060 N. Marine Dr., Portland, OR 97217; rosecityclassic.org. Portlanders love their dogs, and this event—one of the largest dog shows in the United States—allows owners from throughout Oregon and southwest Washington to show off their pets (or vice versa). Four thousand dogs and their breeders attend this dog extravaganza, complete with agility trials, obedience contests, and breed competitions.

⭐ PORTLAND INTERNATIONAL FILM FESTIVAL, various locations; Northwest Film Center; 1219 SW Park Ave., Portland, OR 97205; (503) 276-4310; nwfilm.org. Whether you like to go to the movies or view films, this festival will provide plenty of entertainment. Expect to see a variety of professional, experimental, traditional, and avant-garde films—as well as lectures, talks, and exhibits—during this well-attended event sponsored by the Northwest Film Center. Admission fees vary, but discount passes are available. Movies (as many as 80) are shown in local theaters over a 3-week period. The opening and closing nights feature the Portland premieres of new major movies. Matinee tickets are also available.

⭐ PORTLAND JAZZ FESTIVAL, various locations; (503) 228-5299; pdxjazz.com. The Portland Jazz Festival celebrates our musical heritage with rare insight and wit. The festival is organized around a new theme each year, and so the featured artists vary. But you will hear luminaries such as pianist Randy Weston, local favorites with international reputations such as Dave Frishberg, as well as rising stars such as Portland's Grammy-winning bassist Esperanza Spalding. The Portland Jazz Festival coincides with Black History Month, and many outreach and education events round out this weeklong celebration.

MARCH

⭐ PORTLAND FARMERS' MARKET, Portland State University, 1800 SW Broadway at Montgomery, Portland, OR 97207; (503) 241-0032; portlandfarmersmarket.org. The Portland Farmers' Market, open March through Dec, Sat 8 a.m. to 2 p.m., is only one of many in the region—there are thriving markets all over the city, notably in the Hillsdale, Hollywood, and Interstate neighborhoods, as well as in Beaverton. For a complete list of all the farmers' markets in the city and throughout Portland, check out the excellent Oregon Farmers Market Association website, and you will find one nearby: oregonfarmersmarkets.org.

⭐ PORTLAND SATURDAY MARKET, Southwest Ankeny and Southwest Naito Parkway, south of Burnside Bridge; 108 W. Burnside St., Portland, OR 97209; (503) 222-6072; portlandsaturdaymarket.com. Since 1974 Saturday Market (it is open on Sun too) has been a "must see" for visitors. You can enjoy street theater (some intentional, some not), sample from a range of food booths, and buy everything from candles, macramé, pottery, stained glass and handmade housewares to furniture and toys. The market runs until Christmas. During the holiday-shopping madness, it is as packed as any department store or mall. We still have the Cowichan sweaters we bought there in high school, which are now cult items thanks to *The Big Lebowski*, and now you can have one too.

REED ARTS WEEK (RAW), Reed College; 3202 SE Woodstock Blvd., Portland, OR 97202; reed.edu/raw. This 5-day gala of dance, poetry and prose readings, exhibits, and musical performances includes the work of Reed students and that of important artists from Portland and beyond. There are performances and master classes, and everything is intellectually and aesthetically stimulating and challenging. And the college's Southeast Portland campus is beautiful, with a small but excellent art gallery, a superb performing arts center, and a great bookstore. Exhibitions are open from noon to 6 p.m.; workshops and events begin in the afternoon and linger well into the evening.

SHAMROCK RUN, Tom McCall Waterfront Park, at Southwest Naito Parkway and Southwest Stark, Portland, OR 97239; shamrockrunportland.com. One of Portland's most popular running events, the Shamrock Run attracts more than 35,000 participants. It is a fund-raiser for Doernbecher Children's Hospital, one of the state's most popular and successful organizations. The event includes a Leprechaun Lap, a 1-kilometer run, walk, or jog; the Shamrock Stride, a 4-mile walk; and 5-kilometer, 8-kilometer, and 15-kilometer races. The entry fee varies with the runner's age and selected event but includes a T-shirt and the usual goodies.

SOUTHEAST PORTLAND ARTS WALK, various locations, seportlandart walk.com. Every March, about 100 artists in inner Southeast Portland throw open their studios so you can see them at work and talk technique, as well as purchase some cool art and indulge your curiosity about how these artists decorate their houses and landscape their yards. Every variety of painting, sculpture, ceramics, fiber art, glass art, fine furniture, jewelry, and more is represented. You can download a well-designed map to help you plot your journey on this free, self-guided tour. This event was founded by local artist Rin Carroll Jackson in 2002 as a way to strengthen neighborly bonds. Judging by its massive popularity, the bonds are growing stronger.

AGFEST, State Fairgrounds; 2330 17th St. Northeast, Salem, OR 97301; (503) 535-9353, (800) 874-7012; oragfest.com. Agfest is a celebration of Oregon's largest industry: agriculture. The 18,000 visitors who attend this event will find angora rabbit breeders, grass seed farmers, orchard growers, and multiple other ag-related representatives, who gather here to teach people about their work. Agfest winds throughout most of the fairgrounds, with many activities and events. Children love to follow the elaborate scavenger hunt in the Ag Country display, where they sample Oregon products such as pears and cherries and watch chicks hatch—as well as learn a remarkable amount about their state. Admission is $9 for adults, while children 12 and under are admitted for no charge.

Blossom Time

The Hood River Valley, east of Portland, is prime orchard country, and during late March and all through April, it is blanketed in pink and white blossoms. A drive to see the peach, apple, pear, and cherry blossoms makes a perfect half-day trip, and whether you take the long route over Mount Hood on US 26 or the shorter way (east along the Columbia Gorge via I-84), your drive will be spectacular. Call the Hood River Chamber of Commerce, and they'll send you a blossom-time brochure: (800) 366-3530.

WOODBURN TULIP FESTIVAL, 33814 S. Meridian Rd., Woodburn, OR 97071; (503) 634-2243, (800) 711-2006; woodenshoe.com. Emerging from the gray Oregon winter, hundreds of thousands of tulip bulbs burst into color each spring at several nurseries in this small town just south of Portland. Oregonians flock to the colored fields, rejoicing at this welcome sign that they survived another winter. Visitors can purchase gifts and cut flowers, order bulbs, and dine on local foods. The actual dates vary slightly in response to the severity of the winter, but by mid-April you can usually count on acres of gorgeous blossoms. During the festival weeks there is a $10 vehicle charge per carload of people ($5 if you are on a bike).

FESTIVALS & ANNUAL EVENTS

CINCO DE MAYO, Tom McCall Waterfront Park, between the Morrison and Hawthorne Street Bridges; Portland, OR 97239; cincodemayo.org. Portland is a Sister City to several cities throughout the world, including Guadalajara, Mexico. This is a huge waterfront event celebrating the country's holiday, one of the largest such events in North America. It features Mexican and Latino food, crafts, art, music, and dancing, as well as carnival rides and other festive touches. The entry fee is $8 for those 13 and older, $4 for kids 6 to 12, and $4 for seniors.

CRYSTAL SPRINGS RHODODENDRON MOTHER'S DAY SHOW, Crystal Springs Rhododendron Garden, Southeast 28th Avenue and Woodstock, Portland, OR 97202; (503) 771-8386; rhodies.org. May brings out the full glory of our indigenous rhododendron, and what better way to honor your mom than by walking with her down the lovely, winding paths of the Crystal Springs Rhododendron Garden? The garden features thousands of blooming rhododendrons, azaleas, and other plantings all during Mother's Day weekend in May—a spectacular sight. (See the Parks chapter for more information about Crystal Springs Rhododendron Garden.)

MEMORIAL DAY WEEKEND IN THE WINE COUNTRY, various locations; Willamette Valley Wineries Association; (503) 646-2985; willamette wines.com. This popular self-guided tour of more than 150 vineyards and wineries includes some tasting rooms that are rarely open to the public. Advice, maps, lists of participating vineyards and wineries, and other details (telephone numbers, open hours, etc.) are available on the website above or on their handy mobile app. This event is a unique opportunity to try barrel tastings, reserves, and the special vintages that the winemakers like to hold back. The wineries are open for the festival from 11 a.m. to 5 p.m. on Sat and Sun.

CHAMBER MUSIC NORTHWEST SUMMER FESTIVAL, various locations; (503) 223-3202, (503) 294-6400 (tickets); cmnw.org. Chamber Music Northwest is a highly successful music series that brings together the world's finest musicians to play to sold-out crowds throughout the city. Artistic director David Shifrin, a renowned clarinetist and Avery Fisher Prize recipient, inspires great loyalty in the music community and is able to entice superb artists to reside for the summer in Portland and play together. Ticket prices are

FESTIVALS & ANNUAL EVENTS

reasonable, and series tickets are available, but order in advance for the best seats. Discount prices for rush tickets are available for students and seniors. These concerts are truly worth attending.

⭐**PORTLAND ROSE FESTIVAL**, Portland Rose Festival Association; various venues citywide; (503) 227-2681; rosefestival.org. The Rose Festival draws thousands and thousands of visitors every year and marks the official beginning of the summer season—no matter what the weather is doing. There are more than 100 different official Rose Festival events, including 3 parades, dragon boat races, a carnival on the waterfront, oars of ships from the US and Canadian Navy and Coast Guard, fireworks, concerts, races, and a world-class rose show. The Grand Floral Parade is the culminating event: It includes floats, marching bands, drill teams, clowns, the Rose Queen and her court of princesses, and general festive spectacle. The Rose Festival begins Memorial Day weekend and continues through mid June.

PRIDE NORTHWEST, various locations; (503) 295-9788; pridenw.org. Pride Northwest is Portland's annual gay, lesbian, bi, and trans celebration that includes music, events, a fun run, a pet parade, and the great Pride Parade, which is held on Sun. The Pride Parade, a splendid event, draws more than 50,000 people and is Portland's third largest annual parade. There is also a

Popular Hong Kong–style Dragon Boat races are held during the Rose Festival.

festival of food, crafts, and booths by gay/lesbian–friendly organizations and services.

WORLD NAKED BIKE RIDE, starting at the Park Blocks near the Portland Art Museum; pdxwnbr.org. While the World Naked Bike Ride happens, well, all over the world, readers will not be surprised to learn that Portland is the naked bicycle capital of the world. The World Naked Bike Ride is meant to illustrate the vulnerability of cyclists everywhere, although it is possible that this message is lost on the many spectators. Naked cyclists of every human type ride from the Park Blocks through downtown to the East side and back again. It's a pretty joyful event. Entry fees to the prefunction at the Portland Art Museum are $1 per piece of clothing; otherwise, just show up in all your glory.

JULY

CONCERTS IN THE PARKS, citywide, various locations, (503) 823-PLAY; portlandoregon.gov/parks. Summer in the city: Early evening light softens but still gleams off the river; the current laps gently at the river's banks, a counterpoint to the fading, distant hum of traffic; and music soothes and stimulates the quiet crowd that has gathered at Waterfront Park to hear the Oregon Symphony. Or perhaps the crowd is on its feet and dancing the rhumba at Mount Tabor. Whatever the music and wherever the park, free concerts are held during July (and often into Aug) throughout the city almost every night of the week. You can find concert schedules and locations at the Portland Parks website above: search for "Summer Free For All."

FOURTH OF JULY FIREWORKS, various locations. As in other parts of the country, the Fourth of July celebrates the national birthday. We joke that summer in Oregon begins, however, on July 5—June in Portland can be a rainy month, right up to and including the holiday. We bundle up to watch fireworks anyway; these you will find in downtown Portland at the Waterfront Blues festival (see below), at Oaks Park, and across the river at Fort Vancouver (4th.fortvan.org). This latter event requires some patience for traffic (but worth it), while the other two just require a spot along the river somewhere—the Eastbank Esplanade and the Hawthorne Bridge both make for excellent viewing if you can find a spot.

INTERNATIONAL PINOT NOIR CELEBRATION, Linfield College, 900 SE Baker St., McMinnville, OR 97128; (800) 775-4762; ipnc.org. The Willamette Valley is renowned for its excellent pinot noir, and this celebration

Fireworks over the Willamette celebrate July 4th in style.

features the best wines made from this fine grape. It draws oenophiles from throughout the world for 3 days of tastings, talks and tours, eating, and entertainment. The event encourages you to mingle by dividing participants into 2 groups for activities, which makes for very interesting conversations, especially as the afternoon proceeds. Advance reservations are mandatory—this event sells out fast, even with a ticket price of nearly $1,000. (Tickets are sold starting in Feb.) You can purchase à la carte tickets to selected events on Sat and Sun.

MOLALLA BUCKEROO, The Buckeroo Grounds, 815 Shirley St., Molalla, OR 97038; (503) 829-8388; molallabuckeroo.com. Since 1913, professional riders, ropers, and other persons skilled in the arts of the Western ranch have been coming to the Molalla Buckeroo (that's Oregon-speak for rodeo). Admission prices vary from about $13 to $15, depending on how old you are and where you sit. Matinee prices are discounted. This event includes dances, barbecues, trail rides, parades, and 3 days of professional rodeo, all during the Fourth of July holiday.

★ **OREGON BREWERS FESTIVAL,** Tom McCall Waterfront Park, 1020 SW Naito Pkwy., Portland, OR 97204; (503) 778-5917; oregonbrewfest.com. This popular festival draws 50,000 people to celebrate craft beers from Oregon and beyond. More than 80 brewers offer tastings; many local breweries create special beers that are offered only at this festival. You will also find great food and even craft-brewed root beer for the designated driver. Admission is free, but visitors must purchase a tasting mug for $7; beer tastes are purchased by token, at $1 apiece. The festival runs Thurs through Sun of the last full weekend in July. Note that the Portland International Beer Fest, portland-beerfest.com—a smaller but no less thirst-quenching celebration—is held the third weekend in July.

★ **OREGON COUNTRY FAIR,** 13 miles west of Eugene on SR 126, near Veneta, OR 97487; (541) 343-4298; oregoncountryfair.org. Before there was Burning Man, there was Oregon Country Fair. This event is a wondrous alloy of handicrafts, music, performance art, belly dancing, drum circles, stiltwalkers, alternative ideology promoters, and more. It's a cultural experience unique to Oregon. Order tickets through Ticketswest (ticketswest.com)—none are sold on site. Forty thousand people communing in a small town outside Eugene does create some chaos, so be patient. Consider taking one of the buses that Lane County Transit thoughtfully sends out to the fair site from Eugene. If you do park at the fair, be sure to respect the residents who live near the grounds.

Completely Fair

With their farm animals, 4-H kids, crafts exhibits, carnival rides, and country music, county fairs provide some of the best summer entertainment around.

In May, the Multnomah County Fair is at Oaks Park (call 503-761-7577 for information). In July look for the Hood River County Fair, hoodriver fair.com, and the Washington County Fair and Rodeo faircomplex.com. In August try the Yamhill County Fair, co.yamhill.or.us/fair; the Clackamas County Fair, clackamas.us/fair; and the Clark County (Washington) Fair, across the river, clarkcofair.com. For information about all the fairs in Oregon, visit oregonfairs.org.

THE ST. PAUL RODEO, 20025 4th Street, St. Paul, OR 97137; (503) 633-2011, (800) 237-5920; stpaulrodeo.com. Each July 4 holiday, the rural Willamette Valley town of St. Paul holds one of the best rodeos in the country, with riders competing for prizes in several categories. You'll find food and beverage booths, a carnival with rides and games of chance and skill, Western dancing for grown-ups, lots of music, a traditional small-town Fourth of July parade, and, of course, fireworks. To see the rodeo, you'll need a ticket; these run from about $14 to $30, depending on the luxuriousness of the seat and add-ons to the package. And it's best to order them ahead—they are available through Ticketmaster.

★ **WATERFRONT BLUES FESTIVAL**, Tom McCall Waterfront Park, 1020 Southwest Naito Pkwy., Portland, OR 97204; (503) 282-0555; water frontbluesfest.com. One of Portland's premier events, the Waterfront Blues Festival is held over the Fourth of July holiday and is a tourist attraction in its own right. Hear legendary artists such as Taj Mahal, Mavis Staples, Eric Burdon, and Robert Plant, as well as rising stars, sing away their troubles in beautiful Waterfront Park. This outdoor festival also includes terrific fireworks. Admission is $10 and 2 cans of food for the Oregon Food Bank—all proceeds go to support the Oregon Food Bank—but you can also buy passes that get you priority access, parking, T-shirts, and other special privileges.

THE BITE OF OREGON, Tom McCall Waterfront Park, 1020 SW Naito Pkwy., Portland, OR 97204; biteoforegon.com. The Bite is another local celebration of food, eating, and conspicuous food consumption, and it draws people from all over to eat their way from one end of Waterfront Park to the other. Restaurants from all over the state ply their wares, top chefs show off for one another in a local *Iron Chef*–style competition, and local breweries and winemakers offer their tempting concoctions. The admission charge of $10 for a weekend pass supports the Oregon Special Olympics. Three stages of music and dancing are also featured.

HOOD TO COAST RELAY, starting at Timberline Lodge, 27500 E. Timberline Road, Timberline Lodge, OR 97028; (503) 292-4626; hoodtocoast .com. This 198-mile relay road race, established in 1982, brings teams together to run from Mount Hood to Seaside, Oregon. The race, billed as the largest relay race in the world, attracts more than 12,000 runners. Walking events are offered in addition to running events, and some of the race-walkers are impossibly fast. Because of its popularity, the organizers have a strict registration policy and expect you to register well in advance. But even if you're not racing, the event is fun to follow, whether you're watching the runners speed through Portland or joining them in celebration at Seaside.

★ **PICKATHON,** Pendarvis Farm, 16581 SE Hagen Rd., Happy Valley, OR, 97086; pickathon.com. This delightful roots music festival seeks to maximize the festival-going experience by featuring diverse artists, eco-friendly camping, and a thoughtfully planned venue. It is set on a beautiful farm to the east of the city; the owners of the farm work hand in hand with the event organizers to make this festival one of a kind. Find artists such as Feist, Neko Case, and Kurt Vile among the lineup. There are 7 "stages," outstanding food, and even better music; plus, the festival is very family-friendly (while still being very fun). It's also one of the only such musical festivals to which you can ride your bike.

TUALATIN CRAWFISH FESTIVAL, Tualatin Commons and Community Park, 8535 SW Tualatin Rd., Tualatin, OR 97062; (503) 692-0780; tualatin crawfishfestival.com. As this once-rural suburb grows into a city, it continues to celebrate a tradition dating from 1957. The event is split between the Commons in downtown Tualatin and the Community Park just a short stroll away. This popular event features parades, a 5K race, remote-control boat racing, a pancake breakfast, and many, many booths. You'll find lots of crawfish dishes, including a crawfish cookoff. Many activities are designed just for the children, and there's plenty of entertainment—music, dancing—for adults as well. There's a small admission fee for events at the Community Park, but not for those on the Commons.

ART IN THE PEARL, Northwest Park Blocks, between West Burnside and Northwest Glisan at Northwest 8th Avenue, Portland, OR 97209; (503) 722-9017; artinthepearl.com. More than 100 artists gather here each Labor Day weekend for a lively 3 days of culture and commerce. This arts festival is truly community driven, relying on highly experienced volunteers rather than large corporate sponsorships, and for that reason, it is distinctive. In addition to artists and high-end crafters selling their wares, musicians and theater groups perform on a central stage. You can try out artistic pursuits for yourself in the Education Pavilion, which has activities for children and their grown-up friends.

★ **FEAST PORTLAND,** various locations; feastportland.com. Sponsored by *Bon Appétit* magazine, Feast Portland is a premier festival dedicated to the glory of Oregon food, wine, beer, and spirits. It's also, however, a major fundraiser for charities that feed hungry children—ironically, Oregon ranks high in food insecurity, especially for children. This 4-day extravaganza includes lectures, panel discussions, workshops, special dinners with chefs, and many tastings. You can purchase tickets to individual events (for example, $10 for a lecture; $75 for a special brunch including drink and tip) or for packages ($465 for 5 marquee events). Come on, who wouldn't want to participate in the Sandwich Invitational on a beautiful late summer evening at Director Park (15 chefs, many sandwiches, $95)?

MOUNT ANGEL OKTOBERFEST, throughout downtown Mount Angel, OR 97362; oktoberfest.org. Despite a long history of German settlers, Mount Angel didn't make Oktoberfest a commercial activity until 1966. Now the event lasts 4 days and it's the largest folk festival in the state. There are 4 stages with live music, demonstrations of traditional Bavarian folk dancing, and street dances on Fri and Sat nights. In addition to the traditional Biergarten and Wiengarten, there is a Microgarten with locally brewed beers. For younger visitors there is a Kindergarten with rides and other entertainment. Most events are free; entrance into the entertainment stages and beer gardens will cost from $4 to $14 depending on when you buy it. And yes, it's in September.

MUSICFEST NORTHWEST (MFNW), various locations; musicfestnw .com. MFNW showcases 250 bands over multiple days at more than 20 stages throughout town for 34,000 people. Ground central is Pioneer Courthouse Square, where you'll find artists such as the Decemberists, Wiz Khalifa, and the Smashing Pumpkins. But you can catch lesser-known but equally compelling artists almost anywhere in Portland; festival organizers have commandeered half the stages in town. You can purchase admission to all the events or go à la carte. MFNW includes more than music—there is also TechFest Northwest, which brings together luminaries from the world of design, technology, and start-ups, to add some Apollonian structure to the Dionysian fun of MFNW.

★ OREGON STATE FAIR, State Fairgrounds, 2330 17th St. Northeast, Salem, OR 97301; (800) 833-0011; oregonstatefair.org. The Oregon State Fair is held the last week before Labor Day (which means it sometimes falls in August). The fair has strong roots in the state's rural areas, but in a larger sense, the fair celebrates and honors Oregon's past, acknowledges the present, and recognizes the future. It is good to know people still bake prize-winning cakes, make pickles and jams, raise hogs, and otherwise occupy themselves productively. The fair draws visitors from throughout the state. Preorder tickets are $7 for adults, $3 for seniors and children ages 6 to 12; tickets at the gate may be slightly more. Parking is free, but lots fill early.

★ PICA TIME-BASED ART FESTIVAL, various locations; (503) 242-1419; pica.org/tba. The Time-Based Art Festival is a fun, avant-garde 10 days of performance, hosted by PICA (see the Visual and Literary Arts chapter) and dedicated to celebrating the aesthetics and art practices of the moment. What does that mean for you? Ten days of lectures, workshops, salons, shows, happenings, exhibitions, films, and parties. Because the festival is dedicated to cultivating the new, the forms these events take resist labels. You might find films by cutting-edge artists and performers. Or a discussion of what Homeland Security means for art. Events might be held at toney downtown hotels or under gritty urban bridges. Tickets are sold for individual events or for multiple events; some events are free.

OCTOBER

GREEK FESTIVAL, Holy Trinity Greek Orthodox Church, 3131 NE Glisan St., Portland, OR 97232; (503) 234-0468; goholytrinity.org/cGreek Fest.html. About 15,000 people each year converge on the lovely grounds of this Greek Orthodox church to celebrate Greek food and culture. This popular event, one of the oldest of its kind, draws visitors from throughout northwest Oregon and southwest Washington who come to enjoy Greek music and dancing, arts and crafts displays, and, of course, gorgeous food. At the gate, you'll trade your dollars for Greek talents, which you'll spend on food, icons, and other wonderful things, such as rugs, textiles, jewelry, and other imports from Greece. There is music and dancing, and there are also tours of the beautiful Holy Trinity Church.

HALLOWEEN PUMPKIN FEST, Fir Point Farms, 14601 Arndt Rd., Aurora, OR 97002; (503) 678-2455; firpointfarms.com. Fir Point Farms is a working farm producing flowers and nursery stock, pumpkins, hay, and a variety of fruits and vegetables. At Halloween, Fir Point Farms hosts a hay maze and wagon rides. The grounds are filled with carved and decorated pumpkins, and there are pony rides and other entertainment for children. Rabbits, chickens, and turkeys are on hand for petting and watching, and the farm's goats climb a series of ramps and tree branches to get an aerial perch on the activities. No admission is charged, although there are small fees for rides.

★ **THE MAIZE**, on Sauvie Island at the Pumpkin Patch, 16511 NW Gillihan Rd., Portland, OR 97231; (503) 621-7110; portlandmaze.com. The beloved Pumpkin Patch (see Kids) hosts 2 giant corn mazes each year: one a traditional corn maze and the other a haunted maze—meaning that it is open at night, it's dark, and there are scary things around corners. The traditional maze is fashioned along a contemporary theme—in 2012, it was the television show *Portlandia*. Both are popular; the haunted maze in particular is a favorite outing for teens and the newly dating. A word of caution: It's open rain or shine, and it's Oregon in October, so you should probably wear rain boots because it will be muddy.

OKTOBERFEST, Oaks Park, 7805 SE Oaks Park Way, Portland, OR 97202, at the east end of the Sellwood Bridge; oakspark.com. This Oktoberfest celebration at Oaks Park on the banks of the Willamette River features delicious German sausages and other treats, a sausage-eating contest, oompah bands, polka, and other Germania. For the younger set, a kinderplatz (children's place) complete with Radio Disney is a big draw. Visitors will find traditional German foods, beers, and wines supplemented with local favorites, as well. Admission is $5 for adults, $2 for kids, and $3 for those 62 and older. Be alert: Sometimes this event is held in late September.

Portland's Farmers' Market

Founded in 1992, Portland Farmers' Market features dozens of vendors selling farm-fresh produce, cut flowers and bedding plants, vegetable and herb starts, locally raised organic meat and poultry, smoked and fresh seafood, and artisan breads and cheeses. Much, but not all, of the produce is organically grown. In addition, many vendors offer delicious prepared food featuring local fare. This event is popular with locals, but it is a magnet for tourists as well, who can see, smell, and taste the raw ingredients that make up our exquisite local cuisine.

Open-air markets have been the heartbeat of villages for thousands of years and can still be found around the globe by travelers searching for the real feel of a land and its people. Here in Portland that feel includes the image of mounds of green lettuce heads or a huge tub full of sugar-fried popcorn, the sounds of a fiddle player bowing a jump tune next to a farmer

Local chefs demonstrate novel techniques and recipes every Saturday morning at the Portland Farmers' Market.

Fresh, colorful produce entices thousands of visitors to the market every week.

from the Coast Range town of Alsea bagging up a half-pound of goat cheese. You'll find cinnamon twists, croissants, and pastry here, as well as shiitake mushrooms and organically grown tomatoes. Gardeners can take home honeysuckle starts and dahlia tubers among many other plants. The prepared food booths are run by some of Portland's most innovative and adventuresome purveyors.

As well as the wealth of good food at great prices, the market offers a series of events throughout its season. Chefs-in-the-Market cooking demonstrations let you watch some of the best chefs in Portland cooking with farmers' market produce on Sat at 10 a.m., June through Oct. Monthly celebrations are an important feature of the market because they underscore the seasonal nature of food, from the height-of-summer Berry Festival to the Summer Loaf Bread festival held in August, which brings more than 20 area bakeries to the market, along with a wood-burning demonstration oven, featured bread-baking speakers, and amateur and professional baking contests. In September more than 50 peak-season tomato varieties are sliced and placed on paper plates with name tags along a row of tables. It's your tough assignment to taste them and write down your comments. A Harvest Festival, held in late October, celebrates the season with a pumpkin pie contest, jack-o'-lantern carving, and other fall traditions.

PORTLAND MARATHON, downtown Portland; (503) 226-1111; portland marathon.org. Attracting 9,000 full-course runners and 16,000 total entrants, the Portland Marathon course winds through downtown, across the St. John's Bridge, along the east side of the river, and then returns downtown. While the 26.2-mile run is the centerpiece, this well-organized open marathon includes multiple other events, including a popular half-marathon. The ethos of this event is very Portland—inclusive and friendly. But don't try to run if you are not an official entrant. Spectators and supporters can participate in a sports medicine and fitness fair. The Portland Marathon has a reputation as a true people's race, where anyone can enter. It is, however, a qualifier for the Boston Marathon.

⭐ **WORDSTOCK,** various locations; (503) 549-7887; wordstockfestival .com. Portland is a city of readers, and Wordstock is our annual festival of the book. This gala event brings writers and readers together for 3 days of workshops, dinners, music, readings by best-selling authors and rising stars, a book fair at the Oregon Convention Center, a special Children's Festival, and other fabulous events. Past Wordstocks have featured writers such as Ira Glass, Dave Eggers, Gore Vidal, R. L. Stine, Ariel Gore, Ursula LeGuin, Carl Hiaasen, and Donald Hall. Admission to Wordstock is $7 to $10, depending on your age, but if you're willing to pay significantly more for gala fundraising events, you can mingle with literary stars.

NOVEMBER

CHRISTMAS AT THE PITTOCK MANSION, 3229 NW Pittock Dr., Portland, OR 97210; (503) 823-3624; pittockmansion.org. Perched above Portland's downtown, the Pittock Mansion (see the Attractions chapter) is the grandest of all Portland's mansions. As such it is appropriately decorated and lighted for Christmas. The usual admission fee applies ($8.50 for adults, $7.50 for seniors, and $5.50 for anyone who is 6 to 18), but you'll get the added bonus of seasonal music and other delights.

PIONEER COURTHOUSE SQUARE HOLIDAY HAPPENINGS, Pioneer Courthouse Square, Portland, OR 97205; (503) 223-1613; thesquarepdx .org. Pioneer Courthouse Square hosts many formal and informal holiday events, no matter the weather. The city's Christmas tree is displayed here in the most visited site in Portland. The tree-lighting ceremony happens the day after Thanksgiving, and it is a sight to behold. The city's official menorah is lit nearby when Hanukkah begins. One Portland tradition you must hear (and see) to believe is the annual Tuba Concert. With 100 or more tuba players ranging from symphony members to enthusiastic novices risking badly chilled lips and fingers, the downtown echoes (and echoes) with unique renditions of favorite holiday songs and carols.

⭐ **WINE COUNTRY THANKSGIVING,** Willamette Valley Wineries Association, various locations; (503) 646-2985; willamettewines.com. This popular tour is held the fourth weekend in November, following Thanksgiving Day. Sponsored by the Willamette Valley Wineries Association, the event highlights dozens of wineries and vineyards with new vintages, winery tours, sale prices, and lots of food, crafts, and music. Like the Willamette Valley wine tasting event listed in May, this weekend is a great opportunity to see tasting rooms that are rarely open, get a chance to buy some wine futures, and purchase all your holiday grape beverages.

DECEMBER

HOLIDAY LIGHTS, various locations. In Portland, we put up our lights at Thanksgiving and they stay up for months, because winter nights are long. But during November and December, there are special holiday light festivals that cut through the gloom. Of note are the Festival of Lights at the Grotto, Sandy Boulevard and Northeast 85th Avenue, thegrotto.org; the ZooLights Festival at the Oregon Zoo; and Peacock Lane in Southeast Portland. Residents on Peacock Lane enlist computers and fiber optics to enhance their displays. Some visitors prefer to drive the 2 blocks of display, but the traffic backs up fast. Others park nearby, bundle up, and walk up and down the street to admire the lights and listen to the carolers.

PARADE OF CHRISTMAS SHIPS, Willamette and Columbia Rivers; christmasships.org. Local boat owners form a floating convoy of brightly lit craft, sailing up and down the Columbia and Willamette Rivers each night for several weeks in December. Owners have an informal competition among themselves for the most colorful display and some boats broadcast Christmas carols. All in all, nearly 60 craft participate. Riverside restaurants and bars support this showcase, so it's nice to support them in return by settling in to watch with a tasty beverage at one of them. If the weather is tolerable, try standing on the Hawthorne Bridge over the Willamette as the twinkling fleet sails under the bridge and back.

The Visual and Literary Arts

Portland has long taken a playful approach to art, illustrated in an iconic photo from 1978. In it, a local bar owner, Bud Clark, was photographed by Michael Ryerson facing a statue of a woman by Norman J. Taylor. But Clark was not just looking at the statue: He was wearing an overcoat and flashing it. The poster that was subsequently created was called "Expose Yourself to Art." Not only was it a best-seller, but Bud Clark parlayed it into a successful and influential political career as mayor of Portland.

Echo Gate, *a copper sculpture by Ean Eldred, along the Eastbank Esplanade*

This legacy has remained as Portland evolves into a destination city for the arts. While we have the second-oldest museum building on the West Coast, we are not constricted by tradition, especially in the visual arts. In recent years the city has attracted people who want to make art and who want to start arts-related businesses, and this energy is beginning to have an impact on design as well. Portland is becoming known for its experimental approach to the visual and literary arts, including its innovative galleries, design stars, and overall aesthetic. Events such as the Time-Based Art Festival (see the Festivals & Annual Events chapter) as well as Portland's TedX event in April and Wordstock Literary Festival in October keep the arts scene fresh and alive.

There is some important infrastructure behind all of this experimentation. For example, the Regional Arts & Culture Council (racc.org) is an important source for arts education, advocacy, and stewardship in the Portland metro area, and it's the best place to find out about about Portland's substantial public art program. Likewise, Oregon has a unique cultural trust program (cultural trust.org) that uses state tax credits to support arts and culture. This public-private funding program makes grants to local organizations dedicated to the humanities, arts, history, music, and other cultural institutions. Programs like these provide local artists and organizations the financial stability they need to create freely.

PORTLAND INSTITUTE FOR CONTEMPORARY ART, 415 SW 10th Ave., Suite 300, Portland, OR 97205; (503) 242-1419; pica.org. Dedicated to bringing innovative and relevant contemporary art, music, and theater to Portland, this advocacy group supports visual and performance art across the city. Its Time-Based Art Festival (see our Festivals & Annual Events chapter) is the culminating event of Portland's summer season. PICA has become a major cultural force in Portland, attracting the loyalty of artists and patrons alike. There is a resource room with hundreds of exhibition catalogues, periodicals,

Confluence Project

Lewis and Clark's expedition in 1804 heralded many changes for the people who lived in the Pacific Northwest. As the bicentennial of that journey was celebrated, local Native American tribes and civic groups asked artist Maya Lin, who designed the Vietnam Veterans Memorial in Washington, DC, to help them commemorate this anniversary. The result is the Confluence Project, a series of 7 installations along the Columbia River, designed and shepherded by Lin with the participation of everyone from schoolchildren to respected community elders—including artists, architects, city planners, and even state departments of transportation. The sites are in varying stages of completion, but they include a stunning land bridge at Fort Vancouver, where the Klikitat meets the Columbia River, an installation at the Sandy River delta, and a large, completed project at Cape Disappointment, where the Columbia meets the Pacific Ocean. For more information, directions, and events concerning this remarkable project, visit the project's website: confluenceproject.org.

DVDs, and books on contemporary art, as well as an archive of all past PICA productions. Hours are Mon through Fri, 10 a.m. to 5 p.m.

EVENTS

⭐ **FIRST AND LAST THURSDAYS,** various locations. The 2 major regular events in the Portland visual arts scene are First Thursday and its reverse image, Last Thursday. On the first Thursday of each month, galleries, shops, and museums are open into the evening in the Old Town, Pearl, and downtown districts. This is the traditional opening night for new shows, and throngs of people clog the streets in search of the new, and the free cocktails that go with it. It is great fun, but parking can be maddening. We park in a downtown garage and take the streetcar to the Pearl. Last Thursdays are a kind of Bohemian retort to First Thursdays. This event is held on Northeast Alberta Street and nearby, and it is street theater at its finest, with performers of every variety from fire dancers to a cappella groups mingling with artists, chefs, retailers, and plain old spectators. Last Thursday happens every month, but the summer months, when the street is closed to traffic, are high season.

Galleries and Museums

THE ART GYM, Marylhurst University, 17600 Pacific Hwy., Marylhurst, OR 97036; (503) 699-6243; marylhurst.edu/arts-and-events/art-gym. The Art Gym at Marylhurst is a consistently exciting venue for contemporary artists in and out of school, often out on the cutting edge. Once the gymnasium for this private school, the 3,000-square-foot gallery is large enough to hold sizable sculptures and large installations. The Art Gym is open Tues through Sun noon to 4 p.m.

AUGEN GALLERY, 716 NW Davis St., Portland, OR 97209; (503) 546-5056; augengallery.com. A venerable institution in Portland's art world, Augen Gallery sustains its reputation for eclectic fine art with a large collection featuring not only local artists but internationally renowned masters such as Stella, Hockney, Motherwell, and Warhol as well. Put this gallery on your itinerary when you begin your sampling of art during your First Thursday stroll. Open Tues through Sat, 10:30 a.m. to 5:30 p.m. and by appointment.

★ **BLACKFISH GALLERY,** 420 NW 9th Ave., Portland, OR 97209; (503) 224-2634; (503) 224-2634; blackfish.com. This influential gallery is an important stop on any tour of visual art in Portland. Here, the artwork of the nation's oldest artists' cooperative is displayed during monthly exhibits. Examples of this widely varied effort include abstracts, weavings, and sculpture. The gallery is open Tues through Sat 11 a.m. to 5 p.m.

BLUE SKY GALLERY, 122 NW 8th Ave., Portland, OR 97209; (503) 225-0210; blueskygallery.org. Blue Sky was established in 1975 as the Center of the Photographic Arts to promote the glories of that medium and cultivate innovative talent. Since then, the gallery has been a fierce advocate of local photographers as well as showcasing international artists. The gallery is open Tues through Sat noon to 5 p.m. and on First Thursdays from 6 to 9 p.m.

BULLSEYE GALLERY, 300 NW 13th Ave., Portland, OR 97209; (503) 227-0222; bullseyegallery.com. This impressive gallery is the salon space for Bullseye Glass, an internationally important research firm and manufacturer of art glass. The gallery features the work of locally and globally important and innovative glass artists, focusing particularly on kiln-fired glass. Besides beautiful and interesting shows, they also have lectures and symposia on the role of glass in art and in architecture.

BUTTERS GALLERY, 520 NW Davis St., second floor, Portland, OR 97209; (503) 248-9378; buttersgallery.com. This Chinatown gallery is one of Portland's most respected venues, representing numerous regional, national, and international artists and in every medium: painting, photography, glass, metal, and on and on. Butters is attentive to the importance of display, and their shows are therefore always interesting.

★ COMPOUND, 107 NW 5th Ave., Portland, OR 97209; (503) 796-2733; compoundgallery.com. Part fashion center, part gallery, Compound focuses on what is new in art and graphic design—although they are fond of vintage sneakers and display these as well. The gallery has well-curated shows that embody the zeitgeist of Portland's art world. The store has excellent street fashion, as well as great books, prints, magazines, and other design-focused materials. Their First Thursday shows bring out the beautiful people of Portland's art world. Open Mon through Sat 11 a.m. to 7 p.m. and Sun from 12 p.m. to 6 p.m.

★ DISJECTA, 8371 N. Interstate Ave., Portland, OR 97217; (503) 286-9449; disjecta.org. Disjecta Contemporary Arts Center is an influential exhibition space housed in what was once a bowling alley. This is one of the few venues in the city that accommodate large installations and performance art; their shows are always must-see events. Disjecta also provides studio space for a number of artists, and they have a unique curator-in-residence program to make sure that the future of interesting art in Portland is safe. Open Fri through Sun, 12 to 5 p.m., in addition to its many evening events.

★ ELIZABETH LEACH GALLERY, 417 NW 9th Ave., Portland, OR 97209; (503) 224-0521; elizabethleach.com. One of Portland's premier art scenes, Elizabeth Leach Gallery represents both Northwest and national artists in monthly exhibitions in a variety of media. This gallery features cutting-edge work, and attendance on First Thursday is practically required. Hours are Tues through Sat, 10:30 a.m. to 5:30 p.m.

GUARDINO GALLERY, 2939 NE Alberta St., Portland, OR 97211; (503) 281-9048; guardinogallery.com. This gallery in Northeast Alberta Street has its finger on the pulse of emerging talent, with high-quality exhibits of local painters, printmakers, and sculptors. When you stop by the string of galleries, studios, and shops on Alberta that celebrate Last Thursday, be sure to visit Guardino Gallery. Chat with the Guardinos, who are happy to share their thoughts on the artists on display as well as their own ongoing creative work.

Or you can stop by any time Tues through Sat from 11 a.m. to 6 p.m., or Sun from 11 a.m. to 4 p.m.

LAND, 3925 N. Mississippi Ave., Portland, OR 97227; (503) 451-0689; landpdx.com. Land began as retail website, buyolympia.com, but outgrew its cyberspace and moved into this charming shop/gallery on North Mississippi. It's also the setting for the *Portlandia* sketch "Put a Bird on It." The shop carries a lot of locally produced wares. The second-floor gallery has monthly shows featuring up-and-coming and established contemporary artists; these shows are remarkably representative of the dominant aesthetic of the Portland design vibe. Land is open daily from 10 a.m. to 6 p.m.

LAURA RUSSO GALLERY, 805 NW 21st Ave., Portland, OR 97209; (503) 226-2754; laurarusso.com. One of Portland's largest and most prestigious galleries, Laura Russo Gallery offers classical and controversial artwork by the Northwest's finest artists as well as young talent in a setting that is itself a work of serene art. The gallery is open Tues through Fri, 11 a.m. to 5:30 p.m. and Sat, 11 a.m. to 5 p.m.

★ **MUSEUM OF CONTEMPORARY CRAFT**, 724 NW Davis St., Portland, OR 97209; (503) 223-2654; museumofcontemporarycraft.org. The Museum of Contemporary Craft sponsors permanent and traveling collections of exquisite ceramic, glass, metal, and fiber art. Its permanent collections feature regional stars such as Don Sprague and international artists such as Vladimir Tsivin and Gail Nichols, but you will also find much space devoted to emerging artists. This museum is also in an active partnership with the Pacific Northwest College of Art. Crafts have long been considered fine art in Portland, and this museum displays the highest form of these ideals. Open Tues through Sat 11 a.m. to 6 p.m.; adults $4, students and seniors $3; free if you're under 12.

The award-winning Museum of Contemporary Craft

⭐ **MULTNOMAH ARTS CENTER**, 7688 SW Capitol Hwy., Portland, OR 97219; (503) 823-2787; multnomahartscenter.org. The Multnomah Arts Center—also known as MAC—is in the lovely Multnomah Village neighborhood in Southwest Portland. The focus here is on training people in the visual arts, metalwork, textile arts, ceramics and others programs. There are burgeoning theater, music, and dance departments as well as classroom and hall rentals. It is also home to the Basketry Guild and Portland Handweavers Guild.

NEWSPACE CENTER FOR PHOTOGRAPHY, 1632 SE 10th Ave., Portland, OR 97214; (503) 963-1935; newspacephoto.org. This center is devoted to the photographic image, providing resources for students, artists, teachers, and professionals. It has a wonderful gallery space that shows the work of new and established photographers, but it also offers classes, darkroom space (for those who have not converted solely to digital), and help with access to lighting. They also help out artists by reviewing portfolios and teaching workshops on how to market your wares.

ℹ️ For the latest announcements, reviews, and news about the Portland arts scene, check out PORT at portlandart.net. This site, sponsored by the movers and shakers of the Portland art world, features outstanding writing about what's being shown around town and what to think of it. To gain perspective on design, follow FORTPORT, a blog dedicated to Portland design and culture, fortport.com. This blog is a really useful guide to Portland's TedX talks.

⭐ **PORTLAND ART MUSEUM**, 1219 SW Park Ave., Portland, OR 97205; (503) 226-2811; portlandartmuseum.org. The second-oldest fine arts museum in the Pacific Northwest, it was established in 1892 when business leaders created the Portland Art Association and ponied up dough to collect a group of 100 plaster casts of Greek and Roman sculpture. Now it has more than 32,000 works of art from American Indian artifacts to Monet's *Waterlilies* to Asian art. The museum is open Tues, Wed, and Sat from 10 a.m. to 5 p.m.; Thurs and Fri from 10 a.m. to 8 p.m.; and Sun from noon to 5 p.m. Admission is free to museum members; nonmember price is $10 for adults. Call for information on shows and programs.

QUINTANA GALLERIES, 124 NW 9th Ave., Portland, OR 97209; (503) 223-1729; quintanagalleries.com. A popular stopping spot in downtown Portland since it opened in 1972, Quintana has a bounty of American Indian and Hispanic art. Walking by its windows is a show in itself with a sumptuous display of Northwest tribal masks and totems as well as Pueblo pottery, fetishes, and other crafts from the Southwest. The gallery also has a good collection of photographs by Edward Curtis as well as collector-quality antiques.

TALISMAN GALLERY, 1476 NE Alberta St., Portland, OR 97227; (503) 284-8800; talismangallery.com. Talisman features local artists—those who are well established and those who are on the cusp—in their lively gallery. This gallery also serves as a co-op, supporting the work of its diverse members, whose interests cover the entire spectrum of representational to abstract art, using every medium. It's a must-see on Last Thursdays. It's open Fri through Sun, 11 a.m. through 5 p.m., and from 5:30 to 9:00 p.m. on Last Thursday.

LITERARY ARTS

With Powell's—the biggest bookstore in the country—as a foundation, Portland has one of the most well-read citizenries around, and writers like to visit Portland because people actually attend their book signings and are likely to read the books. The 3 major branches of Powell's (Burnside, Hawthorne, and Beaverton) have author events almost daily. Local colleges—especially PSU, Reed, and Lewis & Clark—also sponsor author events and discussions. The *Oregonian, Willamette Week,* the *Mercury,* and the stores themselves are all good places to check to see who is in town.

Two other important literary events are **Literary Arts Inc.'s Portland Arts and Lectures** series, which features writers with national and international reputations—such as David Sedaris, Ira Glass, Annie Dillard, Adrienne Rich, and Seamus Heaney—who speak at the Arlene Schnitzer Concert Hall to sell-out crowds; and Wordstock, featured in this section.

LITERARY ARTS, INC., 925 SW Washington St., Portland, OR 97205; (503) 227-2583; literary-arts.org. In addition to the Portland Arts and Lectures Series, this busy bunch sponsors Oregon Literary Fellowships, Writers in the Schools, and the Poetry in Motion project. Portland was the first city on the West Coast to launch a Poetry in Motion program, and ours also includes

Wordstock: A Book and Literary Festival

In early October, Portland is at its best—the sun shines a buttery light on the city; the leaves are washed with orange, red, and yellow—and the beautiful fall weather tilts our thoughts toward reading. That's when it's time for Wordstock.

This festival is devoted to all things book-related. It comprises readings, lectures, teachers' workshops, workshops for kids, music, films, discussions, play readings, dances, dialogues, and anything else that can be connected to the word. For the price of a movie and popcorn, you can spend the entire weekend immersed in the world of the book.

Founded by journalist, teacher, and ex-professional-baseball player Larry Colton, Wordstock started out as a way to raise funds for writing programs in schools. It has grown to involve more than 200 writers, more than 100 exhibitors, and thousands of attendees. The *New York Times,* C-SPAN, and major presses join small presses and local cultural organizations; teachers work side by side in master classes; kids practice narratives; ordinary readers listen and talk and read. And writers love this event: They actually request (sometimes to no avail) to be included in the program.

Wordstock features well-known writers such as Timothy Egan and Ursula Le Guin who live in the Northwest, but also local heroes such as Oregon poet and noted teacher Kim Stafford and *Willamette Week* publisher Richard Meeker. An international cast of authors loves to attend as well—for the food, for Powell's, for schmoozing with one another—but mostly for the readers who turn out in large numbers to meet them.

Wordstock takes place at various locations but primarily at the Oregon Convention Center. Call (503) 549-7887 or check wordstockfestival.com for more information.

Also see our Festivals & Annual Events chapter.

poetry from local schoolchildren. Literary Arts also sponsors the Oregon Book Awards at which writers and their friends gather every year to watch as book awards are presented for poetry, fiction, literary nonfiction, drama, and work aimed at young readers.

MOUNTAIN WRITERS CENTER, 2804 SE 27th Ave., #2, Portland, OR 97202; (503) 232-4517; mountainwriters.org. Since 1973 Mountain Writers has been sponsoring readings, lectures, and classes for writers. Its invited speakers have included Nobel Prize–winning writers as well as brand-new voices, from all over the world and from the Portland Metro area. Programs include readings at local colleges and universities—as well as regular readings at the Press Club and TaborSpace—outreach to high school students, residencies in Portland for visiting writers, and sponsorship of visits by writers to rural areas. But it is most well known for its 8-week workshops and short-term master classes. These are open to emerging writers.

> **i** Portland is the home of the literary journal *Tin House*, which also publishes books and sponsors an excellent writing workshop each summer at Reed College. Faculty have included luminaries such as Charles D'Ambrosio, Anthony Doerr, Denis Johnson, Walter Kirn, and Abigail Thomas. The workshop also gives writers opportunities to meet with editors and agents. Find out more at tinhouse.com.

TIN HOUSE WRITERS WORKSHOP, Reed College, 3203 SE Woodstock Blvd., Portland, OR 97202; tinhouse.com/writers-workshop. *Tin House* is an influential magazine and press that may well be more renowned outside the area than it is here—for one reason, they have a publicity office in Brooklyn. They publish major writers, but even more interesting is their summer workshop. This event allows aspiring writers to hang out with important and successful writers at working and social events. But you don't have to be a writer to enjoy this workshop: they have evening readings for which anyone can buy tickets. Readings and workshops are held on the Reed College campus.

Parks

Parks are important in Portland. Many of the most popular attractions are found in parks—and much of the green and civic-minded character of the city is formed and supported by them. So it is not surprising that the Portland Metro area offers an amazing amount and variety of park space, from Forest Park, which, at 5,100 acres, is the largest urban forest in the nation, to Mills End Park, which, at 452 square inches, may be the smallest park in the world. The citizens of Portland consistently vote to expand and maintain our various park facilities, which are therefore popular and well used. The City of Portland Parks and Recreation office manages most parks within the city boundaries; their resources are extensive, and it is easy to get information from them about their broad and deep offerings. They put out a useful catalog each season that gives the details of the tennis lessons, swimming lessons, arts and dance classes, and the innumerable other programs; call (503) 823-7529 to request one, or browse online for a downloadable catalog and to register for classes: portland oregon.gov/parks. This website also has a comprehensive and detailed list of all the parks and facilities in the system. For those of you who like your parks raw, you will find thousands and thousands of acres devoted to wildlife, including Smith and Bybee Lakes, Powell Butte, Elk Rock Island, Marquam Nature Park, Oaks Bottom Wildlife Refuge, and Forest Park. In addition, a regional trail system called the 40 Mile Loop, together with the Willamette Greenway Trail, links more than 220 miles of paths throughout the area, forming a network through and around the city. Maps of this system, which was originally inspired by the Olmsted Brothers, are available from Portland Parks and Recreation on the website (portlandoregon.gov/parks). You can read more about some of these parks and programs in the Attractions and Kids chapters.

The city of Portland is not the only organization that maintains wonderful parks in the area. Metro, our regional government, in addition to establishing growth boundaries, keeping up the zoo, and running the mass transit system, is also responsible for a number of parks and grids of open spaces. You can find out more about Metro's parks by visiting them online at oregonmetro.gov. And the State of Oregon has a fine website that gives a comprehensive look at the parks in the state system, including the reservation system: oregonstateparks .org. General information about all state parks is also available at (800) 551-6949. To reserve campsites call (800) 452-5687.

> **i** The well-organized website for Portland Parks and Recreation provides maps and reservation services and allows convenient online registration for classes. Visit portlandoregon.gov/parks.

But no matter who is running the parks, we love them. Here, then, are some of our favorites.

ARBOR LODGE PARK, North Bryant Street and Delaware Avenue, Portland, OR 97217; (503) 823-7529. Arbor Lodge is representative of many neighborhood parks in Portland, with lots of grassy field for sports, a big off-leash area for dogs, plenty of trees for shade—and a unique feature that makes it distinctive. In this case, it's a play area designed for universal accessibility: Harper's Playground. It opened in 2012, created together by a neighborhood family, whose daughter has a genetic condition that limits movement, and Portland Parks and Recreation. Harper's Playground complements the existing play facilities in a space that is designed to bring together playful spirits of all ages and abilities. Features include climbing walls, a xylophone, and a play area with water and sand. Restrooms are also built with universal access in mind.

BALD PEAK STATE VIEWPOINT, along SW Bald Peak Road, off OR 219, near Laurelwood, OR 97119. Bald Peak is the highest spot in the Chehalem Mountains (elevation 1,629 feet), between Hillsboro and Newberg, and it's a lovely spot to visit if you are touring Willamette Valley wine country. This park was built in the early 1930s by the Civilian Conservation Corps, and it is an alluring spot for a spontaneous picnic on a sunny afternoon (no water, though, so pack your own). Bald Peak offers lovely views of the valley and a number of Cascade peaks in Washington and Oregon, including Mt. Rainier if the visibility is good. Restrooms are available, thankfully.

BATTLE GROUND LAKE STATE PARK, Northeast 249th Street, Battle Ground, WA 98604; (888) 226-7688 (reservations); parks.wa.gov. One of the biggest attractions in southwest Washington, Battle Ground Lake State Park tempts recreators from all over the area who are drawn by 280 acres of swimming, fishing, horseback riding, boating, and hiking as well as 50 campsites. The park is 21 miles northeast of Vancouver; it has a splendid lake in the center of an extinct volcano. The park is open from 6:30 a.m. until dusk from Apr to Sept and from 8 a.m. until dusk the remainder of the year. Summer camping is a breeze with the available kitchen shelters and showers—but remember, this park fills up fast. Kitchens with electricity may also be rented for large groups (20 to 150 people); fees depend on the number of people. Day passes are $10; annual passes good for all the Washington State parks, $30.

★ **BLUE LAKE REGIONAL PARK,** Northeast 223rd Avenue between Marine Drive and Sandy Boulevard, Fairview, OR 97024; (503) 797-1850; metro-region.org. Blue Lake is maintained as a regional park by Metro and is just 8 miles east of downtown Portland, making it easily accessible on summer days. The 64-acre lake has a swimming beach and a special children's "spray-ground" (children under 5 are not allowed in the lake, for purposes of hygiene). But there's lots for everyone—a fishing dock and boat rentals, basketball and volleyball courts, playgrounds, baseball fields, and picnic shelters. The Lake House provides facilities for events. Trails wind their way through the park; these are especially nice for cyclists. The park also hosts numerous programs and events, many of which are geared toward children (see our Kids chapter for more information). You'll need to pay an entrance fee of $5 per car.

CATHEDRAL PARK, North Edison Street and Pittsburgh Avenue, Portland, OR 97203; (503) 823-7529. This park—situated on the banks of the Willamette River and one of Portland's most scenic spots—is named after the tall gothic arches that support the St. Johns Bridge, towering above the park. The park, which has a stage, is home to popular summertime concerts and plays; it also includes soccer fields, a boat ramp, and docking facilities. Cathedral Park is often peaceful, belying its lively history—not only is it the site of the very first plat for the village of St. John's, but it is also suspected to have been a favorite fishing site for the Native Americans who lived here before.

CHAMPOEG STATE PARK, directly off SR 99 West, 8239 NE Champoeg Rd., Saint Paul, OR 97137; (503) 678-1251. Pronounced *"sham-POO-ey,"* Champoeg State Park has much to offer. First, there are the trails that cross the 615 acres; these curl through woods, meadows, and wetlands and are wonderful for running, bicycling, or hiking. Then there's the historical interest: The park is on the grounds of the first settlers' government, and 2 museums and many educational programs help to bring that early history alive. The park is regularly visited by school buses full of children eager to learn what life was like during pioneer days. And finally, it hosts many summertime concerts in its pretty amphitheater. There is a $5 daily day-use fee, but a $30 annual permit grants access to all day-use areas in state parks across Oregon.

Dog Parks

Your dog needs to run, but you live in the city. Where can Fido get plenty of exercise? Portland has 32 parks with off-leash areas devoted exclusively to dog exercising all day, year-round. Wherever the park, you must clean up after your dog or face fines from the city and the ire of your neighbors. Dogs also should be properly vaccinated, licensed, obedient to voice command, and in other ways model citizens. With so many parks now featuring off-leash areas, there is bound to be one near you. These areas are well-marked, so look for the signs or visit portlandoregon.gov/parks and click on the "Recreation" menu for a full list. Or check out their Facebook page: facebook.com/PortlandDogParks.

COLUMBIA PARK, North Lombard Avenue and Woolsey Street, Portland, OR 97217; (503) 823-7529. Healthy competition is a good thing, and when the old city of Albina saw that Portland was developing Washington Park, they were not going to be outdone. They purchased 30 acres on Lombard Street in 1891. Soon after, however, Albina was annexed to Portland. But it took many years before Columbia Park, which was eventually patterned after a park in Berlin, became the handsome, wooded place it is today. In addition to the grounds, the park offers fields for soccer, baseball, and softball, lighted tennis courts, volleyball courts, and an indoor swimming pool.

COUCH PARK, Northwest 19th Avenue and Glisan Street Portland, OR 97209; (503) 823-7529. First thing: It's pronounced "*kooch.*" But however you say it, this little neighborhood park, with lovely trees and a playground, is a draw for residents and for the students next door at the Metropolitan Learning Center. And it is a true neighborhood park, even down to its design and execution, which was largely the work of students and neighbors. Its namesake, Captain John Heard Couch, was responsible for the alphabetized street names of this sector of town, which he developed. The park site was originally the estate of one of Captain Couch's daughters and her family. It has an off-leash area that is very popular with dog-owning neighbors.

⭐ **COUNCIL CREST PARK,** Southwest Council Crest Drive, Portland, OR 97239; (503) 823-7529. High in the Southwest Hills—higher than anywhere else in the city—rests verdant Council Crest Park. This 42-acre site used to host an amusement park, but the traces of that history have vanished, and now it's a quiet neighborhood park with a large water tower. You'll also find trails, natural areas, restrooms, and picnic tables, and a spot for weddings. But the major draw is the view—from here you can see five major peaks of the Cascade mountains: Mount Hood, Mount St. Helens, Mount Jefferson, Mount Adams, and, on a good day, Mount Rainier. It's an excellent spot to regain perspective.

CRESTON PARK, Southeast 44th Avenue and Powell Boulevard, Portland, OR 97206; (503) 823-7529. This green, tree-filled oasis bordering Powell Boulevard is a great place for a summer birthday party or even a quiet, shady lunch. Less than 15 acres, it offers an outdoor swimming pool, a well-equipped playground, group picnic facilities, and restrooms. There is also a handball court, as well as some tennis courts that are best avoided if you really love tennis. The major draw in the summer is the pool: It gets very crowded on warm days and is a favorite for summertime swimming lessons. The park grounds are usually quiet and serene on weekdays. Weekends are a different story; many reunions and parties are held here.

ELK ROCK ISLAND, Willamette River, near SE 19th Avenue and Sparrow Street, Milwaukie, OR 97222. Elk Rock Island is actually part of the Portland Parks system; it's one of the designated natural areas, given to the city as a preserve for natural beauty that would restore the spirits of the citizens. This big volcanic basalt rock—surmised to be the oldest exposed rock formation in the region—is an excellent spot for bird-watching and offers some of the most diverse terrain around. You may spot herons, hawks, kingfishers, and egrets. This park also includes a hiking trail. This park is accessible by land only during the dry months, when the Willamette River is low enough to expose the rocky bridge to shore. The rest of the year, you'll need to get there by canoe or kayak.

⭐ **FOREST PARK,** Northwest 29th Avenue and Upshur Street to Newberry Road, Portland, OR 97210; (503) 823-7529. Forest Park is remarkable for many things, especially its size. At 5,100 acres, it is thought to be the largest urban forest in America. The city bought the property at the end of the 19th century; they had thought about turning it into a park ever since the Olmsted Brothers landscape architecture firm suggested it would be a good use of the property. Today it has more than 70 miles of trails, and it's a haven for 112 species of birds and more than 50 species of mammals, including the humans who love to hike, run, and picnic under its lush forest canopy. You will want to download trail maps from the Portland Parks and Recreation website (portland oregon.gov/parks).

GABRIEL PARK, Southwest 45th Avenue and Vermont Street, Portland, OR 97219; (503) 823-7529, (503) 823-2840 (Southwest Community Center). A large, multifaceted park, Gabriel Park draws enthusiasts from all over the city. Within the 90 acres of the park, you'll find tennis courts, picnic tables, trails, community gardens, sports fields, and 2 off-leash dog areas, one for winter and one for summer (download a map from portlandoregon.gov/parks to find them). Runners can take advantage of both paved and unpaved trails; there is also quite a large skatepark. Gabriel Park is also the home of the Southwest Community Center, which has swimming pools, workout equipment, a basketball gym, and many fitness and other classes.

⭐ **GRANT PARK**, Northeast 33rd Avenue and Ulysses S. Grant Place, Portland, OR 97212; (503) 823-7529. President Grant visited Portland three times, but this park, named in his honor, is now more famous for its Beverly Cleary Children's Sculpture Garden, in which Ramona Quimby, Henry Huggins, and his pooch Ribsy, all born of Cleary's lively imagination, are fixed in bronze. (A few blocks away is the actual Klikitat Street, where Ramona "lived," and the neighborhood where author Cleary herself grew up, attending Grant High School in the 1930s.) The sculptures sit atop a fountain, and in the summer, children play there all day long. At Grant Park you'll also find nice sports fields, tennis courts, and an outdoor swimming pool. The park is next to Grant High School, and you can also use their track (keep the bikes off!).

⭐ **HOYT ARBORETUM**, 4000 SW Fairview Blvd., Portland, OR 97205; (503) 823-7529, (503) 865-8733; hoytarboretum.org. Hoyt Arboretum's 321 forested acres offer unsurpassed arboreal beauty as well as beautiful views of the city, and it's large enough that you can get into some backwoods areas where you aren't bumping into other hikers every time you round a bend in the trail—though it's popular with trail runners, so be careful when rounding those blind corners. Hoyt Arboretum features a collection of conifers, 10 miles of trails, the vestiges of our rural past, and some striking views of the city and the Cascades. We love to take the Fir Trail all the way to the Pittock Mansion. It only takes about 45 minutes, and the view is stunning. (See the Attractions chapter for more information.)

KELLEY POINT PARK, North Kelley Point Park Road and Marine Drive, Portland, OR 97203; (503) 823-7529. This park sits at the confluence of the Willamette and Columbia Rivers, offering views of river traffic as well as Mount Hood and Mount St. Helens. The park is named for Oregon advocate Hall Jackson Kelley, who wrote popular pamphlets urging the settlement of the

Oregon territories before ever visiting them (which he finally did, in 1834). He urged settlers to establish a city at the convergence of the Willamette and the Columbia, but with 20/20 historical hindsight and experience with flooding, it's a good thing he was overruled. Still, the park named in his honor is a fine legacy, providing the anchor for the 40 Mile Loop.

⭐ **LAURELHURST PARK,** Southeast 39th Avenue and Stark Street, Portland, OR 97214; (503) 823-7529, (503) 823-4101. One of the city's oldest parks, the Olmsted-inspired Laurelhurst is among the most popular. Its 34-plus-acres offer a striking variety of trees, shrubs, and flowers as well as a 3-acre duck pond with a small island. There's something for everyone to do here, including running paths, basketball and tennis courts, a large horseshoe pit, and an excellent play structure. The Laurelhurst Studio is here; it's the Eastside conduit for ballet, tap, and other dance programs in the Parks and Recreation system. The park, which began as pastureland for cattle in the 19th century, is gorgeously landscaped; it was once judged as the most beautiful park on the West Coast.

⭐ **LEACH BOTANICAL GARDEN,** 6704 SE 122nd Ave., Portland, OR 97236; (503) 823-9503; leachgarden.org. The Leaches were a couple devoted to plants: John Leach was a pharmacist and his wife Lilla was a botanist. Together they collected more than 2,000 species, some of which they discovered. The Leach Botanical Garden was their estate; its 9 acres have been given over to preserving and studying plant life and maintaining a seed bank, as well as preserving the legacy of the couple who made this lovely, botanically diverse sanctuary possible. The grounds include the garden, the manor house, and natural areas. Garden and guided tours are free, and special tours are given by appointment. (For more information see the Attractions chapter.) It's closed on Mon.

⭐ **MILL ENDS PARK,** Southwest Naito Parkway and Taylor Street, Portland, OR 97204; (503) 823-7529. Mill Ends Park is reportedly the smallest park in the world, though it looks more like a planter. It was named after a column by journalist Dick Fagan, who could see it from his office. The plot was supposed to hold a lamppost, but for whatever reason, the city neglected to install one. Fagan grew tired of looking at the weeds, took action by planting flowers, and then used the "world's smallest park" as a theme, writing occasionally of the leprechauns who spent their leisure time there. It became an official park in 1976 and now is one of the features that keeps Portland weird. It lies in the crosswalk, so ensure your personal safety before attempting a closer look.

MT. SCOTT PARK, Southeast 72nd Avenue and Harold Street, Portland, OR 97206; (503) 823-7529, (503) 823-3183. Harvey W. Scott was an early settler, the editor of the *Oregonian*, and by all accounts a force to be reckoned with (you can see him in statue form, pointing west, at the top of Mt. Tabor). Mt. Scott Park is named for him. The park encompasses 12 arboreal acres with a playground, softball field, tennis courts, and picnic benches. The Mt. Scott Community Center, on the grounds of the park, offers a beautiful lap pool and a fun leisure pool with a great water slide, current channel, and imaginative built-in water toys as well as a separate spa. The facility also has meeting rooms, gyms, classes, an auditorium, and a roller-skating rink.

MT. TABOR PARK, Southeast 60th Avenue and Salmon Street, Portland, OR 97215; (503) 823-7529. Mt. Tabor sits atop an extinct volcano and it affords some of the best views in the city: east to Mount Hood, north to

Harvey Scott points the way from Mt. Tabor Park.

The vintage reservoirs at Mt. Tabor Park, with downtown Portland and the West Hills on the horizon

Mount St. Helens, and west to downtown and beyond. Many paths, paved and unpaved, wind through the park, and the hilly terrain makes the park a favorite with runners, hikers, cyclists, go-karters, and anyone who likes a good view and a vigorous climb. The 190-acre park also offers basketball courts, a large off-leash area, lighted tennis courts, group picnic facilities, an excellent playground, and an outdoor amphitheater. Birders may be spotted early in the morning. They are on to something—a sunrise at Mt. Tabor is spectacular and worth the struggle out of bed.

PENINSULA PARK AND ROSE GARDENS, North Albina Street and Rosa Parks Way, Portland, OR 97217; (503) 823-7529. Portland emerged as a city at a historically auspicious moment for parks, and Peninsula Park demonstrates why. Its formal design was characteristic of its early-20th-century era; it is the site of the city's first public rose garden, and the gazebo bandstand is a Portland Historic Landmark and a National Heritage Historical Structure. And its playground, as well as the community center (a city first), made Peninsula Park quite novel when it was finished in 1913. It is also an early example of urban renewal. Previously the site had been home to a roadhouse and a racetrack. The rose garden is still important, with 2 acres of roses—almost 9,000 plantings. The park also has all the usual park amenities.

Close-up

Plaza Blocks

This tiny park consists of two adjacent city squares. In 1974 the squares were designated Historic Landmarks; they have been public spaces for about 150 years. Chapman Square, the southern square, was donated to the city by early Portland attorney William Chapman, while Lownsdale Square was contributed by Daniel Lownsdale, who arrived in Portland in 1845. The squares were originally popular sites for public oratory and other gatherings—a tradition that is revived from time to time, as when Occupy Portland made its camp here in the fall of 2011. These squares have a quaint history—at one time, the idea was that women and children would gather at Chapman Square, while the men would have Lownsdale to themselves. Lownsdale Square is the home of the Soldiers' Monument from 1906, a granite pillar supporting the likeness of an infantryman. This soldier represents Oregon's contribution to the first major force of American troops dispatched overseas, the Second Oregon United States Volunteer Infantry. Two small cannons at the base of the monument are from Fort Sumter; they honor the Northern and Southern soldiers killed during the Civil War. A large bronze elk stands alert right in the middle of Main Street, between the two squares. It's actually a fountain, built in 1900 at the behest of then-mayor David Thompson. It's hard for modern residents to imagine that the fountain, which has a special drinking trough for horses and dogs, was initially regarded as monstrous by some local residents (notably the Exalted Order of Elks). Later residents objected to its placement in the middle of the road, but it appears that, unlike its natural predecessors, the bronze elk is here to stay. Chapman and Lownsdale Squares; Southwest 4th Avenue and Main Street, Portland, OR 97204; (503) 823-7529.

RIDGEFIELD NATIONAL WILDLIFE REFUGE, Northwest 269th Street (Washington SR 501) at I-5, exit 14, Ridgefield, WA 98642; (360) 887-4106; fws.gov/ridgefieldrefuges/complex. This 5,218-acre wildlife sanctuary features pasture, woodlands, and marshland. Much of the wildlife that sustained the area's Native American population and the later European settlers is still found here. The refuge's population includes deer, coyotes, nutria, foxes, rabbits, beavers, and otters—as well as large flocks of migratory birds and waterfowl that travel the Pacific Flyway and either stop and rest in the preserved wetlands or decide to spend the winter there. This is a day-use-only area. Though hiking and fishing are allowed, fires and off-road vehicles are not. Open from dawn to dusk all year long, the refuge is free to all ages, but leave Fido at home. (Bicycling, horseback riding, and ATVs are also not allowed.) There is a $3 day-use fee.

SELLWOOD PARK, Southeast 7th Avenue and Miller Street, Portland, OR 97202; (503) 823-7529. Tall, well-spaced trees distinguish this pretty park, which is a crowd pleaser for its sports fields, excellent playground, and wonderful round swimming pool. The park has both sunny, grassy, open spaces and shady, cool refuges. On the bluff above Oaks Bottom and the Willamette River, you'll get pretty river views as you peer between the trees. Trails link Sellwood Park to Oaks Bottom and Oaks Park. The unusual pool is outdoors, so it's open only during the summer, but it is popular. An abundance of picnic tables encourage large groups—it's a favorite spot for parties, spring through fall. The off-leash area is down the hill from the main park, along the river. Bring towels; it can get muddy.

SPRINGWATER CORRIDOR, Southeast Ivon Street to Boring, OR. Springwater Corridor is a 20-mile rails-to-trails route comprising the southeast part of the 40-Mile Loop, following Johnson Creek east. It begins at Southeast Ivon Street near the Willamette River and ends in the town of Boring. The mostly flat route is a popular trek especially for cyclists and people riding horses: It's mostly blacktop or chip-sealed surface, with thin gravel for the last 4 miles. The trail takes you through city neighborhoods, farmland, wetlands, and nature reserves. An excellent history and map of the trail is available here: 40mileloop.org/trail_springwatercorridor.htm.

TRYON CREEK STATE PARK, 11321 SW Terwilliger Blvd., Portland, OR 97219; (503) 636-9886. This pristine natural area is within the city limits, which is the reason so many school field trips are held here—that, and the fact that so much native wildlife can be found here. One of the few streams in the city that steelhead use for spawning is found here, and the native trillium plant grows abundantly. Tryon Creek State Park has shady trails perfect for biking and walking, and lots of signs tell you about what you're seeing. Much of the park is wheelchair accessible. Day camps are a staple of summer life at Tryon Creek, and guided tours are available as well as a gift shop. There is no fee to use Tryon Creek.

Close-up

Washington Park

The crown jewel of the city's park system, 160-acre Washington Park is one of the oldest, best-loved, and most well-used parks in Portland, offering beautiful scenery; summer concerts; statuary; playgrounds; water reservoirs; fantastic views of Mount Hood, its foothills, and the Willamette Valley; and some of the region's premiere attractions. This is the home of the famed International Rose Test Garden, with more than 400 varieties of roses; the Japanese Gardens; and the Oregon Zoo. Besides these world-renowned sites, and the lush trees, shrubs, flowers, and ferns, the park is a treasure trove of history and a tribute to prescient urban planning. Washington Park has been a city property since 1871, when 40 acres were purchased for the development of a park—at a time when most of the city was still wilderness. Early residents thought the city was crazy. By the turn of the 20th century, however, Portland was glad to have the park, and never more so when they hired John C. Olmsted, whose distinguished firm also designed New York's Central Park, to advise them on their own park system. The Olmsteds envisioned for Portland a series of parks that would be linked together with greenways all across the city. But they also made some specific suggestions for Washington Park, including the preservation of the natural habitat in addition to formal plantings.

While the major attractions of Washington Park are obvious, some of the minor ones are just as interesting. The first public statue of a woman is here—it's the bronze *Sacagawea,* the intrepid Shoshone who made it possible for Lewis and Clark to navigate the West, which was commissioned for the Lewis and Clark Exposition in 1905. Women all over the nation contributed money to pay for this statue. The park is also home to an arresting Lewis and Clark memorial, consisting of a granite shaft with the seals of the states of Oregon, Washington, Montana, and Idaho at its base; the foundation stone for this memorial was laid in 1903 by Theodore Roosevelt. Washington Park's attractions also include the World Forestry Center, the Oregon Vietnam Veterans Living Memorial, and the Portland Children's Museum. And if you have children, don't miss the fanciful play structure just south of the Rose Garden. This bright and inventive gem has slides, bridges, swings, sand, musical toys, ropes, and other enticing figures. The park is at the western end of Southwest Park Place, Portland, OR 97205; (503) 823-7529.

WALLACE PARK, Northwest 25th Avenue and Raleigh Street, Portland, OR 97210; (503) 823-7529. Wallace Park is a busy little park next to Chapman Elementary School, containing basketball and tennis courts, softball and soccer fields, and a playground. A major feature, however, is the flock of Vaux's Swifts that stops annually on its migration south for the winter. Beginning in late August they gather every evening near sunset. As more arrive, they begin to circle a large chimney at Chapman school, which they have adopted as a roost site—and then all at once rush into the chimney in a funnel cloud of bird. The local red-tailed hawks have also noticed the swifts, making for high drama. Note: Wallace Park does not have a parking lot, and parking in this neighborhood is limited.

⭐ **WATERFRONT PARK (GOV. TOM MCCALL WATERFRONT PARK),** Southwest Naito Parkway and the Willamette River from Steel Bridge South to River Place, Portland, OR 97204; (503) 823-7529. This city park showcases the Willamette River and hums with activity on sunny days. Hugging the west bank of the river, Waterfront Park extends from Southwest Clay Street to the Steel Bridge, 22 blocks in all; it's the site of many Portland events from the Rose Festival to the Brewer's Festival to the Blues Festival, in addition to the throngs of joggers, bikers, and those out for leisurely lunchtime strolls along the pleasant waterside pathway. There are basketball courts, fountains, statuary, and opportunities to sightsee, both for people-watchers and those more interested in the scenic views of barges and cruise ships passing under the bridges. See the Festivals & Annual Events and Attractions chapters for more on this fabulous park.

Itineraries

THREE DAYS IN PORTLAND

You can have many adventures while you're in Portland—there is a lot to do and it's easy to get around. The following suggestions will help you structure your visit.

Day 1: The Flavor of Portland: Nature and Culture

Start your day with a **Voodoo Doughnut**—if you go early, you can avoid the lines. Try some coffee from **Courier** or **Spella Coffee,** or **Stumptown,** if you're feeling old school. Properly fueled, make a visit to the **International Rose Test Garden** (rosegardenstore.org), which will give you a beautiful view of the area amidst the 8,000 rose varieties grown there. Then try a visit to the nearby **Japanese Garden** (japanesegarden.com), world renowned for its classical style. Head back downtown and stop for lunch at **Higgins Restaurant** (higginsport land.com), the iconic restaurant that started Portland's food revolution. After lunch, hop on the streetcar and pay a visit to **Powell's City of Books** (powells .com), the largest bookstore of new and used books in the world. It takes up an entire city block; get a map so you don't lose your way. Spend the rest of the

Saturdays in Portland

If you're here on a Saturday, you will want to take in two essential Portland experiences: the Portland Farmers' Market and the Portland Saturday Market. The Portland Farmers Market (portlandfarmersmarket.org) brings together farmers, artisan food purveyors, cheesemakers, ranchers, chefs, and others in an insanely popular and festive weekly celebration of regional bounty. The prepared food is plentiful; shipping for many items can be arranged. Likewise, the also popular Portland Saturday Market (portlandsaturdaymarket .com) sells wonderful hand-crafted items every week, Mar through Dec. It is the perfect place to find an interesting souvenir to remind you of your time in the City of Roses.

The Japanese Garden is one of Portland's most popular stops.

afternoon wandering through the **Pearl District,** taking in shops, galleries, and public parks, before a predinner cocktail at the **Teardrop Lounge.** Have dinner at **Paley's Place** or **Little Bird,** two other westside Portland restaurants.

Day 2: Portland's Greatest Cultural Hits

Portland's art scene always garners national attention. Here's a suggested itinerary. Begin with the **Oregon Historical Society** (ohs.org), which will ground you in local culture and history. Next, cross the Park Blocks to the **Portland Art Museum** (pam.org), renowned for its collection of native and northwest art, in addition to European masters such as Monet. Just to the west of the museum, board the Portland streetcar to the **Pearl District** and **Old Town,** where you will find many of the most influential galleries in Portland. These include internationally known **Bullseye Glass** (bullseyeglass.com), **Elizabeth Leach, Froelick,** and **Augen,** all near the **Museum of Contemporary Craft** (museumof contemporarycraft.org), which is one of the oldest museums dedicated to high crafts in the United States. End your museum crawl with a visit to the **Lan Su Chinese Garden,** (portlandchinesegarden.org), a gorgeous specimen of an authentic classical Chinese garden. Have dinner at the **Deschutes Brewery** or another nearby restaurant, and take in a show at the **Gerding Theater** or the **Artists Repertory Theatre.**

Day 3: Hike the 4T Trail—Trail, Tram, Trolley, and Train

This 4-mile hike might be the quintessential walking tour of Portland. You start at one of Oregon's most popular attractions, wander through lovely residential areas, explore the urban forest, travel along the river, and experience the hills, and all on the best parts of the public transportation network. You begin by either riding the MAX to the **Washington Park** station or parking near the **Oregon Zoo,** then cross US Highway 26 to the **Marquam Trail,** which you follow along the top of the west hills, through neighborhoods and trails, to **Council Crest Park,** the highest point in the city. After taking in the comprehensive view from Council Crest, you descend along a wooded and cool trail through an urban forest to **Oregon Health & Science University.** From there, you board the **Portland Aerial Tram,** taking it down to the **South Waterfront.** This connects you to the Portland streetcar, which takes you to the MAX and back to the Oregon Zoo. This trail gives you spectacular views of the Cascades when it's clear. From Council Crest and the Tram, you can even see Mt. Rainier if the day is fine.

The trail is a little tricky in places—be sure to use the map and wear sturdy shoes (find a map at 4t-trail.org). Also be sure the tram is operating on the day you plan to hike; occasionally it's closed for maintenance (and on Sunday during the winter season). You can ride the Aerial Tram for free—there is no cost for riding downhill, though it's $4 to ride back up. Once you're at the bottom of the hill, before you board the streetcar, you may want to get an espresso at the counter in **OHSU's Center for Health and Healing** at the bottom of the tram or explore the ever-growing list of shops and restaurants on the **South Waterfront.**

An Afternoon in Portland

What if your meeting ends early but your plane leaves late? If you just have an afternoon in Portland, you should get a bite to eat at the food carts on Southwest 10th and Alder, then take the streetcar to Powell's and walk around the Pearl District. Or, if it's clear, ride the streetcar in the other direction to the Portland Aerial Tram to take in the view.

EAST SIDE EXPLORATION

Portland's east side is a paradise for tax-free shopping and fine dining. Here's how to make the most of it. Start with breakfast at **Slappy Cakes** or the food cart **It's Fried Egg I'm in Love** (Belmont and 43rd). We would send you to **Tasty n Son's** but you don't have time for that kind of line!

After breakfast, travel north to the **Mississippi neighborhood** (mississippi ave.com). This adorable area filled with vintage shops, specialty food stores, clothing boutiques, art galleries, and other friendly shops will make you so happy there is no sales tax in Oregon.

After you have blissed out on shopping, travel south to the **Oregon Convention Center,** where you can make a pilgrimage to "Host Analog." This unique living sculpture was created by artist Buster Simpson. He used a 1,000-year-old log and its accompanying microbes from a wind-fallen Douglas fir tree that he found east of the city, in the Bull Run watershed (which provides Portland's water). He built an irrigation system so that this log would continue to evolve along its original path, misting the log every 15 minutes to keep it going. As a result, multiple species have made themselves at home on this urban nurse log.

Having contemplated the borders of nature and culture, it might be time for a stop for lunch at **Olympic Provisions** (olympicprovisions.com/southeast/about-us) or **Bunk Bar** (bunkbar.com), both notable for their amazing sandwiches. Next, walk through Portland's **Distillery Row** (distilleryrowpdx.com/distillery-row-map), where you can taste excellent whiskeys, aquavits, gins, and other spirits microdistilled in Southeast Portland. At that point, a long walk up **Hawthorne Boulevard** (thinkhawthorne.com) might seem like a good idea; here you will find more outstanding independent shops, including yarn and fabric stores, vintage shopping, music stores, gifts, beautiful clothing, more specialty food shops, and two branches of Powell's—one devoted exclusively to home, garden, and cookbooks and related wares.

---

i If you want to go extreme Portland, consider a Pedal Bike tour (pedalbiketours.com/bike-tours/portland .shtml): They offer everything from a food-cart bike tour to tours of wine country, the Oregon coast, and the Columbia Gorge. They also offer a special bike tour of Portland's extinct volcanoes, Mt. Tabor and Rocky Butte.

End your day at one of the fantastic restaurants on nearby Division: **Pok Pok, Xico, Bar Avignon, Ava Gene's, Sunshine Tavern,** or any of the others that you find. And try **Salt & Straw** for dessert.

MOUNT ST. HELENS NATIONAL VOLCANIC MONUMENT

Johnston Ridge Observatory (West Side), 24000 Spirit Lake Hwy., Toutle, WA 98649; fs.usda.gov/mountsthelens; (360) 274-2140. Mount St. Helens was once known as "the Mount Fuji of America" because its symmetrical beauty was reminiscent of the famous Japanese volcano. But on May 18, 1980, after nearly two months of smaller earthquakes and steam eruptions, Mount St. Helens began a series of massive, explosive eruptions after an earthquake with a magnitude of 5.1 struck at 8:32 a.m. Within seconds, the volcano's unstable and bulging north flank slid away in the largest landslide in recorded history, triggering a destructive blast of lethal hot gas, steam, and rock debris that swept across the landscape at 684 miles per hour. Temperatures reached as high as 572 degrees Celsius, melting snow and ice on the volcano and forming torrents of water and rock debris that gushed down river valleys leading from the mountain. Within minutes, a massive plume of ash thrust nearly 12.5 miles into the sky, where the wind carried about 490 tons of ash across more than 22,000 square miles of the western United States and, in trace amounts, around the world.

The lateral blast, which lasted only the first few minutes of a nine-hour continuous eruption, devastated 250 square miles of forest and recreation area, killed thousands of animals, and left 57 people dead. The eruptions and huge avalanche removed about 4 billion cubic yards of the mountain, including about 170 million cubic yards of glacial snow and ice. The eruption also caused mudflows so severe that they blocked the shipping channel of the Columbia River 70 river miles away.

The volcano periodically spewed steam and ash for several years, eventually settling down enough for the region to rebuild. In 1982 President Ronald Reagan designated 110,000 acres around the volcano as Mount St. Helens National Volcanic Monument. Trails, campgrounds, and visitor centers were established to accommodate the thousands who visited each year.

Now Mount St. Helens is one of the most popular day-trip destinations in the Pacific Northwest. It is an easy, scenic 2.5-hour drive from Portland. There is a lot to do and see on this trip, so start early in the morning and pack some ice and refreshments in the cooler. Take I-5 north to exit 49 (the Toutle/Castle Rock exit), which will lead you onto Washington SR 504 (Spirit Lake Memorial Highway). Continue driving east past some of the most striking scenery in the Northwest, from the washed-out stretches of the Toutle River to the white carcasses of the fir trees that laid themselves down before the awesome power of the volcanic blast. SR 504 winds around the north fork of the Toutle River, and overlooks along the road offer views of the crater, Castle Lake, Coldwater Lake, and the mountain's northwest lava dome.

Hoffstadt Bluffs Rest Area offers a spectacular view of the landslide that preceded the blast. **Elk Rock Viewpoint** offers another stunning view into the still sediment-choked Toutle River Valley.

Just 5 miles farther up the road from Coldwater Ridge, SR 504 ends at **Johnston Ridge Observatory** (milepost 52; 360-274-2140). Only 4 miles from the volcano's crater, this wheelchair-accessible-site affords views of the inside of the crater and its dome. It was named in honor of brave geologist David Johnston, who was keeping watch over the mountain for the US Geological Survey and whose final words warned the world of what was to come. This magnificent center is a fitting tribute. The center also offers an incredibly high-quality movie about the eruption, along with many fascinating, interactive displays and kiosks.

Other monument highlights include **Windy Ridge** and **Spirit Lake,** which rose 70 yards as a result of the blast. Consult with visitor center staff about selecting the best route.

You will need a pass to visit the tourist centers at the monument. These can be purchased at any of the visitor centers. Adult multiuse passes are $8; children 15 and under are free. Discounts for seniors are also available. The monument is open year-round, though Johnston Ridge and some of the viewpoints and trails are closed by snow from Oct through May. The visitor centers may be on limited schedules during the winter. If the volcano is active, it may be closed to climbers, though barring a major eruption, the other monument sites tend to remain open.

Excellent picnic and day-use areas are plentiful, but there are few places to purchase food. No overnight accommodations are available on the grounds of the monument, but nearby towns offer lodging, camping, and supplies.

For the most spectacular views of the crater, try to go on a sunny, summer day. But do remember that it is the Northwest, and even sunny days can bring clouds to the mountaintops.

On October 1, 2004, the volcano awoke from its slumber, emitting steam and erupting ash to signal a new phase of geological activity, which is ongoing, rebuilding the dome of the mountain. A volcanic eruption puts daily cares in perspective like nothing else, and despite the potential danger, residents have been enthralled by the reminder that Mount St. Helens has a mind of its own.

MOUNT HOOD-COLUMBIA GORGE LOOP

When friends visit from out of town and ask what they should do, we send them to the Columbia Gorge. The gorge showcases our region beautifully, with its dramatic cliffs, tumbling falls, and the mighty Columbia rolling along despite the obstacles we have put in its way. Extending the tour by adding the rich farmland of **Hood River** and the drive over the archetypical **Mount Hood** deepens that sense of place, so precious to Oregonians. Here, we recommend an optimal tour of the region, one that you could drive in a day or that you could lengthen with an overnight stay. You can also reverse the drive or easily cut it short. The total length of the journey will be something between 100 and 160 miles, depending on where you stop, where you linger, and where you detour.

These days, cars and trucks race along I-84 at great speed. But before the freeway, drivers had to rely on the road that is now the **Columbia Gorge Scenic Highway.** This narrow, winding road, with its many moss-covered bridges, was dedicated in 1916 by President Woodrow Wilson. One can only imagine the harrowing journey it must have been when it was the principal route east from Portland. Now it is quieter and less crowded, though on summer days you can still find yourself crawling through the shady forest behind an ambitious RV.

To reach the gorge along this route, begin by taking I-84 east to Troutdale to exit 17 and follow the signs designating the Scenic Highway. The road takes you through Troutdale, along the swift Sandy River, until you turn up and onto the rural bluffs that overlook the Columbia. Just past the little town of Corbett, you will find the **Portland Women's Forum,** a pretty wayside that provides a spectacular view east of the Columbia Gorge, particularly Crown Point, Rooster Rock, and Beacon Rock, and north into the Washington Cascades.

Just east of the Portland Women's Forum is the road to **Larch Mountain,** a 29-mile detour (round-trip) that leads to some of the most breathtaking views of the Cascades in the entire area. The road winds through fields and forests until you get to a large parking lot, where an easy, paved trail takes you to a special viewing area that tells you which peaks you are seeing—on a clear day, this can mean a view north all the way to Mount Rainier. Closer in you'll see Mount St. Helens, Mount Adams, Mount Hood, and Mount Jefferson, as well as the verdant, rolling foothills of the Cascades. Larch Mountain also provides picnic areas and other hiking trails, and it's a popular place to watch the Perseid meteor shower in August. (The road may be closed in winter—its final elevation is 4,050 feet.) A note of caution: The Larch Mountain detour is slow going, so it may not be for everyone. And don't bother if the cloud cover is thick. But the payoff is worth it if you have the time and if the weather is cooperative.

Returning to the highway, turn right to continue down the Scenic Highway. After a number of hairpin turns, you will find yourself at **Crown Point Vista House,** a pretty stone building that affords views west and east of the river and the Gorge. Crown Point is especially popular at sunset, when the river washes west into a red and orange sky underlined by the lights of the city and the view east fades into soft purple twilight as the cliffs grow dim. (See the Attractions chapter for more on Crown Point Vista.) East of Crown Point Vista, the highway turns into the forest and provides access to—and views of—the dozens of waterfalls that trickle and gush from the cliffs above on their urgent errand to meet the Columbia below. Many of the biggest falls have waysides, trails, and parks that invite you to explore and linger. **Latourell Falls,** easily accessible via a paved, 150-yard trail, plummets from a basalt outcropping 250 feet above. **Bridal Veil** and **Wahkeena Falls** are next, and then you will arrive at **Multnomah Falls.** Multnomah Falls—at 620 feet, the second-highest waterfall in the United States—is a premier attraction in the state (and indeed warrants a special exit from I-84, in addition to being accessible via the Columbia Gorge Highway). Most visitors are content to view the falls from the viewing area behind the **Multnomah Lodge** (503-695-2376; multnomahfallslodge .com), a beautiful historic building that houses a restaurant, gift shop, and information center. For the information center, call the US Forest Service at (503) 695-2372. Some visitors venture a bit farther, taking the paved path first to the bridge beneath the falls and then to the top of the falls (1 mile, uphill).

But if you want to hike the entire 3.25-mile loop, you will be rewarded with a verdant walk that takes you along the ridge just west of the falls and past Upper Wahkeenah Falls, before dropping back down to the parking lot. To follow this loop, from the paved overlook spur, you'll continue along the unpaved trail, across the stone bridge, until you reach the junction for the Perdition Trail. Bear right along this trail along the ridge for 1.2 miles. The trail has a number of stone staircases, and just past the steepest and longest set, you will meet the Wahkeenah Trail. Take this, staying to the right and passing Upper Wahkeenah Falls. You'll meet with pavement again about half a mile before Wahkeenah Falls; then stay on the path above the highway for another half mile, until you reach the Multnomah Falls parking lot.

Resuming your trip, the next stop on the Columbia Gorge Highway is **Oneonta Gorge.** Here the reward of the trail, should you choose to take it, is a walk behind the falls. Horsetail Falls is next, before the highway connects back to I-84 at milepost 35.

Once you are back on the freeway, the next destination is the **Bonneville Dam** (541-374-8820), the oldest Army Corps of Engineers project along the

Dramatic Multnomah Falls, at 620 feet, is worth a visit.

Columbia River. It's fun to watch the salmon struggle up the fish ladder along the dam or to throw chow at the fry in the nearby **Bonneville Hatchery.**

About 2 miles past the Bonneville Dam is the town of **Cascades Locks,** as well as the **Bridge of the Gods,** an impressive steel toll bridge that takes you across the Columbia into Washington and to the **Columbia Gorge Interpretive Center** (990 SW Rock Creek Dr., Stevenson, WA 98648; 509-427-8211; columbiagorge.org). This museum, designed to resemble a sawmill, offers an absorbing thematic history of the gorge based on who lived here and what they did. It is a good complement to the **Cascade Locks Museum,** back on the Oregon side (1 NW Portage Rd., Cascade Locks, OR 97014; open daily May through Sept, noon to 5 p.m.; 541-374-8535; cascadelocks.net/about-us-historical-museum.php). This little museum was formerly the home of a lockman. It dates from 1905 and features many fascinating artifacts and photos from life along the river 100 years ago. In front stands the Oregon Pony, the first steam locomotive on the Pacific coast and the first west of the Missouri. Cascade Locks was built around the site of the navigational pass that allowed boats around a series of Columbia River rapids. Since the building of the dam, of course, these rapids have been submerged, but Cascade Locks is a great stop because of its historic museums, its park, its summer stern-wheeler tours and its two restaurants: **Charburger** (714 Wanapa St.; 541-374-8477), which offers cooked-to-order burgers, home-baked pies and cookies, and striking views of the Columbia; and its neighbor, the **East Wind** (541-374-8380), an old-fashioned drive-in with excellent soft-serve ice cream.

Back on I-84, your next stop will be **Hood River.** Just west of town, at exit 62, is the historic and luxurious **Columbia Gorge Hotel** (4000 W. Cliff Dr., Hood River, OR 97031; 541-386-5566; columbiagorgehotel.com), famous for its dining room views and its lavish 5-course farm breakfast. The pretty grounds sit atop a waterfall that plunges 208 feet.

Hood River is known for two things: windsurfing and orchards. For a span of 70 miles east and west of Hood River, windsurfers swoop and glide through the chilly Columbia waters, taking advantage of the wind that gusts persistently through the gorge. Hood River is a pleasant little town, with many charming shops, art galleries, and restaurants. Other stops might include the **Hood River Hotel** (102 Oak St., Hood River, OR 97031; 541-386-1900 or 800-386-1859; hoodriverhotel.com), an appealing 1913 vintage building that houses a good restaurant. Also try the **Full Sail Brewery,** home to some of the finest beer in Oregon (or anywhere). Guided tours are available daily on the hour from noon until 5 p.m. for those older than 13. And all ages are welcome at the pub if they are eating. Pub hours are noon to 8 p.m. daily. The brewery is found at 506 Columbia St., Hood River, OR 97031 (fullsailbrewing.com; 541-386-2247).

Hood River is a good place to turn around and head back to Portland along I-84. But if you decide to explore further, you will be rewarded.

Follow the main street of Hood River as it angles southeast on SR 35 into the lovely **Hood River Valley,** home to thousands of acres of orchards and farms. Less than a mile from town, as the highway clings to the hillside, turn up the road marked by the sign designating a panorama point. This will take you to a vista point, with much of this beautiful valley laid before you. Two terrific times to visit the Hood River Valley are during the **Hood River Blossom Festival,** held in mid-April, and the **Hood River Harvest Festival** in mid-October. But at any time the trip through this pocket of traditional farmland is a journey beyond life in the city.

After leaving the valley SR 35 starts to curve around the eastern slope of **Mount Hood.** Soon you begin to catch close-up glimpses of Mount Hood's glacial cap, and if you use your imagination, you can sense the wonder felt by pioneers who opted to take a path around the mountain instead of rafting down the dangerous Columbia. Just before the confluence of SR 35 and US 26, a historical marker announces that you are crossing **Barlow Pass,** named for Sam Barlow, a trailblazer who found a way down the mountain and set up a toll road. Barlow charged $5 per wagon and 10 cents per head of cattle for those hardy and brave enough to slide and rope their wagons down the muddy slopes and treacherous canyons that are now traversed by US 26. Another historical marker shortly after the Barlow Road marker is a poignant reminder of the cost of this detour. The **Pioneer Woman's Gravesite** is a short distance from the road; there you can also view intact wagon ruts near the gravesite.

Once on US 26 heading west, there are a number of spots of interest. One is **Trillium Lake,** a picnic site and fishing hole stocked with rainbow trout. To get there take FR 2656 a couple of miles before reaching Government Camp. If it's ski season, you can go to **Timberline, Summit Ski area,** or **Mount Hood Ski Bowl** for some world-class downhill action. **Timberline Lodge** (503-272-3311; timberlinelodge.com) is worth a visit whether or not you ski and even if no snow is on the ground. This attractive lodge, made of hand-hewn logs and great stones, is a National Historic Landmark built in 1937 as part of the Works Progress Administration (WPA). It stands as a monument to the talents of its builders and to its era. The lodge also features an outstanding restaurant, as well as several cafes and other eating areas. (If you are taking two days, it would make an excellent halfway stop.)

After descending from the ski zone, you'll come to **Welches,** a mountain town with lodging, shopping, and dining. You might also want to stop here at the **Mount Hood Information Center** for information on just about everything going on around the mountain.

One last site to see is the **Philip Foster Farm and Homestead** at 29912 SE Oregon Hwy. 211, Eagle Creek, OR 97022 (503-637-6324, philipfosterfarm.com). Follow US 26 west to SR 211 in Sandy, and drive south for 6 miles to the hamlet of **Eagle Creek.** This national historic site served as many as 10,000 emigrants on the Oregon Trail. Nearing the end of their journey, they ate 50-cent dinners of steak, potatoes, coleslaw, and biscuits at Foster's farm. Foster was an entrepreneurial fellow as well as a restaurateur, and he anticipated and met the needs of weary pioneers. Here they could stock up on fruit, grain, and other supplies and their livestock could partake of the Foster family's hay, before proceeding west and south into the Willamette Valley. Today you'll find a working farm complete with house, barn, garden, orchard, and blacksmith shop. Visitors are invited to help with chores. There is also a picnic spot and a general store. Hours are Fri through Sun 11 a.m. to 4 p.m. June through Aug and just Sat and Sun during Sept.

> **i** For maps, trails, and other information on the Columbia Gorge, call the Columbia Gorge National Scenic Area offices at (541) 308-1700 or visit fs.usda.gov/columbia.

NORTHERN WILLAMETTE VALLEY'S WINE COUNTRY

In the 1960s Oregon wine pioneer David Lett started planting grapes in the Dundee Hills west of Portland, and everyone thought he was crazy. But he had observed something important. Roughly in the same latitude as Burgundy, the great wine-producing province in France, Oregon's northern Willamette Valley has a cool marine climate, rich soil on the southern slopes of rolling hills, and a long, gentle season with ample sunny days. Now, decades later, Oregon wines hold their own against the best wines in the world.

But don't take our word for it. Taste these remarkable varieties yourself by taking a tour of northwestern Oregon's wine region. It's a delightful drive through some of the state's most bucolic countryside. Many of the wineries are open to visitors, and some are near fine restaurants and inns along one of the most popular tourist loops on the West Coast.

Plan for a journey that starts in the morning, looping out into wine country and back to Portland by evening. Visit the **Oregon Winegrowers' Association** website at oregonwine.org (or 1200 NW Naito Pkwy., Suite 400, 503-228-8403). We cannot emphasize enough how essential this resource is—it provides a comprehensive listing of all the wineries in the valley (and in Oregon). You can also preorder brochures from the **Willamette Valley Winegrowers Association** at willamettewines.com; these have information on winery tasting rooms, maps, and other features. Give yourself time to plan a good route and be sure to designate a driver. It will make your trip much better. (If you are not into a DIY wine tour, then we highly recommend utilizing the resources of the Portland Visitors Association. They have a list of commercial wine tour vendors available at travelportland.com). There are 155 wineries in the northern Willamette Valley alone—but not all of them are open to the public or have tasting rooms. So planning is essential.

Once the planning is out of the way, you can get on the road. Below is an example tour of the northern Willamette Valley that hits three of the founding vineyards as well as sampling those of more recent vintage.

Start by visiting **Ponzi Vineyards** (ponziwines.com), one of the most important winemakers in the valley. Take I-5 to SR 217 and on to SR 210 for 4.5 miles to Vandermost Road. Turn left and head south, following signs to 14665 SW Winery Lane. Here, with the exception of January and holidays, visitors are welcome to sample the wines of the pioneering Ponzi family, who have been instrumental to the establishment of Oregon's wine industry and to its continued success. The Ponzis were one of the first to grow grapes in the region, just a little after David Lett. They continue to produce stellar wines, as well as being true community leaders and supporters of young growers. Their tasting room is spacious and attractive, and the grounds offer bocce courts in addition to the views of rolling countryside—bocce being one of the two great games one can play with a wineglass in one hand (boules is the other).

The next leg of the journey, the longest, will take you through about 30 miles of beautiful farmland and vineyards—both large estates and small craft wineries such as **WillaKenzie,** noted for its Burgundy-style wines—to the **Carlton Winemakers Studio** (winemakersstudio.com). This handsome LEED-certified building holds the tasting room for about 8 local winemakers, including pinot star Andrew Rich. The studio also offers classes and events. To get there from Ponzi, you will follow Southwest Winery Lane back to Southwest Vandermost Road, turn right, and take the first left onto SR 210/Southwest Scholls Ferry Road. You should be heading west. After about 2 miles, you'll make a left turn to stay on SR 210/Scholls Ferry Road. Stay on this road—it will turn into SR 219/Southwest Hillsboro Highway, and you'll follow SR 219 for nearly 10 miles. You will turn right at East Illinois Street in Newberg, then quickly turn left at North Main Street, and then turn right onto SR 240 West, the Yamhill-Newberg Highway. You'll continue on this road, and then turn left to stay on SR 240 West. When you come to the junction of SR

47, turn left and follow this road south to Carlton. You'll turn right at West Lincoln Street; the Carlton Winemakers Studio is at the intersection of Lincoln and Scott (801 N. Scott St.).

After you chat with the winemaker on duty at the Carlton Studio, head south to the tasting room for **Eyrie** (eyrievineyards.com/journal), David Lett's visionary winery, in McMinnville, about 7 miles to the south. You'll backtrack on Lincoln Street to SR 47, and follow it to West Main Street. Turn left at Main (still on SR 47—there will be a sign for McMinnville), and then follow SR 47 through the second right onto South Pine Street. This street will turn into the Tualatin Valley Highway, but you will still be on SR 47. Stay on this road until you reach SR 99W; take a slight right, continuing to follow the signs for McMinnville. Stay on 99W, driving southwest, until you reach Northeast Lafayette. Turn left (following the sign for Bayton—Salem), and follow Northeast Lafayette for almost 1.5 miles until Northeast 10th Ave. You'll find Eyrie in an unprepossessing building at 935 NE 10th Ave. Eyrie is noted for not only the first pinot noir plantings in the Willamette Valley but also the first pinot gris plantings in the United States. David Lett's international-medal-winning pinot noir wines were the catalyst that turned the valley into the winemaking hub it is today. In 1979, French winemaker Robert Drouhin was so amazed by Lett's third-place finish in a blind-tasting competition in Paris that he held a new contest the following year. This time, Lett's wine came in second. (The Drouhin family soon set out for Oregon themselves, and now they are one of the top producers in the area.) David's son Jason Lett now runs the family business, still producing elegant pinots and other varietals, and numerous rising winemaker stars have apprenticed with him and his father.

McMinnville is a pretty college town and the home of the **International Pinot Noir Celebration** (see the Festivals & Annual Events chapter). It has good tasting rooms, wine bars, and restaurants featuring local wines and food, as well as some quite good shopping. **Nick's Italian Café** (521 NE 3rd St., McMinnville, OR 97128; reservations 503-434-4471; nicksitaliancafe.com) would be a pleasant stop for lunch.

Next up is **Erath Winery** (erath.com), which is famous not only for the excellence of its pinot noirs, but also for bringing French grape clones to the valley in 1974. Until then, the small grape-growing community had been working almost exclusively with California grapes. If the Oregon climate was more like the Burgundy region of France, why not use French clones? From Eyrie, backtrack onto SR 99W and turn right. (If you are in downtown McMinnville, make your way toward 99W Forest Grove/Portland.) You'll travel about 9 miles east on 99W to the outskirts of Dundee. At Southwest Niederberger Road you will turn left off the highway (it will say CR 78 on the right). Stay on Southwest Niederberger Road for about 0.5 mile and turn right on Northeast Warren Road. After about 0.7 mile, take a left on Northeast Worden Hill Road. Erath has a friendly tasting room with a patio that offers gorgeous views across the Willamette Valley.

Complete your tour by heading back onto 99W and into **Dundee** or nearby **Newberg,** each of which has several outstanding restaurants. In Dundee, you must choose between **Tina's** (760 SR 99W; 503-538-8880), which is a highly rated place that specializes in local, seasonal dishes; and the charming **Dundee Bistro** (503-554-1650; dundeebistro.com) at SR 99 and 7th Street. To get to either of these restaurants from Erath, drive southeast onto CR 12/Northeast Worden Hill Road. Stay on CR 12. Turn left at Southwest View Crest Drive and then right at Southwest 7th Street. If you want to go to Tina's, turn right at 99W—the restaurant will be just to the right; if you want to go to the Dundee Bistro, turn left into the parking lot just before the highway.

If you want to head to Newberg from Erath, stay on CR 12 until you reach 99W, and turn left onto the highway. Take 99W north until Newberg. Here, you'll need to make a choice. You can turn right at South College Street and head to the **Painted Lady** (201 S. College St.; 503-538-3850; thepainted ladyrestaurant.com). This superb restaurant is in a beautifully restored Victorian house and serves fine seasonal Northwest cuisine. Or you can head to the luscious **Allison Inn and Spa,** featuring **Jory Restaurant** (2525 Allison Lane; 503-554-2526 for the dining room; theallison.com). Instead of turning on South College, you'll stay on 99W; it will veer to the left, becoming East Portland Road. Turn left at North Springbrook Road. You'll reach a traffic circle; stay straight to remain on North Springbrook. Turn right to stay on North Springbook (if you don't turn, you will be on East Mountainview, which you don't want to do). Take North Springbook until Allison Lane, on the left.

At this point, your designated driver may wish to stop driving and savor some wine at Jory—or perhaps the luxurious spa treatments and rooms at the Allison. You could stay over and the next morning enjoy an alternative view: **Vista Balloon Adventures** (800-622-2309; vistaballoon.com) in Newberg offers aerial tours in hot-air balloons for around $200. This is a lovely way to see wine country—though a little far from the tasting rooms.

In any case, whether you stay the night or head home, to return to Portland from either Dundee or Newberg, take 99W through Sherwood and Tigard, all the way back to I-5.

About 100 miles west of Portland, you will find some of the most spectacular coastline in the world. To get there, take US 26 west, following the signs that direct you toward the ocean beaches.

When you reach US 101, turn north toward Astoria if you want to visit **Fort Clatsop,** the site of Lewis and Clark's winter encampment. This historical re-creation is as entertaining as it is educational. Astoria, a few miles north of Fort Clatsop, is a delightful working harbor at the mouth of the Columbia River. Or turn south on US 101 for **Cannon Beach.** By now you're probably ready for lunch, and Cannon Beach, a lively beach town, has many shops and restaurants, as well as beautiful hotels and spas. Cannon Beach is the home of the famous **Haystack Rock** (at 235 feet high, the third-tallest coastal monolith in the world).

A bit farther south, you'll encounter **Neahkahnie Mountain,** with a trail leading to its summit. Neahkahnie is an excellent viewing area for whales in the spring and fall.

Continuing south, you'll pass through Manzanita, Nehalem, and Wheeler. Manzanita, which lies just west of US 101, has especially good beaches, and all three towns are filled with charming shops. Next you'll reach the fishing villages of Garibaldi and Bayside and on to Tillamook. Just to the west of this friendly blue-collar burg is the **Three Capes Loop,** a 35-mile byway off US 101 between Tillamook and Neskowin. As you cruise through gentle, misty dairy country, you'll get far enough west to check out Cape Meares to the north, Cape Lookout midway, and the last cape right next to Pacific City, Cape Kiwanda.

Just a short way down the coast is Neskowin, a sweet little town with a pretty beach in the shadow of Cascade Head, a looming monolithic outcrop favored by hikers seeking solace in a genuine rain forest. After beachcombing at Neskowin, drive a few more miles south to the junction of US 101 and SR 18.

Here you have a choice of directions. You can continue south along the coast, past Lincoln City on to **Newport** with its fascinating **Oregon Coast Aquarium, Hatfield Marine Science Center,** historic **Nye Beach,** and scenic **Yaquina Head lighthouse** and bird-watching station. It's an easy, if long, journey back to Portland from Newport either by backtracking to SR 18 or heading east on US 20 to Corvallis and then on to I-5 and north. But it will make for a long day, so you may want to plan for a stay-over in one of the many hotels and motels along US 101.

Or you can choose to take SR 18 and angle back to Portland, stopping for some great food at the **Otis Cafe** at Otis Junction, 2 miles east of US 101 (541-994-2813; otiscafe.com). Just past Otis you'll enter the **Van Duzer Corridor,** a stretch of ancient firs that frame the road with their verdant grandeur. Beyond the forest, and past the Spirit Mountain Casino and a broad valley dotted with barns and farmhouses, you'll cruise through Yamhill County and on to Portland.

APPENDIX:
Living Here

In this section we feature specific information for residents or those planning to relocate here. Topics include real estate, education, and more.

Relocation

Portland is repeatedly honored across the nation as being one of the best places to live. Its setting among mountains, farmland, and rivers contributes to its desirability, and so does its solid economy and unfrenzied style of life. Yet above all, we are a city of neighborhoods. And this may be the true secret of Portland's charm, the source of its community feeling. Government agencies such as Metro, nonprofit organizations such as the Coalition for a Liveable Future, neighborhood associations, far-sighted real estate developers, and plain old unaffiliated citizens keep the neighborhood spirit alive and provide a foundation for its strength to grow. After you've had a look at some of our neighborhoods, we'll turn to the topic of real estate and let you know about ways to find your own place in our beautiful metropolitan area. And we'll tell you other important facts about moving to the area.

NEIGHBORHOODS

Researchers predict that the Portland Metro area will increase to up to 4 million people in by 2060. All these new people will have to live somewhere, but we also need to protect forests to clean the air and water (and the spirit), and we need to preserve the farmland to feed all these new residents. Our unique tri-county government, Metro, plays an important role in determining land use policies, and because its officials are elected, these policies ideally reflect the wishes of citizens. This unusual tri-county government helps to protect open spaces, to allow for coordinated transportation management, and to stabilize development by encouraging population density instead of suburban sprawl.

Metro and the kind of planning it embodies is not without its critics from both sides of the political spectrum. Developers rankle under the land-use plans, while environmentalists worry that the urban growth boundary actually encourages growth by requiring a certain amount of urban space to be dedicated to development. The best hope is that the competing interests will work in fertile tension with each other. For example, Metro's encouragement of affordable housing and mass transportation have sparked some of the most innovative developments in the nation. Orenco Station, which was built in Hillsboro specifically to take advantage of the light-rail line, has been dubbed "America's Best Master Planned Community" by the National Association of Home Builders. This assemblage of cottages, Craftsman retros, apartments, and row houses reverberates with an old village way of life. Similarly, highly accoladed projects such as the Belmont Dairy, Irvington Place, Albina Corner, and the Division 43 micro homes, which reclaimed underused urban space and now provide attractive, mixed-use facilities and affordable housing for lower- and middle-class residents, might never have happened without the productive constraints of land-use planning.

Old or new, upscale or down-home, Portland's neighborhoods embody the *genius loci* of the city. From the friendly, front-porch lifestyles of St. Johns to the funky old Victorian houses of inner Southeast Portland to the stately manors of the Dunthorpe district to the shiny and light condos in the South Waterfront, Portland is home to a healthy

Portland housing features a mixture of new city development and older neighborhood homes.

array of diverse and distinct communities. We have 95 formally recognized neighborhoods in the city of Portland alone. This chapter is meant to serve as a broad overview of Portland Metro area neighborhoods. In the first section of this chapter we try to give you a feel for Portland's four distinct areas—Southwest, Northwest, Southeast, and North/Northeast—and also to introduce you to Vancouver and at least some of the communities outside Portland's formal borders.

Southwest Portland

The heart of Southwest Portland is the downtown area. Not only is it the home of many businesses, cultural organizations, government agencies, and public spaces, it is also the home of many residents, who like the urbane atmosphere and the proximity to work and nightlife. Portland's downtown is a mecca for shoppers, with department stores such as Nordstrom, Macy's, and Saks Fifth Avenue, as well as the Pioneer Place shopping center, all within several blocks. Pioneer Courthouse Square is a popular meeting place and offers a wide range of free, live entertainment during the noon hour. But despite the tempting stores, the impressive statues, and the well-designed business towers, nothing defines downtown Portland as well as the Willamette River.

In the early 1970s the city underwent a huge renewal project, ripping apart a four-lane highway along the west bank of the Willamette and transforming it into beautiful Tom McCall Waterfront Park. It is the site of numerous concerts, festivals, and celebrations as well as a showplace for community events. Eight blocks west, Park Blocks, a 25-block boulevard of trees, grass, flowers, fountains, and statues, offers another urban refuge for workers, shoppers, and students. Nearby are many of the city's most important cultural and recreational facilities, including the Portland Art Museum, the Oregon Historical Society, the Performing Arts Center, and the Arlene Schnitzer Concert Hall. Just outside the inner city is Washington Park, home to the Metro Washington Park Zoo, the tranquil Japanese Gardens, the World Forestry Center, and Hoyt Arboretum.

Beyond the park's boundaries to the south and west are several of the most established, picturesque, and tree-lined of all the city's neighborhoods. Collectively referred to as the "West Hills," each of these neighborhoods nonetheless has distinctive features. For example, Arlington Heights, one of Portland's most scenic neighborhoods, just west of downtown above the city center, gives residents easy access to the spectacular International Rose Test Gardens and all of Washington Park. The houses here tend to be older, and the architecture diverse—one house is a miniature replica of Canterbury Castle in England. Arlington Heights's neighbor, Portland Heights, also displays diverse architectural styles. Ranging from Victorian cottages to the latest contemporary dwellings, these houses are noted for their lovely gardens and spectacular views. Nestled amid the Southwest Hills, Council Crest affords extraordinary views of both the city and the western valleys. Farther west, on the other side of the hills, you'll find Multnomah Village, named by *Money* magazine as one of Portland's best neighborhoods. This charming neighborhood offers the grace of older houses and the vitality of the newer ones; but all houses are tempered by a hint of the rural past—it wasn't formally annexed until 1954, and some of the most desirable houses yet repose on unpaved roads. Multnomah Village itself is a notable shopping and business district that offers a congenial center to village life. (See the Shopping chapter.)

More Southwest Neighborhoods

CORBETT-TERWILLIGER AND LAIR HILL

On a 4-mile-long ribbon of land along the west bank—one of the most scenic segments of the Willamette River—you'll find the Corbett-Terwilliger and Lair Hill neighborhoods, directly south of downtown Portland. Residents here are indirectly responsible for preserving the character of our city. Years ago, when urban renewal crept its way to the north end of these older neighborhoods, a backlash resulted in establishment of the South Portland–Lair Hill Historic Conservation District, the first protected historic district in Portland. This was an appropriate gesture, given that Portland's very first building, a cabin constructed by William Johnson in 1842, was built in what became this neighborhood, near Southwest Gibbs and I-5. Some residents later balked at the construction of the Portland Aerial Tram, which glides above this neighborhood, but the new development on the South Waterfront seems to be a net positive for this neighborhood. The houses in this pretty urban neighborhood are mostly older Victorian-style structures, but there are intriguing modern structures as well.

HILLSDALE NEIGHBORHOOD

Hillsdale is just 3 miles from downtown Portland, but its location in the Southwest Hills gives parts of it an almost rural feel. Hillsdale's commercial district evolved in the 1940s along old dairy-cow pastures, and after the war, as suburban-style houses were built in the area, the virtues of things such as sidewalks were forgotten. Now Hillsdale residents are guiding developments to foster accessibility and community. Southwest Terwilliger Boulevard, one of Portland's favorite scenic routes for bikers, pedestrians, and cars—and the product of community planning efforts—is a hallmark feature along with Oregon Health and Science University, one of the major employers in the state. This area is very popular with young families, since the neighborhood schools are very good.

HAYHURST NEIGHBORHOOD

A unique feature of the Hayhurst neighborhood area is the Alpenrose Dairy, which continues to operate as a dairy, as well as serving as a community center offering sports fields, picnic facilities, entertainment, and bicycle racing. In a sense, Portland's most familiar dairy symbolizes the wholesomeness of this middle-class area, which is made up mostly of single-family houses and is creating ways to accommodate growth while preserving its distinctive neighborhood character and livability. Hayhurst School and its nature learning garden and Pendleton Park with its neighborhood planting projects are some of the community-friendly features of this neighborhood. This is another family-friendly area—schools are good, backyards are large.

GOOSE HOLLOW

Goose Hollow's name goes back to the 1870s when women who lived there raised flocks of geese. Early residents of the district were the barons who guided the destiny of the region from its raw pioneer days through the prosperity of the 1890s and the following war years. But while Portland boomed between 1970 and 1990, Goose Hollow slumbered. However, since 1991, Westside light rail and high-density planning have spurred unprecedented developments, pumping more than $50 million in improvements into the 3.2-square-mile district. Bordered by downtown, Washington Park, the University District, and Burnside Street, the western end of the district is hilly and residential, while the eastern portion is flat and commercial. Served by the MAX line, this neighborhood has seen handsome new apartments and condominiums in recent years, along with attractive new commercial spaces, infusing the area with new life.

The South Waterfront District

One of Portland's newest residential areas, the South Waterfront District has been built upon reclaimed industrial land along the banks of the Willamette, south of downtown. Here you will find gleaming glass towers with luxury condominiums, as well as colorful new apartment buildings for the economically diverse—the neighborhood is reminiscent of Pacific Rim cities such as Vancouver, British Columbia, and is defining itself as the leading edge of Portland development. Built on landfill along the Willamette on a parcel that was once used for building ships, the South Waterfront district is anchored by Oregon

Floating houses—known here as "houseboats"—line portions of the Willamette and Columbia Rivers.

Health and Science University's Center for Health and Healing and the Portland Aerial Tram, as well as a new campus that combines research and education programs of OHSU, Portland State, and Oregon State. Alongside these are new parks and schools, shops, restaurants, and cafes. It's popular with retirees at the beautiful Mirabella retirement community (see Retirement) and with medical students, who "commute" by walking a few blocks to the tram, which whooshes them up to OHSU's main campus on Marquam Hill, a 3-minute ride away. And there are plenty of families moving in, taking advantage of the urban amenities of this neighborhood, including the easy commute to downtown via streetcar. The residents of this neighborhood are defining themselves with a strong community voice; they are deeply involved in shaping the character of the neighborhood.

Northwest Portland

Northwest Portland offers panoramic views of the mountains, the Willamette River, and the city. Northwest Portland is a delightful blend of old and new and of classic and Bohemian, and community interaction is extremely high in this area as residents and neighbors strive to create a secure and friendly living environment. Northwest Portlanders find boutique shopping, art galleries, coffee, and culture within easy walking distance. Well-built and beautifully reconditioned Victorian houses, huge fir trees, and lush parks and gardens provide an old-world feel, while above the city, contemporary mansions in the Forest Heights neighborhood demonstrate that American dreams of progress are still alive. The heart of Northwest Portland is the Nob Hill and Alphabet Blocks neighborhood—the commercial and residential areas north of Burnside along Northwest 21st and 23rd Avenues. Though many of its three-story Victorian estates have been converted into condominiums, this neighborhood has retained its elegance and appeal, and there are many handsome apartment buildings dating from the early 20th century, with their vintage features intact. The numerous shops on Northwest 21st and 23rd Avenues offer unusual and distinctive wares, though chain stores like Pottery Barn and Gap are slowly encroaching. Still, this is one of the toniest areas of the city—also one of the most densely populated, and popular with young professionals.

Excellent hospital facilities, fine schools, many banks, good grocery stores and restaurants, and a highly efficient public transit system that includes the streetcar system add to the desirability of Nob Hill. Possessing a wide range of socioeconomic diversity, the area supports an impressive variety of employment, volunteer, and recreation opportunities. And it's moments away from Washington and Forest Parks as well as downtown.

More Northwest Neighborhoods

PEARL DISTRICT

Money magazine designated the Pearl District as one of the best places to live in the best city to live in. This is remarkable because not long ago the area was a grimy, downtown postindustrial wasteland. Today it is one of the most fashionable locations in the close-in city. Extensive renovations and adaptive use of historical and other structures have led to lofts, row houses, new restaurants, theaters, art galleries, and new retail activity. Also, a flurry of important new urban creative-commerce entrepreneurs, ranging from small Internet service providers to internationally known advertising and multimedia companies, are staking out territory here.

In addition, the Pacific Northwest College of Art, PICA, the Museum of Contemporary Craft, and other arts organizations have chosen the Pearl as their home. Well-clad entrepreneurs sip coffee next to spiky-haired students; art supply stores and antiques shops vie for attention; cool lofts with cityscape views perch above truck-loading ramps. The atmosphere in the Pearl is a heady brew of past and future productively engaging. Important retail and residential developments include the Brewery Blocks (on the site of the old Henry Weinhard Brewery), between Burnside and Northwest Davis, as well as an innovative

Charming houses are found throughout the city.

restoration project by Ecotrust. The latter, the Jean Vollum Natural Capital Center, 907 NW Irving, holds a major Patagonia retail shop in addition to other shops and offices. This restored brick building is constructed with eco-friendly timber and energy-efficient spaces. Its roof is planted with native vegetation that keeps the building cool and filters rainwater.

Want to know more about Portland's neighborhoods? Check out the useful website sponsored by the Office of Neighborhood Involvement Programs and Services: portland online.com/oni.

The Pearl District draws urbanites young and old, and more recently, families with children. The North Pearl area in particular has concentrated on family-friendly housing, including larger and affordable apartments near beautiful Jamison Square and equally attractive Fields Park. Many of the newest shops and cafes are taking advantage of this new demographic trend. The work in progress here should give hope to cities everywhere.

OLD TOWN–CHINATOWN NEIGHBORHOOD

As its name implies, Old Town–Chinatown is one of the pioneer neighborhoods of Portland. Besides serving as the Chinese District, the city's early docks and railroad station were teeming with sailors on shore leave and loggers from the nearby woods, creating colorful—if rowdy—city scenes.

This neighborhood, which lies just east of the Pearl District, serves as a gateway to downtown Portland. Art, music, culture, great ethnic food, unique architecture, small businesses, major corporations, and residents of all income levels thrive here. Numerous social service agencies harmoniously coexist with for-profit businesses. The diversity of the residential population is reflected in the housing, which ranges from single-resident hotels to upper-end apartments and lofts. The Chinese and Japanese cultural roots of the area are manifested in old buildings as well as new developments, particularly in the Classical Chinese Garden on Northwest 3rd and Everett.

Southeast Portland

The east side of Portland has seen a renaissance during the last decade. Expansive renovation, busy commercial activity, and general vigor have ignited the return to the city of many former suburbanites and the reclamation of the city by confirmed urbanites who always understood the virtues of established

RELOCATION

neighborhoods with beautiful parks, good schools, and appealing architecture, especially in the close-in neighborhoods. These neighborhoods offer a reduced commute time and greater access to cultural life than the suburbs. The Hawthorne and nearby Belmont Districts, which are subdivided into many distinctive neighborhoods such as Richmond, Sunnyside, Buckman, and Mt. Tabor, are filled with single-family houses and mixed-use apartment buildings. Bakeries, coffeehouses, boutiques, music shops and bookstores, pubs, and restaurants are within walking distance of many houses, buses run frequently, and street life is abundant. Similarly, the neighborhoods of Eastmoreland, Westmoreland, Sellwood, and Laurelhurst have vibrant retail districts along with their single-family houses.

Surprisingly—given its proximity to downtown—inner Southeast Portland has taken longer than other neighborhoods to complete its revival. It might be because its early renewal efforts lost momentum, or it might be because much of it is industrial, but for whatever reason, its renovation seemed to stall. It remained purely industrial.

That is now changing, and there are signs of mixed development. The Eastbank Esplanade opened up the east side of the river to pedestrians and cyclists, and they love the subtle promise of the west views of the Willamette and the

The Eastbank Esplanade provides a bike- and pededtrian-friendly way to connect eastside neighborhoods.

city skyline. By connecting all the bridges from the Steel Bridge to the Sellwood Bridge, the Esplanade seems to have shaken things up and people are looking at this chicly industrial area once again. For example, more influential restaurants opened in the past several years in inner Southeast Portland than in any other neighborhood—the chef behind nationally acclaimed Le Pigeon chose a renovated storefront in Southeast Portland for his restaurant, and new restaurants seem to open weekly along Southeast Division, home to renowned Portland chef Andy Ricker of Pok Pok, Whiskey Soda Lounge, and Sen Yai. Southeast Belmont is is a mecca for coffeehouses—Stumptown Coffee has two of them there. Lower Burnside—home of the Doug Fir Lounge, the Jupiter Hotel, and Biwa—is another growing neighborhood. The enterprising folks who have started businesses there took advantage of the fact that the area had been stuck in a time warp and used it to their advantage, since everything comes around again eventually. Technically, LoBu straddles both Southeast and Northeast Portland, but in terms of spirit and aesthetic, it is Southeast all the way.

More Southeast Neighborhoods

INNER SOUTHEAST PORTLAND

The core of inner Southeast Portland comprises three commercial streets— Hawthorne, Belmont, and Division—that run from the Willamette east (in the case of Division, all the way to Gresham). These business districts are filled with independent, DIY businesses, from food carts to yoga studios to high-end design. The neighborhoods that surround these innovative and entrepreneurial districts are likewise independent-minded, and you will find many sustainable organic gardens, ecoroofs, alternative public and private schools, and architect-designed chicken coops, along with young families, old Italian grandparents, urbanites, and professionals living in single-family turn-of-the-century homes and brand-new condominiums all in a glorious mélange.

Hawthorne Boulevard supports high-density housing that meshes with retail activity, fashioning one of the city's premier shopping and living districts. This street intersects the Sunnyside and Richmond neighborhoods. Pedestrian-friendly and lined with gift stores, period clothing shops, and distinctive restaurants, this district is bordered by the Central Eastside Industrial District, home to the Oregon Museum of Science and Industry to the west and the base of Mount Tabor, an extinct volcano and one of the city's most beloved parks, to the east.

The houses on Mount Tabor's west side are large, older, and upscale. Belmont, which also ends on Mount Tabor, used to hold the streetcar line, and you will see gorgeous estates at the east end of the street, where well-to-do Portlanders built them at the beginning of the 20th century, taking advantage of the streetcar to get them to their firms in the city. Further west, Belmont, which is the core of the Sunnyside neighborhood, is filled with bustling coffeeshops, bars, and stores.

Division is rapidly refreshing itself, with some of the city's best new restaurants and bars opening along this bustling route and a new master plan for the street in the works. Attractive new live-work spaces are also being built to take advantage of its proximity to downtown. This renewed focus on Division is fitting—in some ways, the neighborhood revolution in Portland began here in the early 1970s, when the state of Oregon proposed, essentially, to turn Division into a freeway. Citizens banded together to stop it, prompting officials to rethink the freeway scheme in general. Eventually, this freeway revolt led to strong neighborhood associations, alternative transportation plans, and a new ethos for the city, including removing the old freeway downtown. These citizens didn't just stop a freeway; they created a revolution.

HOSFORD-ABERNETHY

Also called Ladd's Addition, this neighborhood was settled in the mid-1800s. In the southeast sector, Hosford-Abernethy is one of Portland's oldest neighborhoods. The Ladd tract—one of the nation's first planned communities, with sidewalks, paved streets, electricity, and a streetcar line—began developing early in 1900. After World War II many of the residents abandoned the neighborhood in favor of the suburbs, and the area declined. Beginning in the 1970s hundreds of historic houses have been restored, bringing back its sense of neighborhood, and now it might be considered an exemplar of good planning. One hundred years later, this neighborhood has some of the most valuable property in the city.

i Each April *Portland Monthly* magazine (portlandmonthlymag.com) devotes itself to describing the climate of real estate and emerging trends—and gives their stamp of approval to the 20 top neighborhoods and why they consider them such, including statistics on commute times, crime rates, and other information of interest. This popularity contest—of great interest to homeowners all over town—is not available online, but you can buy back issues from the website.

Retail storefronts, schools, parks, churches, community gardens, movie houses, live theater, restaurants, and coffee shops are within easy walking distance, but the centerpiece is still Ladd Circle's beautiful garden and the little shops that surround it, which provide the neighborhood with a meeting place and a focus. This neighborhood also hosts one of the liveliest food cart pods, at the corner of Southeast Hawthorne Boulevard and Southeast 12th Avenue (see the Dining chapter).

SELLWOOD–WESTMORELAND

Historic Sellwood is known for its Antique Row, composed of more than 50 antiques and other attractive stores tucked into the neighborhood of Victorian houses and turn-of-the-20th-century architecture. Where Sellwood meets the river, you'll find Oaks Bottom, home to the Oaks Bottom Wildlife Sanctuary, a refuge for herons, beavers, ducks, and other marsh animals and birds. Here, the neighborhood meets the Willamette, with houseboats docked along the river's edge. Sellwood is also renowned for its strong community spirit. Westmoreland is graced with one of the city's most beautiful parks, as well as its own healthy retail district, including the wonderful Moreland Theater, an independently owned movie theater that is a true community hub. Most of the houses in this neighborhood are single-family dwellings, from small bungalows and old Victorian cottages to some houses that are impressive in their scale and architecture. Many of these can be found along the ridge above Oaks Park. Families like this neighborhood, its good schools, and beautiful parks.

EASTMORELAND

Eastmoreland is a lush residential neighborhood. Quiet and tranquil, it is bordered by the Eastmoreland Golf Course, Reed College, Crystal Springs Lake, and the Crystal Springs Rhododendron Gardens. Houses are large, expensive, and handsome. Public schools are top-notch. Eastmoreland claims on city surveys to be the happiest neighborhood in all of Portland.

LAURELHURST

Laurelhurst is a pretty neighborhood with a variety of house styles, most of them well landscaped with mature plantings and offering some of the most desirable property on the east side. The neighborhood is bordered by Belmont to the south, and it has its own charming retail district on Burnside between Southeast 28th Avenue and Southeast 32nd Place. Its anchor, however, is the gorgeous, Olmsted-designed Laurelhurst Park (see the Parks chapter for more information).

North & Northeast Portland

Many Oregonians regard this section of Portland as an area of tremendous opportunity. Here, Portlanders are rightfully proud of their old, well-established neighborhoods featuring lovely houses and elegant, historic mansions. And that pride has been refreshed, since many intense redevelopment activities are pumping new life and vitality into this section of the city, making it a more exciting and appealing place to live, work, and visit.

Beautiful older houses line the tree-shaded streets in the Northeast neighborhoods of Beaumont, Irvington, and Alameda. Some of the houses in the Alameda neighborhood, especially those along the periphery of the ridge, afford good views of the Willamette River and the downtown skyline. Alameda and Irvington share schools and shopping districts, and both are among the most highly prized neighborhoods in town.

Attractive shopping areas draw people from around the region, and so does Portland's Convention Center, between the Lloyd District and the river. The MAX train stops outside the center's north entrance and also serves the adjacent Rose Quarter, a 43-acre complex featuring the Memorial Coliseum arena, the Moda Center arena, the One Center Court entertainment complex, and 4 parking garages. The Rose Quarter hosts a variety of sports events, including the Portland Trailblazers, the Portland Winter Hawks, college basketball, and indoor soccer. Around Lloyd Center, the Northeast Broadway Business District is blossoming, and just east, the delightful Hollywood District offers a wonderful blend of affordable housing and great small shops. Grant Park is another popular neighborhood. With the eponymous park at its center, this tree-lined area of pretty single-family houses, many of which were built in the 1920s and 1930s, has great schools, an incredibly convenient location, and a superfriendly vibe.

Other neighborhoods farther north, such as Hayden Island, St. Johns, and Kenton, offer their own distinctive charms. These areas, rich in character and history, are blessed with many well-tended parks and green spaces. The Woodlawn neighborhood is undergoing new development around its Dekum Triangle area, with excellent coffee shops and restaurants complementing the refurbished and affordable houses.

More North Portland Neighborhoods

BOISE-ELIOT NEIGHBORHOOD

Formerly the city of Albina, which was established in 1872 and annexed to Portland in 1891, the Boise-Eliot neighborhood in inner Northeast Portland started out as a community of European immigrants, then became the foremost residential and cultural centers of the African-American community, and now it is a diverse and multicultural neighborhood—and above all, youthful.

From 1960 to 1990 the area lost more than half its housing to urban renewal projects such as the building of Legacy Emanuel Hospital, conversion to business and institutional use, and neglect. This neighborhood is now one of the most vital and popular, especially with first-time homebuyers and young families.

No place is this more evident than North Mississippi and North Williams Avenues. Both historic and innovative, these streets have undergone a renaissance. This neighborhood was a vibrant hub in the early 20th century, complete with its own streetcar line. But history passed it by and left it with vacant lots and buildings, crime, and deterioration. After suffering generations of neglect, North Mississippi Avenue is now filled with young entrepreneurs who are bringing the deserted storefronts to life and filling the vacant lots with gardens and new buildings. Cafes, art galleries, bakeries, flower nurseries, antiques stores, food carts, and other indie enterprises are revitalizing the street, and many of these urban pioneers make their homes here as well, living above or next to their businesses. Unlike many neighborhood improvement projects, this one has been specifically designed to protect its longtime residents from the unintended consequences of gentrification—though this is not always as successful a message as planners had hoped—but overall, Portland views North Mississippi as a model for future urban renewal. Likewise, North Williams has blossomed. It's a major biking arterial, and shops and restaurants are sprouting up like a vegetable garden in June, bolstered by designation as an official Urban Renewal Area. Housing prices remain affordable—so far.

CULLY NEIGHBORHOOD

Just east of the lovely Kennedy School and the Alberta arts scene, the Cully neighborhood is blossoming. Another neighborhood defined by revival and renaissance, especially along Alberta Street, this area also has houses with nice big yards, as well as new markets, cafes, and services. Once noted for having the least amount of park space per capita in town, the Cully neighborhood has a new greenspace, Cully Park, that is at the center of this renewal. Cully Park has trails, exercise equipment, off-leash areas for dogs, and a community garden designed by local school kids. It also has a neighborhood produce farm and CSA, the Cully Neighborhood Farm.

OVERLOOK NEIGHBORHOOD

Nestled along a high bluff above the Swan Island industrial area and Willamette River Overlook in North Portland, the Overlook neighborhood was once the home of many shipyard workers. Today it has drawn a diverse ethnic population, reflected in an elementary school population among whom 22 percent study English as a second language.

This historically rich district is home to a large Kaiser Permanente health care facility, as well as the Kaiser Town Hall, a cherished neighborhood meeting place. It also features popular Overlook Park; Saint Stanislaus Church and Polish Hall, the site of a yearly festival and repository of cultural heritage; the Interstate Firehouse Cultural Center, a recycled firehouse used for a wide variety of community activities; and the Overlook Community Center. With its beautiful older homes, it is undergoing a major gentrification boom. There's a New Seasons up the street at Killingsworth, a trendy Overlook Farmers Market in the summer, and lots of new shops and restaurants.

ST. JOHNS–CATHEDRAL PARK NEIGHBORHOOD

At the tip of the North Portland peninsula near the confluence of the Columbia and Willamette Rivers lies Cathedral Park and adjacent St. Johns, one of Portland's oldest communities. Once an independent village, it still has the feel of a small community, especially in its bustling retail district. The industrial area surrounding St. Johns is a source of employment for residents but also a point of conflict as the community struggles to protect its livability and adjacent natural resources. The St. Johns Bridge, the jewel of Portland's bridges, is the area's most visible landmark, and the graceful arches of its base give Cathedral Park its name. The popular park represents a 10-year effort by the locals to preserve some of the riverfront for public use. The area is also home to Smith and Bybee Lakes, both unique natural and recreational resources.

More Northeast Portland Neighborhoods

CONCORDIA NEIGHBORHOOD

A large, northeast Portland neighborhood dating back to the turn of the century, Concordia was once considered a suburb. Now indisputably urban, this neighborhood is an exemplar of urban renewal. Thanks to the efforts of the neighborhood association and enterprising entrepreneurs, the commercial spine of this area, Alberta Street, is a vital, thriving artery. Concordia University, for which the neighborhood was named, is just 3 miles from downtown and continues to play an important role in the area's positive changes.

A showcase of these positive developments is the old Kennedy School, a neighborhood landmark since 1915. Declared surplus decades ago by the school district, the building slowly deteriorated over the years as competing interests wondered what to do with it. Portland's McMenamin brothers solved the problem by converting it into a huge attraction, complete with pubs, a bed-and-breakfast inn, and a movie house. (See our Accommodations chapter.) The beneficial effects of the Kennedy School development have helped to revive the real estate market in the area and have spilled over into nearby neighborhoods.

SABIN NEIGHBORHOOD

Sabin is another highly diverse residential neighborhood comprising mostly older houses that has gentrified mightily since 2000. In recent years the non-profit Sabin Community Development Corp. has developed more than 100 units of housing for very-low-income families in the area.

In other endeavors, Sabin hosted Portland's first multicultural festival and stages an annual Alberta Street Festival on the revitalized Alberta Corridor. Tree plantings and murals add to the friendliness and attractiveness of the area. Retail activity is starting to take off, and urban pioneers are buying their first houses in this area, where handsome old houses may still be reasonably priced.

HAZELWOOD/GATEWAY NEIGHBORHOOD

Along the old Barlow Trail, one of the earliest pioneer routes across the Cascade Mountains into Portland, is Hazelwood. This neighborhood stretches throughout eastern Portland along Burnside, and most of the area's housing was built during the post–World War II development boom of 1946 to 1960. Some of these developments include high-quality projects such as Cherry Blossom Park. Hazelwood, like most of the outer east area, remained unincorporated until it was annexed to Portland in the 1980s. As the city's population increases, it feels less remote—especially since the MAX line runs through the middle, making it quick and easy to get downtown. Distinctive features of Hazelwood include the East Portland Police Precinct, Midland Branch Library, the Gateway Apartments mixed-use project, Midland Park with plantings by local students, and the blossoming Gateway business area.

i Community newspapers are the glue that holds the neighborhoods together. Neighborhood association meetings, traffic plans, and discussions with local legislators and officials combine with personal essays, advertisements, and advice columns to provide community spirit and critical information for residents. Look for papers locally in stores, coffee shops, and kiosks—and see the Media chapter for more information.

Vancouver

At the stroke of midnight on January 1, 1997, with the Eastside annexation, Vancouver, which sits across the Columbia River directly north of Portland, became the fourth-largest city in the state of Washington and the second-largest city in the Portland Metropolitan region. In the blink of an eye, Vancouver increased in size from 26 square miles to more than 44 square miles and nearly doubled its population from 68,000 residents to 128,000.

The seat of Clark County, Vancouver is one of the fastest-growing regions in the United States. This burgeoning high-tech port and city was established as a fur-trading center by the Hudson's Bay Company in 1825. The trading post and historic Fort Vancouver, surrounded by a fertile plain, soon became the commercial center for the Pacific Northwest. Although neighboring Portland's superior port facilities make it the leading city of the area, Vancouver's role remains essential to the economy and character of the region.

Outlying Areas

West of Portland

BEAVERTON

Midway between Mount Hood and the Oregon coast, Beaverton is 7 miles west of downtown Portland in Washington County at the crossroads of US 26 and SR 217. With a population of more than 90,000, and its status as the second-largest city in Washington County (total population of nearly 530,000), this suburb of Portland has its own distinctive culture.

Spread over 15 square miles, the town features many shopping areas, including Beaverton Mall, Beaverton Town Square, and Washington Square. Tree-lined streets highlight the clean neighborhoods, while a 25-mile network of bike paths and trails connect its well-groomed playgrounds and green spaces. Building activity is vigorous.

In the city itself there are 100 parks—one within a half-mile of every house—encompassing 1,000 acres and offering 30 miles of hiking trails. Beaverton is relatively prosperous and its school district is one of the most esteemed in the state—and Nike corporate headquarters are here.

HILLSBORO

Incorporated in 1876, the city of Hillsboro has grown from a tiny farming community into a modern city of more than 90,000 residents and is the largest city in Washington County. Originally called Hillsborough, the city was named for David Hill, one of the pioneers who crossed the Oregon Trail and became one of the state's original legislators.

About 20 minutes due west of Portland, Hillsboro is spread out over 19 square miles in the heart of the Tualatin Valley. Hillsboro lies within the 9,000-acre Sunset Corridor, one of Oregon's fastest-growing economic development regions and the home of Intel and other high-tech firms. Many impressive facilities have sprung up in Hillsboro, including one of the highest-quality corporate parks in the United States: 319-acre Dawson Creek Park, which contains 7 lakes, fountains, promenades, and more than 5 miles of pedestrian and bicycle trails.

TIGARD AND TUALATIN

Tigard and Tualatin are the southwest outposts of the metro area, both characterized by major new commercial, industrial, high-tech, and residential development. Just under 50,000 residents live in Tigard; many commute to Portland, but others work in nearby electronics or computer firms. It's a young town—a third of its residents fall in the 20 to 44 age demographic. Tualatin had 750 residents in 1970. It now has more than 26,000. Its gazillion new housing developments are big hits with families—there are more children than 20- to 44-year-old adults here. As with Tigard, many people find work close to home in business services, manufacturing, and other modern forms of employment; there also remains a great deal of agricultural work in the area.

East of Portland

GRESHAM AND TROUTDALE

Once a land of berry fields and farmland, Gresham has blossomed into a bustling city of 106,000 residents while still retaining its small-town appeal. The state's fourth-largest city, Gresham sits at the east end of the MAX light-rail system, providing its residents with cheap, efficient transportation into downtown Portland. Situated in eastern Multnomah County and encompassing 22.5 square miles, Gresham is the metropolitan area closest to the Columbia Gorge and Oregon's year-round playground, Mount Hood National Forest. Its downtown area is particularly appealing and easy to navigate. Colorful, pedestrian-friendly, and well-designed, it offers a wide variety of restaurants, retail shops, and services in a concentrated area. Gresham also maintains an excellent educational system, including its notable Mount Hood Community College. Troutdale lies just west of the Sandy River, with about 14,000 residents. It is the official gateway to the Mount Hood recreation area, with an old-fashioned downtown area and pretty riverside houses.

South of Portland

LAKE OSWEGO AND WEST LINN

These two riverside residential cities are pretty and quiet, with reputations for fine schools and well-to-do inhabitants. Lake Oswego, with a population of more than 36,000, retains its beautiful older English cottage- and Tudor-style houses built in the first half of the 20th century, but today most people live in contemporary houses, many of which are in developments. However, you can find the vestiges of its sleepy rural history evident in the properties that still boast horse pastures and chicken coops. Spectacular houses line pretty Lake Oswego, the manmade body of water that lends its name to the town. The neighborhood associations are busy and active. Lake Oswego is alluring to many people, but there's only so much of it to go around, so its neighbor West Linn has seen much growth in the past decade. In fact it's grown about 40 percent since 1970—but its residents still number only about 25,000 people. Both towns are a short commute from downtown Portland, traffic permitting.

Oregon City

This historic city 10 miles south of Portland was founded in 1845. Oregon City was the first incorporated city west of the Rocky Mountains, and when the city of San Francisco was originally platted, its papers had to be filed at the federal courthouse in Oregon City. Because the town awaited at the end of the Oregon Trail, and because Oregon City was the place where pioneers refreshed and restocked before traveling to their new farms south in the Willamette Valley, it became known as Pioneer City.

For decades the city thrived as a mill town, but today its economy is becoming much more diversified, and its population is about 32,000—and growing. The downtown area, nestled on the banks of the Willamette River, is still a beehive of commercial, retail, and community activity.

MILWAUKIE & GLADSTONE

Small-town charm, life on the waterfront, easy access to big city amenities—all these describe Milwaukie, the City of Dogwoods. Situated between Oregon City and Portland on SRs 99 East and 224 in Clackamas County, Milwaukie, a city with 20,000 residents, has been named as one of the 50 best places in the nation to raise a family. Milwaukie and neighboring Gladstone (population 12,000) provide clean environments, good transportation, excellent schools and health care, and many cultural and recreational opportunities. Many shopping centers, industries, and commercial businesses flourish near this modest-to-upscale area.

REAL ESTATE

If you are new to Oregon and looking to buy a house in the Portland area, you may be surprised at the cost. People really like living in this area, and houses in the Portland Metro area are priced higher than the national average. It is still difficult to find a decent single-family house in the city for less than $200,000, even though housing prices are still recovering from the crash.

The market in Portland seems to be returning to historical norms in which real estate was meant to be a long-term investment whose main purpose was not to generate cash but to provide a home. Like most of the rest of the nation, Portland's real estate market has declined since its peak in 2007, but as of this writing, the market is making a strong comeback: Prices are increasing, the inventory and time on market are both low, and investment buyers with suitcases full of cash are putting pressure on prices. Average prices are now about 14 percent lower than the 2007 peak. Mortgage rates are still comparatively low, however. While this is a glimmer of good news for buyers, houses in the inner core of the city are still desirable, especially in a city that prizes both public transportation and easy commuting, as well as one that is as obsessed with neighborhoods as Portland is. Being within a walk of 20 minutes or less to shops and restaurants is a very Portland value, so houses surrounding such districts will tend to have higher prices.

Education & Child Care

Portland's solid sense of community, reinforced by consistently high marks for its quality of life, makes it a fine place to raise a family. But even here, child care can be difficult to find, especially for infants and toddlers, and choosing a school causes much soul-searching among parents of future kindergarteners and of families moving into the area. Parents are often bewildered by the number of decisions they must make in choosing the nature and scope of their children's care and education. To make those decisions easier, we survey the territory for you. And you may also be interested in other local resources. Two free publications, *Metro Parent* and *Portland Family*, offer regular updates on child-care facilities in the area and on local schools. Another good source is *Portland Monthly*, which compiles extensive data from the state on local public and private schools. And informal networks through community centers, libraries, religious organizations, and word of mouth can put parents in touch with good caregivers and schools.

EDUCATION

Philosophers tell us that there is no education without growth. Oregonians have seen a lot of growth in the past decade—and that has influenced education and been an education in itself. The institutions devoted to education have also had to contend with growth. As a result they are multifaceted and diverse—they include state and private universities, community colleges, and public and private elementary, middle, and high schools.

The metro area has more than 200 public schools and a robust selection of private institutions. In both public and private schools, you may find a selection of special-needs facilities as well as experimental settings where students are challenged in different ways, from learning other languages to designing business plans. The schools in Oregon are generally well regarded, despite recent and ongoing fiscal trials. It's a testament to parents and teachers alike that the public schools remain relatively strong in spite of the financial turmoil, although recently, the high-school graduation rate in Oregon has come under scrutiny. Portland is also the home of Portland State University, one of seven universities run by the Oregon University System, as well as the site of a commendable list of private colleges. Among these are Reed College, Lewis & Clark, Marylhurst College, and the University of Portland. And Oregon Health and Science University holds a significant place in the Portland skyline. It is devoted to teaching and training medical professionals and research scientists, and it is responsible for innovative research in the fight against cancer and other diseases.

Community colleges play a major role in the area's educational scene. Indeed, Portland Community College has more students than any other college in the state. All the community colleges offer a broad range of programs for a broader range of students, whose reasons for attending are various and idiosyncratic. You will find newly graduated high school students who plan to transfer to a four-year college, students wishing to earn their high-school diplomas, students returning to college after a number of years, students who are pursuing some kind of professional training, and students who just want to take a sculpture class or two. Besides Portland Community College, which has satellite campus sites around the area, you will also find Mount Hood Community College in Gresham, Clackamas Community College in Southeast Portland, and Clark College in Vancouver.

What Parents Need to Know

If you're moving to Oregon with school-aged children, visit the useful website sponsored by the Oregon Department of Education—it features school report cards, information about Oregon's standards, and other helpful data: ode.state.or.us. And even if you live here already, you'll find the parents' page of the Portland Public Schools website to be of infinite help, with information on everything from magnet schools to school menus: pps.k12.or.us. The Beaverton school district site can be found at beaverton.k12.or.us/home.

CHILD CARE

State Programs & Initiatives

The Oregon Commission for Child Care (OCCC), oregon.gov/employ/ccc, an advisory board to the governor, studies the issues concerning the development of accessible, affordable, and high-quality child care and makes legislative recommendations based on its findings. The OCCC has become a major player on these issues since its inception in 1985, and one of its notable successes has been the creation of a program for child-care resource and referral, the Child Care Division of the Oregon Employment Department. This division certifies child-care centers through criminal history checks and inspections of facilities.

It also registers family child-care businesses, though it does not inspect them. (Family child-care providers are still required to undergo criminal background checks and a certain amount of training.) The division sponsors mentoring and training programs for providers, working closely with the Center for Career Development in Childhood Care and Education at Portland State University.

Child Care Resource & Referral Network

The Child Care Division of the Oregon Employment Department has also developed the Child Care Resource and Referral (CCR&R) agencies (oregon childcare.org). These community-based agencies strive to provide all parents with as much information and as many options for quality child care as possible. The CCR&R agencies direct parents toward resources for child-care screening as well as to other community resources, including child-care provider support groups. Although the CCR&R programs are extremely busy, and you must leave a message on a recording, they generally return calls within a reasonable amount of time and are quite helpful. CCR&R staff are knowledgeable and will answer questions about a wide range of topics and dispense information about child-care accreditation, local workshops for providers, and information about scholarships to help cover training and accreditation fees. Your local CCR&R representative can also meet with you and provide a personal consultation to address concerns about your child-care situation, health and safety matters, child development issues, activities for children, and even technical information regarding business development, taxes, and zoning. CCR&R resources are considerable, including a lending library of videos, books, toys, and equipment, so don't be afraid to ask for help or advice. Check the website to find the one nearest you.

Child-Care Providers

Finding someone to care for your child can be remarkably stressful, but surveying the territory will make things a little easier. Regardless of what option seems to best suit your needs, you should start your search for child care early. A range of care is available, but a lot of other parents are looking for qualified help for their child-care needs, and waiting lists are not unusual. It takes time to find the right person or center for your child and your family.

Work and school may help you with your child-care needs. Since Oregon gives employers good tax breaks when they subsidize child care, many employers keep their workers happy by offering this benefit. If you're still working on your degree, Portland Community College (pcc.edu/resources/child-care) and Portland State University (hgcdc.pdx.edu) campuses have lovely, though limited, child-care programs for students and staff. Likewise, some employers offer some childcare subsidies or discounts. Check with your benefits office to see your options.

Doulas & Early Care

Child care begins early for some of us. Many Portland parents find the transition to their new roles goes more smoothly with the help of a doula, a professional family helper who provides nonmedical assistance to new parents at home. Doulas may show anxious parents how to hold, bathe, dress, and feed the new little one; they may take care of the house or older siblings; they may aid with nursing; in general, they help to keep things peaceful and calm. Since hospital stays for postpartum women are notoriously abbreviated, a doula could be just the person to ease you through the surprise of new parenthood. You can find doulas in a variety of places. Your ob/gyn may have some contacts, and midwives are very good sources; often midwifery practices include them on staff.

Sometimes all you need is the support of other parents. Hospitals and health-care organizations will often run programs for new parents and their infants. Hosted by nurses or other health-care professionals, these free or low-cost forums allow you to ask questions about breast-feeding, child development, and other issues. Just hanging out with the other parents is comforting, especially when you find out they all feel the same way that you do. Check with your hospital or health care plan to see whether they offer such programs, and on the web look in the Craig'slist community section under Child Care, where parent support groups may be listed as well as discussion forums for parents (portland.craigslist.org). And don't forget the power of the spoken word: Most of the people we know found their groups informally, through their childbirth education classes, friends of friends, story time at the library, the baby swings at the park, the Baby Gap store at the mall, or interesting conversations about baby acne at the local Starbucks. Later, when the babies get bigger, these groups are invaluable resources for setting up casual babysitting co-ops.

Nannies

If you read the *New York Times*, you might worry that hiring a nanny will require you to sign away not just your first-born child but his or her entire inheritance. However, this is still Oregon, and while nannies are expensive, they are still affordable for many families. In fact, nanny care is growing in popularity, for it may be the least disruptive to the family. Nannies can be full- or part-time; they can live in your house or in their own; they can be temporary or long-term. Nannies have widely varying responsibilities and duties, such as housework, meal preparation, and picking the children up from school and driving them to sports or extracurricular functions. You should make it clear what duties the job entails and spell them out in a contract.

Two good sources for nannies are **Northwest Nannies** (503-245-5288; nwnanny.com) or **Care Givers Placement Agency** (503-244-6370; cgpa .com). Both agencies can find you temporary or permanent full- or part-time help. Care Givers will also help you find temporary emergency child care; contact them in advance, if you think you might be subject to emergencies, to see how their system works. While the nannies we have known have been trustworthy, reliable, and resourceful, nannies are not licensed in Oregon; going through an agency may afford you some protection since the agency screens the applicants and expects them to have some training. If you want to take on the job of performing background checks yourself, however, Craigslist (portland.craigslist.org) can be a fantastic resource for finding child-care help.

Day-Care Centers & Family Care

Day-care centers are open 52 weeks a year, are licensed by the state, and are usually staffed with a number of teachers who are supervised by a director. They can charge up to several thousand dollars per month for full-time care, depending on the scope and number of children you enroll. Caregiver–child ratios are strict and vary with the age of the child. Day-care centers are becoming increasingly specialized and are more competitive than ever. These centers, which according to state law must provide at least 35 square feet of space per child, can be quite large and usually offer lots of recreational and educational activities to help children acquire new skills as they burn off their seemingly endless supply of energy. There are hundreds of day-care facilities in the area. Many families choose one close to either home or work, but wherever you live and work, you'll have to sort through the facilities to find one that coheres with your outlook on things. As you might expect, the kind of care and theory behind it varies widely; we have pretty much everything here, from Waldorf-based philosophies to Montessori philosophies to Piaget's philosophies, and everything in between. Many day cares incorporate religious themes. Some of the nationally known chains that operate in Portland are the Learning Tree, Kindercare, La Petite Academy, and Children's World, but there are many locally grown centers for you to probe.

In-home, or, as the state refers to it, "family" day care, is ubiquitous throughout Oregon and involves taking your child to someone's home for care. In-home day-care operations must be registered with the state and can provide care for up to 10 children at a time. Be sure that you check the qualifications of anyone you hire to care for your children in his or her home and ask to see the paperwork. As with day-care centers, strict requirements for ratios of caregivers to children apply. Also, operators and employees must undergo criminal background checks, and new training requirements demand that they have an overview session, are trained in CPR, maintain a food handler's certification, and are trained to prevent child abuse and neglect. They must also carry household insurance. The Child Care Resource and Referral network listed above can refer you to providers.

Drop-in day care is a godsend for emergency babysitting—and it's useful for visiting families when the parents would like to enjoy, say, a dinner with adult beverages or perhaps house hunt in an unimpeded fashion. One popular and well-located site is **WeVillage:** The Pearl, 424 NW 11th Ave., Portland, OR 97209; (503) 935-5590; wevillage.com. Another is **Grandma's Place,** with several locations: Clark Family Center, 2740 SE Powell Blvd., Portland, OR 97202, (503) 249-7533; Rose Quarter, 1730 N. Flint St., Portland, OR 97227, (503) 281-6800; and Center Village, 5845 NE Hoyt, Portland, OR 97213; (503) 238-0123; grandmasplacedaycare.org.

> **i** Saturday Academy (503-200-5858; saturdayacademy .org) is an award-winning, innovative enrichment program for kids in grades 4 through 12. Area professionals share their labs, equipment, and expertise to teach hands-on experimentation and critical thinking in science, math, writing, and other subjects. Saturday Academy has been awarded many National Science Foundation grants among other honors. Scholarships are available.

Extended-Care & Summer Programs

Many Portland schools, both public and private, offer extended-care programs after and before school for children whose parents have incompatible work schedules, and these programs often run during school breaks as well. The public schools have contracts with 18 state-certified, nonprofit providers, who run programs in 62 elementary schools. Two additional schools have child care within a safe walking distance (that is, a distance that could be covered by a child in kindergarten). Your child's school can give you information about these programs, or you can call the **Portland Public Schools Child Care** coordinator at (503) 916-3230.

In addition to extended care within the schools, you'll find other weekday programs that take care of children until their parents can. **Boys and Girls Clubs** are helpful in this regard; they have four clubs in the area and run summer programs in addition to their extended-care programs. Their administrative office in Southeast Portland, at 7119 SE Milwaukie, (503) 232-0077, is a well-equipped facility that keeps kids busy with all kinds of wholesome activity, from basketball to photography. The number for the club is (503) 238-6868. Other locations include the Wattles Club, 9330 Harold St., (503) 775-1549; the Blazers' Boys and Girls Club, 5250 NE Martin Luther King Jr. Blvd., (503) 282-8480; and in Hillsboro, at 560 SE 3rd Ave., (503) 640-4558. You can find them online at bgcportland.org.

The **YMCA of Columbia-Willamette** has multiple regional centers and in-school programs for child care, education, and extended care. The YMCA offers flexible and affordable day care and does a great job of keeping youngsters involved in stimulating and challenging activities. These fully licensed and well-staffed centers are conveniently located on both sides of the river and offer full- or part-time options for busy parents. In addition, the YMCA manages a half-dozen Child Development Centers for six-week-old infants up to five-year-old children. You can reach them at (503) 327-0007 or ymca-portland .org.

Portland Parks and Recreation and summer day camps, both covered in the Kids chapter, can also help you take care of your child. Summer day camps are a popular form of "child care." Devoted to activities such as basketball, dance, computer or language training, art lessons, theater, monitoring baby animals at the Oregon Zoo, or an array of other things, they provide care for the kids and peace of mind for their parents. OMSI sponsors the Northwest Kids Summer Camp Expo in April; this free event brings together dozens of high-quality summer camp programs so you can find the right one for your child. Finally, Portland Parks and Rec sponsors many after-school and school-break programs throughout the city. These offerings change regularly and vary according to the season; download a catalog at portlandonline.com/parks.

Retirement

Portland is a particularly agreeable place for retirement whether you are moving here specifically for that purpose or you have lived here your whole life. And that's because civic life is still celebrated here. We have a sophisticated, affordable, and reliable mass-transit system that is sympathetic to the needs of seniors, an outstanding public library, world-class health care, a fine public parks system, and most of the other amenities that make life worth living. The temperate climate ensures that there usually won't be too many very hot or very cold days. In the interest of full disclosure, however, we should let you know that many seniors in the area spend part of the year in warmer climates such as Palm Springs and save their Portland time for the months from June through Oct, when the weather is especially good. We have noticed, however, more and more seniors retiring to Portland permanently and choosing to live downtown, with its convenient access to the streetcar and other transportation, as well as outstanding restaurants, shopping, and the arts. And we are not the only ones who have noticed: Since 2006, Portland State University's Institute on Aging has been working with the World Health Organization to define what makes an "age-friendly city"—the first US city to participate in this groundbreaking project. It turns out that access to nature is one of the most important features, which the city has in abundance. Other important features include good public transportation, housing that is close to shopping and services, and a culture of friendliness. In the intervening years, Portland has been designated an "age-friendly city," along with New York—the only two designated cities in the nation to date.

Affordable housing is a critical component for age-friendliness, and we have some work to do in this arena. Nonetheless, there are excellent housing opportunities for seniors in the area. You will find communities devoted solely to seniors, as well as neighborhoods that have a balance of all ages, whichever you prefer. If you live independently but are ready to give up such tasks as mowing the lawn and maintaining a house, you'll have a wide variety of choices available. And this is also true if you need more help than just having the lawn mowed. Portland is comparatively expensive when it comes to real estate, especially in the heart of the city, which has the most accessible services. However, if you look hard you can usually find something well priced. Many charming, well-planned, affordable housing communities are being built all across the region; some of these are close to the MAX and streetcar lines.

As in most places in the United States, Portland offers a variety of housing options for seniors, depending on their needs, everything from adult care homes, memory care, in-home nursing, and residential care to assisted living and retirement communities. An outstanding resource documenting the many options available is the Senior Resource Network, theseniorresourcenetwork.com. They provide a good overview of the types of housing options available, but more importantly, they have a referral and placement service to help ensure a good fit.

CHOOSING A RETIREMENT COMMUNITY

Our retirement communities offer independent apartment, house, or condominium living, along with support services such as weekly housekeeping. Some locations offer one or more meals per day. Many of these places contract with private home health agencies to provide extra assistance to residents for which there are additional fees. In general these retirement communities are not licensed as care facilities, but some locations offer floors or sections that are licensed to provide a higher level of care. There is no financial assistance available to help cover the cost of housing in nonlicensed retirement communities.

In the Portland area alone, there are more than 100 retirement communities—one for every taste and budget. Some have buy-in fees and long-term leases, some rent apartments by the month. Some have swimming pools, health spas, and tennis courts; others focus on providing activities such as bridge

Research and Retirement

A unique senior facility is emerging in the South Waterfront district: **Mirabella** in Portland. This innovative continuing care retirement community is designed to allow residents to "age in place"—in chic condominiums with amenities such as a penthouse dining room atop the 30-story building. A major component is its relationship with Oregon Health and Science University, which uses its world-class researchers and caregivers to address multiple dimensions of the aging experience in order to improve care. Many residents have become involved in research projects related to aging, not just participating in trials but also serving in advisory roles in this exciting collaboration. To learn more, call Mirabella at (503) 245-4742 or visit their website at mirabellaretirement.org/portland/index.htm.

> ## Elders in Action
>
> Elders in Action advocates for seniors in large ways and small. Not only do they help individuals find resources in their community, but they also provide workshops on how best to use these resources, advocate for policy changes that benefit seniors, and guide businesses and local governments in making senior-friendly services and products. You can find them at 1411 SW Morrison, Suite 290, Portland, OR 97205, (503) 235-5474, or online at eldersinaction.org. They also have a very busy Facebook page.

clubs, group outings, and community meals. Many offer different levels of care should you ever need them. Most retirement centers will be delighted to send you a brochure and arrange a guided tour. Expect to pay from $1,000 to $3,500 and above per month.

While many of the retirement communities are designed for seniors without serious medical problems, many of them do provide continuing care when needed. Some of the following communities are designed to meet the increasing care needs of an aging resident by providing independent apartment living supplemented with an on-site health-care facility, usually licensed by the State of Oregon Senior and Disabled Services office. The residency agreement includes a contract, and tenants pay a large entrance fee (or buy-in) in addition to monthly rates. Before making a decision on any retirement community, check with Senior and Disabled Services at (800) 282-8096 or oregon.gov/DHS/spwpd/Pages/index.aspx. They can tell you about any complaints made against the place you are considering. If you are in the market for Alzheimer's care or other intensive, continuing-care facilities, we suggest you also check the above link to the Oregon Department of Human Services website—it has a comprehensive guide to long-term care and provides a list of local offices that can help you find placement.

RESOURCES FOR SENIORS

HOME REPAIR & WEATHERIZATION, Community Energy Project, 422 NE Alberta St., (503) 284-6827; communityenergyproject.org. The Community Energy Project (CEP) helps seniors on a fixed income enjoy a warmer home and lower utility bills during the winter months. They install vinyl storm windows that roll up and down easily, weather-strip doors, caulk and eliminate drafts throughout the home, and save money and energy by insulating water heaters and pipes. The CEP also helps seniors with minor repairs and adjustments such as installing safety bars, repairing stairs, installing carbon monoxide and smoke detectors, and other services that will improve quality of life and safety. Homeowners as well as renters are welcome to call, and all services and materials are provided free of cost.

HOME REPAIR PROGRAM, Washington County Aging Services Department, 328 W. Main St., Hillsboro, OR 97123; (503) 846-8814; co.washington.or.us/HHS/DAVS. This program for low-income seniors can provide assistance for accessibility improvements such as ramps, wider doorways, grab bars, lower counters, and security devices. Other improvements for homeowners may include heating, plumbing or electrical repairs, and roof and siding upkeep.

HUMAN SOLUTIONS ENERGY ASSISTANCE PROGRAMS, 12350 SE Powell Blvd., Portland, OR 97236; (503) 548-0200; humansolutions.org. This program helps low-income families and seniors stay cozy while reducing their utility bills during winter months. Human Solutions also provides other safety net service programs and low-income housing.

REBUILDING TOGETHER, 5000 N. Willamette Blvd., Portland, OR 97203; (503) 943-7515; rtpdx.org. This well-established nonprofit agency donates material and labor to do extensive remodeling on homes owned by low-income seniors. They accept referrals in the fall and winter and do the work in the spring, investing more than $1 million in the repair of 50 to 60 homes each year.

Legal Help

Before you call your attorney, you may want to check *Legal Issues for Older Adults*, published by the Oregon State Bar Association. It is a fine reference guide, providing legal information on issues ranging from Medicare to age discrimination, and it includes valuable insights on safety, insurance, and landlord-tenant rights. To order, call (800) 452-8260, or check it out online at osbar.org. A printed copy costs $10, but you can download it for free.

LOAVES AND FISHES/MEALS ON WHEELS, 7710 SW 31st Ave., Portland, OR 97219; (503) 736-6325; loavesandfishesonline.org. Since 1969, Loaves and Fishes and their army of caring volunteers have carried out their mission "to enrich the lives of seniors and assist them in maintaining independence by making nutritious food, social contacts, and other resources easily available." In addition to wellness and community programs, Loaves and Fishes provides more than one million low-cost, nutritious meals to senior citizens in the Portland Metro area each year. In addition, each day Meals on Wheels delivers thousands of hot meals throughout the metro area to homebound seniors who are at least 60 years of age or have a spouse 60 or older. They have 35 sites, and you can have meals delivered or eat at the sites themselves, with transportation provided. Although the suggested donation for a meal is $3, no one is turned away. Besides offering balanced and carefully planned meals and fellowship, Loaves and Fishes sponsors numerous activities and parties throughout the year, especially on the holidays. Loaves and Fishes centers offer a lot more than hot meals—companionship, spiritual fellowship, and ethnic meals and celebrations make the centers a hub of activities for a wide range of elderly clients. To find your nearest Loaves and Fishes, call the central line, listed above, or take advantage of their comprehensive website.

SENIOR CITIZENS COUNCIL OF CLACKAMAS COUNTY, 812 7th St., Oregon City, OR 97045; (503) 657-1366; seniorcouncilofclackamasco .org. The Senior Citizens Council offers a variety of services, including grocery delivery, home care, help with medical equipment and oxygen tanks, and information and referral assistance. They also provide guardian and conservatorship services for elderly citizens who may be vulnerable.

STORE TO DOOR OF OREGON, PO Box 4665, Portland, OR 97208; (503) 200-3333; storetodooroforegon.org. This volunteer agency shops for and delivers groceries to the disabled and senior citizens throughout most of Multnomah and Washington Counties.

RECREATION & EDUCATION

Portland Area Senior Centers

Senior centers around the Portland metro area are oases of hospitality, compassion, and fun for many senior citizens. Besides offering such wide-ranging activities as ballroom dancing, bingo nights, Bible classes, and knitting and

RETIREMENT

The South Waterfront district, including the Mirabella retirement complex, from the upper deck of the Portland Aerial Tram

crocheting sessions, they are a place for seniors to meet longtime companions as well as to make new friends and learn about different cultures.

In addition to providing recreational and educational activities, the centers also function as information and referral sites, and periodically provide health and cholesterol screenings, tax and legal assistance, flu shots, and referrals for medical and mental health needs. At many senior centers, volunteers are available to help with a variety of in-home services, shopping and transportation, and other needs. Some of the principal senior and aging and disability services (ADS) locations are as follows, though there are a number of others as well:

ADS Central Office, 421 SW Oak St., Suite 510, Portland, OR 97204; (503) 988-3620

ADS Mid-County Office, 10615 SE Cherry Blossom Dr., Portland, OR 97216; (503) 988-5480

ADS Southeast Office, 4610 SE Belmont St., Portland, OR 97215; (503) 988-3660

Hollywood Senior Center, 1820 NE 40th Ave., Portland, OR 97212; (503) 288-8303

Neighborhood House, 7688 SW Capitol Hwy., Portland, OR 97219; (503) 246-1663

North/Northeast Office, 5325 NE Martin Luther King Jr. Blvd., Portland, OR 97211; (503) 988-5470

Outlying Areas:

Elsie Stuhr Center, 5550 SW Hall Blvd., Portland, OR 97005; (503) 629-6342

Hillsboro Community Center, 750 SE 8th Ave., Hillsboro, OR 97123; (503) 648-3823

Lake Oswego Adult Community Center, 505 G Ave., Portland, OR 97034; (503) 635-3758

West Linn Adult Community Center, 1180 Rosemont Rd., West Linn, OR 97068; (503) 557-4704

PORTLAND PARKS AND RECREATION COMMUNITY CENTERS, various locations; (503) 823-7529; portlandonline.com/parks. The Portland Park Bureau's community centers offer a variety of programs and a good number of them are designed specifically for senior citizens. Many of the centers have swimming pools; most have fitness centers and basketball and volleyball courts. Community centers provide more than instruction and classes—they are hubs of social activity. Contact the Parks office to have a complete catalog sent to you. Also see the Senior Recreation Program, below.

SENIOR RECREATION PROGRAM, Portland Parks and Recreation, 426 NE 12th Ave., Portland, OR 97232; (503) 823-4328; portlandonline .com/parks. Activities ranging from piano lessons and ceramics classes to getting started with Facebook to hikes on Mount Hood are available at low cost through the Portland Parks and Recreation's Senior Recreation Program. There are also a variety of excursions and day trips planned throughout all seasons of the year. Some are close, such as trips to see the Swan Island dahlias and to ride the Canby Ferry; others are all-day affairs at the Oregon coast or treks up to Silver Star Mountain in Washington. The year-round seniors program provides many great opportunities to meet new friends while staying in good physical condition. Wilderness hikes—to destinations such as Lewis River Falls, Blue Lake, Mount Adams, and Devil Rest Trail in the Columbia Gorge—are offered every weekend during spring and summer months. The program is progressive, giving novices a chance to build up stamina and strength. Other activities

RETIREMENT

include dances to big band orchestras, visits to area golf courses, art classes, yoga training, and computer classes. Activities are held at park sites throughout the city. The service will also help golfers obtain an identification card for reduced greens fees at city of Portland courses. The one-time cost for the card is $10. A handy seasonal catalogue is available online and in print. (Be sure to check out the Parks chapter for more information on the vast offerings of this wonderful park system.)

TRANSPORTATION

The senior centers in the Portland Metro area provide a wide variety of services, including help with transportation needs in their area. But they can only do so much, so many other agencies and volunteer groups have stepped up to fill the gaps in transportation services for seniors.

AMERICAN RED CROSS, 3131 N. Vancouver Ave., Portland, OR 97227; (503) 284-1234; redcross.org/or/portland. Providing nonemergency transportation to seniors throughout Multnomah and Washington Counties, the American Red Cross will gladly help with almost any request in return for a modest $1.50 donation. This helpful service is available on weekdays from 9 a.m. until 4 p.m., but they stay very busy and it is best to schedule your ride up to 2 weeks in advance.

NEIGHBORHOOD HOUSE AGING SERVICES, 7780 SW Capitol Hwy., Portland, OR 97219; (503) 246-1663; nhpdx.org/WhatWeDo/seniors .html. Neighborhood House offers many programs for seniors, but among the most important are the services that help coordinate transportation to medical and dental appointments in southwestern Multnomah County.

PROJECT LINKAGE, 2200 NE 24th Ave., Portland, OR 97212; (503) 249-0471; metfamily.org/project_linkage.htm. Through its 175 volunteers, this agency assists elderly people living in Northeast and Southeast Portland with a wide range of transportation needs, as well as yard work, housekeeping, minor bookkeeping and bill paying, shopping, and home maintenance.

RIDE CONNECTION, 847 NE 19th Ave., Suite 200, Portland, OR 97232; (503) 528-1720 (office), (503) 226-0700 (transportation services); rideconnection.org. The mission of the nonprofit Ride Connection is to keep seniors mobile for as long as possible. They coordinate a network of more than 30 transportation providers so the elderly and disabled can get where they need to go. This innovative program has won many accolades for its approach to service.

Oregon State Services for Seniors

The **Oregon Department of Human Services (DHS)** is the state agency that assists older adults, persons with disabilities, and their caregivers, and they are dedicated to helping people live dignified and independent lives. The division Seniors and People with Disabilities (SPD) serves as a clearinghouse for all kinds of information, from how to find a nursing home to how to find discounts on travel. You can reach the state office of SPD at 500 Summer St. NE, Salem, OR 97301, (503) 945-5921, (800) 282-8096 (voice/TTY). Their website, oregon.gov/DHS/spwpd, is easy to use, comprehensive, and features many links to local, state, and national organizations.

VOLUNTEER OPPORTUNITIES

If you have the time, many agencies, services, and hospitals in the Portland Metro area would be grateful for your volunteer services. Check with your professional organizations too. But here are just a few places to get you started.

AARP EXPERIENCE CORPS, Metro Family Services, 2200 NE 24th Ave., Portland, OR 97212; (503) 232-0007, ext. 211; metfamily.org. This program offers seniors the chance to mentor and tutor children.

ELDERS IN ACTION, 1411 SW Morrison St., Portland, OR 97205; (503) 235-5474; eldersinaction.org. Elders in Action, as noted above, is a vigorous volunteer group dedicated to making life better for seniors.

RETIRED AND SENIOR VOLUNTEER PROGRAM OF MULTNOMAH COUNTY, Metro Family Services, 2200 NE 24th Ave., Portland, OR 97212; (503) 232-0007, ext. 222; metfamily.org. The Retired and Senior Volunteer Program provides multiple opportunities to put your experience to work in the service of others.

RETIREMENT

Media

The media landscape in Portland, like everywhere, is transforming before our eyes. The city's major newspaper, the *Oregonian*, is losing subscribers for the dead-tree edition but has a large online following. Local television stations have active, high-traffic websites. Weekly newspapers and monthly glossy magazines continue to have loyal readership; online magazines start and fold—but new ones keep coming. In the face of this experimental churn, it's too early to tell where we are headed.

NEWSPAPERS

Daily Publications

The Columbian, columbian.com.

The Daily Journal of Commerce, djcoregon.com.

The Oregonian, oregonlive.com.

Nondailies

The Asian Reporter, asianreporter.com.

Beaverton Valley Times, beavertonvalleytimes.com.

The Business Journal of Portland, bizjournals.com/portland.

Catholic Sentinel, catholicsentinel.org.

> **i** If you hike or bike to the summit of Mount Tabor at the east end of Southeast Hawthorne, you'll see a statue of Harvey Scott, editor of the *Oregonian* from 1865 to 1910. Scott, with his arm outstretched and finger pointed accusingly at the objects of his editorial wrath, once said, "Write so the hod carrier will understand you."

Portland is a city of neighborhoods, and reading the neighborhood newspapers is indispensable for finding out the scoop on local businesses and events—as well as the political issues that might affect you directly. Find them at coffee shops, grocery stores, restaurants, and sidewalk kiosks wherever you are.

Gresham Outlook, pamplinmedia.com/gresham-outlook-news.

The Hollywood Star, thehollywoodstar.com.

The Mid-County Memo, midcountymemo.com.

The Northwest Examiner, nwexaminer.com.

The Portland Alliance, theportlandalliance.org.

Portland Mercury, portlandmercury.com.

Portland Observer, portlandobserver.com.

Portland Tribune, portlandtribune.com.

The Sellwood Bee, readthebee.com.

The Skanner, theskanner.com.

The Southeast Examiner, southeastexaminer.com.

Street Roots, streetroots.org.

Willamette Week, wweek.com.

MAGAZINES

1859, Deschutes Media, LLC, 70 SW Century Dr., Suite 100-335, Bend, OR 97702; (541) 550-7081 (office); 1859oregonmagazine.com. This beautiful glossy is notable for its Oregon-wide perspective on lifestyles, history, and culture.

EDIBLE PORTLAND, 721 NW 9th Ave., Suite 200, Portland, OR 97209; (503) 467-0781; edibleportland.com. This quarterly publication covers the food scene in Portland, from locally renowned home cooks to gardening to new restaurants to local agriculture.

JUST OUT, PO Box 10609, Portland, OR, 97296; (503) 828-3034; justout .com. This glossy monthly magazine covers current events and social-political issues affecting the area's gay and lesbian community.

METRO PARENT, PO Box 13660, Portland, OR 97213; (503) 460-2774; metro-parent.com. This user-friendly guide for parents offers a variety of thoughtful articles pertaining to the overall well-being of children.

NORTHWEST PALATE, PO Box 10860, Portland, OR 97296; (503) 224-6039; nwpalate.com. This bimonthly, glossy, consumer magazine focuses on gourmet food, wine, entertainment, and travel in the Pacific Northwest.

OPEN SPACES, PMB 134, 6327-C SW Capitol Hwy., Portland, OR 97239; open-spaces.com. *Open Spaces* quarterly provides intelligent commentary on the major issues facing the Pacific Northwest, giving voice to a variety of perspectives and opinions.

OREGON BUSINESS MAGAZINE, 715 SW Morrison St., Suite 800, Portland, OR 97205; (503) 445-8805; oregonbusiness.com. Founded in 1981, and with a circulation of 20,200, this highly polished publication covers the business scene all over Oregon and southwestern Washington.

OREGON HOME, 715 SW Morrison St., Suite 800, Portland, OR 97205; oregonhomemagazine.com. *Oregon Home* is a glossy magazine published

i Blogging is very Portland—it's the essence of the do-it-yourself spirit. Some of our favorite Portland blogs—in addition to the ones already mentioned in other chapters—are Lost Oregon (lostoregon.org), which covers Portland's history and rapidly changing built environment; Good Stuff Northwest (goodstuffnw .com), a compendium of delightful Oregon things; and Silicon Florist (siliconflorist.com), which usefully covers the start-up scene.

i For a really useful guide to Portland Metro area radio, check out pdxradio.com—you'll find information on the format, call letters, and other tips on the local airwaves, including historical notes and details on finding good Internet radio.

bimonthly that is devoted to houses in Oregon—how they are decorated and lived in.

PORTLAND FAMILY MAGAZINE, 8630 SW Scholls Ferry Rd., #304, Beaverton, OR 97008; (503) 336-0250; portlandfamily.com. Besides tackling serious issues such as education, health and wellness, and child development, *Portland Family Magazine* (*PFM*) keeps a calendar of events and describes events and fun activities that parents and their kids can enjoy together.

PORTLAND MONTHLY, 921 SW Washington St., Suite 750, Portland, OR 97205; (503) 222-5144; portlandmonthlymag.com. This monthly magazine provides outstanding coverage of all things Portland, from real estate and restaurants to fashion and fund-raisers.

TELEVISION

KATU-TV Channel 2 (ABC), katu.com.

KGW-TV Channel 8 (NBC), kgw.com.

KOIN-TV Channel 6 (CBS), koin.com.

KOPB-TV Channel 10 (PBS), opb.org.

KPDX-TV Channel 49 (FOX), kpdx.com.

KPTV-TV Channel 12 (FOX), kptv.com.

Index